A VERY BRITISH STRIKE

Also by Anne Perkins

RED QUEEN
The Authorized Biography of Barbara Castle

ANNE PERKINS

A VERY BRITISH STRIKE

3 MAY–12 MAY, 1926

MACMILLAN

First published 2006 by Macmillan
an imprint of Pan Macmillan Ltd
Pan Macmillan, 20 New Wharf Road, London N1 9RR
Basingstoke and Oxford
Associated companies throughout the world
www.panmacmillan.com

ISBN-13: 978-1-4050-4996-2
ISBN-10: 1-4050-4996-0

Photographic Acknowledgements
Empics – 5. Gallacher Memorial Library, Glasgow Caledonian University
Special Collections and Archives – 7. Getty Images – 1, 3, 4, 6, 8, 9, 10, 13, 14, 15, 16, 17, 18, 19,
20, 21, 23, 25, 26, 27, 28, 29, 30, 31, 32, 33, 34, 35, 36. TUC Collections – 2, 12.

1 3 5 7 9 8 6 4 2

A CIP catalogue record for this book is available from
the British Library.

Typeset by SetSystems Ltd, Saffron Walden, Essex
Printed and bound in Great Britain by
Mackays of Chatham plc, Chatham, Kent

FOR MARK

Contents

ACKNOWLEDGEMENTS

Many people have helped and encouraged me on my way. First and foremost, Georgina Morley at Pan Macmillan, who had the original idea and with my agent, Bill Hamilton, chivvied me into action. The wonderful people at the London Library, as well as those at the British Library and at the National Archive at Kew, made research a pleasure. The Museum of Labour History, and the omniscient Steve Bird, offered more advice. Christine Coates at the TUC library at London Metropolitan University was kind and helpful. I am extremely grateful to Sir Nicholas Wall for allowing me to use his mother's schoolgirl diary. Rosie Anderson's imagination, intelligence, experience, and diligence at the National Archive were indispensable as the deadline drew near; Robert, Eleanor and Catherine Rogers all played differing but important roles in and out of the Palace of Westminster. David McKie generously sent me Sir Wyndham Childs' memoirs. I am very grateful to John Barnes and Martin Kettle for making time to read the manuscript, although of course only I am to blame for errors of fact and judgement. The *Guardian* kindly continued to allow me to work on an erratic schedule. At home, Cecily and Izzie were wonderfully understanding, and Mark, as ever, offered unflagging encouragement.

Preface

This book was conceived in the protracted aftermath of 9/11, and like so much else written in the last four or five years it bears the imprint of peacetime's most devastating act of terror. The moment in 2001 when the image of the World Trade Center's twin towers crumbling was etched on to the West's collective retina left the governing classes of every free country floundering. The conundrum facing politicians was not what to say, although that was hard enough, but the more fundamental problem of what to do.

So when I began to think about the General Strike of 1926 and found it shaped by the actions of governments terrified by a barely comprehended revolutionary movement, it was impossible to ignore the contemporary parallels. Just at the time when it became clear that one part of the response to 9/11 was to be an erosion of civil liberties, I started reading of the constant threat and occasional use of wide-ranging emergency powers in the early 1920s, allowing arrest without charge and detention without trial.

The event that so terrified Western democracies in the 1920s was the Bolshevik revolution of October 1917. After it, as after 9/11, nothing could be the same again. Of course there are limits to the parallels that can be drawn, but the argument that it slammed into Western democratic tradition with the same force as did the attack on the Trade Center's twin towers sheds unexpected light on the enduring nature of the constraints binding governments that must sustain a popular mandate while trying to combat an enemy largely unseen and little understood. There is the same tendency to reach for the apparatus of state repression while trying to calculate what can effectively be conceded; the question of where to confront and how to appease, the debate about inclusion and exclusion and the limits of democratic acceptability – and perhaps above all the uses and abuses of an idea of national identity – were all as familiar eighty years ago as they have now become again.

Meanwhile, the National Archive began to open up intelligence files from the period immediately after the First World War. Requests, latterly permitted under the Freedom of Information Act, obtained many more. The files revealed how little politicians knew for sure, but how much they were prepared to guess at, as they felt their way through a fog of anxiety tainted by the anticipation of political advantage. Meanwhile, operating in a similarly disorienting murk, Tony Blair's government was revealed to have made selective use, amounting to misrepresentation, of intelligence material in order to manipulate public opinion into supporting the disastrous invasion of Iraq.

As I finished writing, London itself became the target for suicide bombers, terrorists who had been born and had grown up here in Britain. Ordinary commuters were murdered by their fellow citizens. More than fifty people died in what most of us fear might not be the high tide of the response to a clash of economic and cultural ideas. On one level, after 7/7 the parallel has to stop. During the General Strike there was little violence, and the only casualties were the result of tragic accidents. But a tiny proportion of those involved in the strike did have violent intent, and it was not only diehard Conservatives who feared that, as it had in Russia, a general strike would precipitate revolution and bloody civil war.

For eighty years since, the Left has found in the strike the grit in the shell of political debate. Communist and para-Communist websites continue to promote their condemnation of the great betrayal of the workers by their leaders with as much vigour as they did in the pamphlets they published in the months and years immediately after the strike ended. For those who do not use the Internet to pursue minority political interests, grainy newsreel footage, and radio archive material emitting the strangled vowels that made the BBC's early announcers sound as if they were soon to be garrotted, keep alive the sense of the strike as a defining moment in modern British history.

The General Strike is the subject of constant re-examination and reinterpretation. Thirty years ago, at a time of chronic industrial unrest, a new generation of academics and writers examined the growth and impact of industrial politics. Now, the strike's eightieth anniversary is dominated by the fear of terror and of the political management – and sometimes exploitation – of that fear. It is this entirely different context that justifies another study of this brief moment in British history.

This is not a work for an academic audience. I hope to inform and interest a new generation in an event that was a product of its time but which reveals a timeless interplay of forces. It is a political account rather than a study of the strike as an industrial cataclysm. Part I seeks to outline the political context: the fear of Communism, the rise of mass democracy, the collapse of the Liberal Party, and the advent of a Labour government. These events created the atmosphere of fear and uncertainty in which a general strike became possible. Dense details of negotiations and pay scales, of profits and contracts, should be sought elsewhere. It reflects contemporary preoccupations with the nature and weapons of influence, for the strike coincided with the development of mass-circulation newspapers and the birth of the BBC. In Part II, the story of the nine days the strike lasted, I have used many accounts – diaries and newspapers, the comments of ordinary people, as well as official papers – that vividly convey what participants and observers thought at the time. I have tried to bear in mind that diaries in particular are dangerous sources to take authoritatively, for the charm of their individuality has to be balanced by the self-glorification of their intent. Memoirs are even less reliable and normally a good deal duller to read, but they have their place if only to reveal what participants wished later they had done at the time.

This book has been great fun to write; I hope that readers will share at least some of that pleasure.

ANNE PERKINS
Semley 2005

Chronology

1900   Labour Representation Committee formed

1906   Labour Party formed after 22 Labour Representation Committee MPs elected in Liberal landslide

Asquith becomes PM

1908   Ramsay MacDonald becomes Labour Party chairman

1914   Triple Alliance formed of dockers', miners' and railwaymen's unions

First World War begins

1916   Lloyd George becomes Liberal Prime Minister of a coalition that comes to be dominated by Conservatives

Mines taken into government control as wartime measure

1917   February: first Russian Revolution

October: Bolsheviks take power in Russia

1918   First World War ends

Coalition wins 478 seats in 'khaki' election

Labour wins 63 seats; MacDonald, pacifist, loses seat

1919   Sankey Commission on future of coal industry set up to investigate demand for nationalization, six-hour day and 30 per cent pay increase

Sankey reports narrowly in favour of nationalization; Lloyd George ignores recommendation, although working day cut to seven hours and pay increased

Bloody Friday: 'general' strike in Glasgow followed by rioting

Police strike in Liverpool, more riots

Labour conference votes in favour of 'Direct Action' to end Allied military intervention against Russian Revolution

Threat of national rail strike leads to government establishing Supply and Transport Committee

1920 Labour and TUC delegation declare Bolshevik regime 'a dictatorship'

August: *Jolly George* incident, when dockers refuse to load ship carrying arms against Russia; formation of councils of action uniting Labour movement against intervention

Ernest Bevin, 'the dockers' KC', wins improved pay and conditions

Postwar boom tails off

Triple Alliance revived to support miners' pay claim; government concedes subsidy

TUC votes to establish General Council to improve cooperation between trade unions in industrial disputes

1921 March: government announces it will return mines to private sector

June: unemployment reaches two million; does not fall below one million until 1940

Emergency Powers Act passed, giving extensive powers to government to arrest and detain without trial

Triple Alliance invoked in support of miners against owners' demands for pay cuts

21 April: Black Friday, when transport workers desert miners because miners will not negotiate. Miners stay out until their defeat in July. Over following two years, pay cuts imposed on railways, in engineering and textile industries

1922 Lloyd George Coalition collapses

General election: Conservatives 345, Labour 142, Liberal and National Liberal 116 seats; Andrew Bonar Law becomes Prime Minister

MacDonald re-elected and becomes Labour leader

Transport and General Workers' Union formed, with Ernest Bevin as its first general secretary

Stanley Baldwin replaces Bonar Law as Conservative leader and Prime Minister

1923   General and Municipal Workers' Union formed

Baldwin seeks popular mandate to introduce tariff barriers to try to protect British industry

December: Baldwin calls general election and loses overall majority: Con. 258, Lab. 191, Lib. 159 seats

1924   January: Labour takes power as minority government and threatens to use emergency powers against transport workers.

Autumn: abandons sedition prosecution against Communist J. R. Campbell and is defeated in the Commons

A. J. Cook becomes general secretary of Miners' Federation

TUC elects left-wingers to General Council

Labour conference bans dual membership of Labour and Communist Parties

29 October: Labour loses election after publication of 'Zinoviev letter' purporting to show MacDonald pro-Bolshevik

Election result: Con. 419, Lab. 151, Lib. 40 seats

1925   Special Branch intercepts 'Strike Strategy in Britain' document

Return to Gold Standard overvalues sterling and forces up cost of exports while reducing cost of imports; more pay cuts predicted

Walter Citrine becomes acting general secretary of the TUC

July: Mine owners demand pay cuts; Miners' Federation rejects cuts and invokes the Triple Alliance. TUC threatens General Strike

30 July: Red Friday; Baldwin agrees to nine-month subsidy and establishes new Royal Commission under Sir Herbert Samuel to investigate coal industry

Red scares dominate newspaper headlines

October: arrest, trial and conviction of twelve leading Communists

1926   6 March: Samuel Commission report recommends reorganization of coal industry but lacks clarity on contentious issue of district pay awards; accepts inevitability of pay cuts

Mine owners demand pay cuts and reintroduction of eight-hour day

Miners' Federation rejects terms and refuses to negotiate: 'Not a minute on the day, not a penny off the pay'

29 April: TUC special conference opens in London; miners appear to accept TUC should conduct dispute

30 April: lockout begins as miners continue to reject owners' terms

1 May: TUC conference authorizes General Strike to start at midnight on Monday 3 May

TUC tries to negotiate through government until late on 2 May, when talks break off after *Daily Mail* production interrupted by some trade unionists objecting to editorial content

3 May, midnight: the General Strike begins

PART ONE

1

A THREAT TO THE STATE

The struggle for economic possession is bound to come.

Ernest Bevin, September 1924[1]

This is the way the world ends
Not with a bang but a whimper.

T. S. Eliot, 'The Hollow Men', 1925

EARLY IN 1925, a fat envelope posted in Leeds was intercepted before it reached its destination, a terraced house in a Doncaster suburb. The address was written in an irregular hand, as if an effort had been made to disguise the writing. The contents of the envelope were passed from the Postmaster General's office to the CID, where they were copied and forwarded to General Sir Wyndham 'Fido' Childs, Assistant Commissioner of the Metropolitan Police, head of Special Branch. There they were copied again. This time they went to the Prime Minister, the Lord Chancellor, the Foreign Secretary and other cabinet ministers, a circulation list that indicated the significance of the intercept. The thirty-five-page document found in the envelope was headed 'Strike Strategy in Britain'. 'The Art of Civil War as far as Britain is concerned,' concluded its anonymous author, 'must basically rest upon the advance guard ... bringing about a General Strike and a general revolutionary combat.'[2]

That October, police raided the headquarters of the Communist Party of Great Britain. Together with busts of Lenin and other heroes of the Russian Revolution (and, curiously, the ballcock from the lavatory), the headquarters at King Street in Covent Garden yielded up extensive evidence of plans to shape the policy, through infiltration and propaganda, of the TUC and the Labour Party. Most of the evidence came from humbly phrased letters addressed to superiors in Moscow; the Party in Britain saw itself as the obedient subsidiary of Soviet power. There were plans to insinuate party members into the police, to incite mutiny in the armed forces, to destabilize industry and to mobilize the unemployed.

Later that month, in the most overtly political trial of twentieth-century Britain, twelve leading Communists were convicted under an ancient piece of legislation, the Incitement to Mutiny Act of 1797. In court, the prosecution set out a bleak Communist future built upon strife and bloodshed, mutiny and insurgency. The defendants argued that this depiction of their aims belonged in the fantasies of 'popular lady novelists'. An ill-judged reference to the 'Frenchy revolutionaries' of 1789 as 'respectable middle class citizens whose views on private property were not dissimilar to those held by the Conservative Party'[3] left the judge, a former Conservative MP, unimpressed. Using 'harsh words' about the Communist Party, he sentenced the twelve defendants to between six and twelve months' imprisonment. When the General Strike began six months later, the most influential Communist leaders were still in prison.

Only eight years earlier, in 1917, mutinies and strikes had heralded what might now be judged the most cataclysmic event of the twentieth century: the Russian Revolution. The fear it created lingered like a cloud of volcanic ash, altering the world's political climate. To a large extent, Britain's General Strike in 1926 was an almost accidental by-product of the fear of revolution; in a calmer atmosphere, there might have been no catalyst, no spark to ignite the unstable mixture of declining industries and burgeoning ideas about the political uses of industrial strength in a nation that had lost its faith in the inevitability of benign progress and was struggling to recover its status as the world's superpower.

Winston Churchill, who was to draw down the iron curtain across Europe after the Second World War, defined this era as 'The Aftermath', of war as well as of revolution, in which 'a poisoned Russia; a Russia of armed hordes smiting not only with a bayonet and with cannon, but accompanied and preceded by swarms of typhus-bearing vermin ... slew the bodies of men, and political doctrines ... destroyed the health and even the soul of nations'.[4]

British politicians watched anxiously as the European political landscape was redrawn. War, revolution and the spread of democracy toppled emperors, kings and governments across the continent. The February Revolution in Russia had been a welcome end to a corrupt and despotic tradition. 'A spring-tide of joy has broken out all over Europe,' the Labour leader Ramsay MacDonald had declared. On May Day 1917, seventy thousand Clydeside workers marched in support of the provisional government in Russia. But in October that year, the Bolsheviks had captured power; and in July 1918 in Ekaterinburg, the Czar and his family, first cousins to George V, who had denied them asylum in England, were murdered.

In Britain support for the revolutionaries now became muted. For a time the Russian civil war, in particular its expansion into Poland, had appeared to threaten peace in Europe. In Germany, Kaiser Wilhelm, another of George V's cousins, abdicated and Communist uprisings burgeoned in another year of revolution. By the mid-1920s the exigencies of the Versailles peace treaties, with their demand for financial reparations, had bankrupted the German economy. In Italy, in October 1922, in response to a general strike, Mussolini became the first European Fascist leader. And, having occupied and then retreated from the coalfields of the Ruhr in order to take in kind the reparations Germany could not pay in cash, France fell to the Left at the election of 1924.

The people's century in Britain had begun with the formation of a workers' party, initially called the Labour Representation Committee, in 1900. Six years later it became the Labour Party and, although the electoral gains were slender, its share of the vote trebled as the electorate expanded from six million in 1910 to twenty-one million in the 'khaki' election of 1918. A grateful nation returned the Lloyd George Coalition by a landslide: just sixty-three Labour MPs were returned for a 22 per cent share of the vote: a tenth of the seats for a fifth of the vote. It was by no means certain, despite being the biggest of the parties of the Left, that Labour's arguments for parliamentary Socialism would capture the new electorate. And it was not only the Conservative classes that were disturbed by nightmares of revolution. Fabians like Beatrice Webb, apostles of gradualism who initially questioned the need for a workers' party, agonized over the working class's 'capacity and patience to go peacefully forwards'.[5] Webb reported London gossip among the ruling classes and foreign diplomats who believed that great hardship and poverty were certain, and revolution itself possible.

In 1918 the Labour Party adopted a Fabian programme, 'Labour and the New Social Order', built on a minimum wage, democratic control of industry, full employment and redistributive taxation. But by 1922, Ramsay MacDonald, was toying with the idea of some kind of centrist grouping with the Lloyd George Liberals to isolate his party's left wing. Some saw in MacDonald's aristocratic charm another Kerensky, whose attempt to create a liberal democracy in Russia had been swept away by Bolshevism. They feared his ambition for a new progressive party was, like Kerensky's, also doomed to fall to the fervour of the authentic working classes. Such alarm was only exacerbated by the creation in 1920, on the instructions of Lenin, of the Communist Party of Great Britain.

Men back from a war to which many had been reluctantly conscripted understood organization better, had become more confident in formulating and seeking their rights and less trusting of authority. King and country had demanded that they be ready to make the ultimate sacrifice; now they wanted the land fit for heroes that they had been promised.

The TUC was originally founded in 1868 as a forum for ideas about trade unions, but had rapidly developed into an organization for lobbying parliament, a process conducted through a parliamentary committee. In 1900, the desire for its own political representation led the TUC to become the main sponsor of the Labour Representation Committee, but it remained little more than a loose federation of unions which met annually. Meanwhile, trade union membership was reaching new peaks: in 1920, a total of 45 per cent of the workforce belonged to a union, a record not reached again until 1974, and six and a half million of them were affiliated through their unions to the TUC, another peak not equalled until after the Second World War. The unions modernized and merged: the Amalgamated Engineering Union was formed in 1921, the Transport and General Workers' Union in 1922 and the National Union of General and Municipal Workers in 1924. By the mid-1920s, despite the rapid decline in union membership that accompanied the slump after 1920, each had well over a quarter of a million members and a corresponding potential to cause severe economic disruption. All of these, however, were overshadowed by the 900,000 members of the Miners' Federation.[6]

In 1920, the same year the Communist Party was launched, the Trades Union Congress decided it needed a stronger centre, and voted to create a General Council, with a permanent general secretary, to impose some element of national coordination on the six and a half million working men and women the TUC represented. In some quarters, this new body appeared a potential rival to Westminster. In 1924 an ambitious young electrician from Liverpool, Walter Citrine, became deputy general secretary, and within a year the early death of the general secretary, Fred Bramley, saw him promoted to the top job. Citrine, a man of spats and briefcases, was born the youngest of six children of a hospital nurse and a sailor with an appetite for drink that left his son a lifelong teetotaller. Sailors were not paid between voyages and the Citrine family was often poor; Walter left school at twelve, joined the electricians' union in 1911 and within three years had become a full-time official. 'Tall, broad-shouldered, with the manners and clothes and way of speaking of a superior bank clerk', was Beatrice Webb's rather lofty description of him in 1927, although she also acknowledged that he was the TUC's first 'really able' general secretary. 'He is loquacious, naively vain and very disputatious, self-conscious and sensitive ... expects too much relative to his faculties.'[7]

At a time when parliamentary democracy seemed unresponsive to working-class aspirations for a greater share in the country's prosperity, ideas for alternative ways of reflecting the national will – most of which started by considering the question of control of the means of production – were being eagerly debated. Guild Socialists argued for ownership through craft or trade unions. Syndicalists, who like Guild Socialists rejected the Marxist model of state ownership, favoured ownership through industry-wide unions, an idea that for the first quarter of the twentieth century was fashionable across Europe and the United States.

To men faced with hostile employers in whose interests government worked, 'Direct Action' – strikes and demonstrations – to achieve working-class objectives was an appealing prospect. Early in 1920, the TUC allied with Labour MPs and individual trade unions to try to stop the government sending arms to Poland to use against the Bolshevik regime in Russia. The campaign opened with the London dockers refusing to load a ship, the *Jolly George*. No arms were sent, and the unions claimed a victory. Uniting both industrial and political wings of the Labour movement, a 'council of action' was set up that declared the 'industrial power of the organized workers' would be used to defeat any military plans. More councils of action, regarded by the Communists as embryonic Soviets, sprang up around the country. At a meeting in Downing Street, the trade unionists told Lloyd George that they would not only oppose the shipping of arms and equipment, but war itself, and said in terms: 'It is not merely a political action, but an action representing the full force of Labour.'[8] Later in the month a special TUC delegate conference gave unanimous approval for the use of industrial power to win world peace, accepting that it 'transcends any claim in connection with wages or hours of labour'.

England was developing a bad conscience about its heroes,

home from the war to a land where too many of them found only low wages, poor housing and limited opportunities for education. The Christian economist R. H. Tawney was applauded for his book *The Acquisitive Society*, indicting the unjust and immoral capitalist world. A handful of Hilaire Belloc's 'Distributionists', who rejected both Socialist and capitalist models in favour of universal and equal property ownership, retired to the country to live on three acres and a cow. Disappointingly for Belloc, they were artists rather than the urban poor he had envisaged.

In the years from 1919, a bewildering number and variety of strikes by workers responding to inflation and the postwar boom soured the country's early euphoric days of peace. Three times as many working days were lost to industrial action between 1919 and 1921 as in the years before the war, which had themselves been unusually disrupted. Many believed they were living in a revolutionary era that must be approaching a climax. A 'general' strike in Glasgow provoked riots; a crowd put at sixty thousand gathered outside the City Hall in George Square, the police charged and the strikers fought back with bricks, bottles and iron bars. One of the strike leaders was felled by a blow from a police baton as he emerged from City Hall. Terrified that the revolution had actually begun and fearing the Scottish regiment based in Glasgow might mutiny, Lloyd George's government swiftly despatched troops from England.

Although there was rarely such violence after Glasgow's 'Bloody Friday', railway workers, dockers, miners and engineers were all engaged in industrial disputes in the following two years. But there was no real enthusiasm for revolution among trade union leaders. J. H. (Jimmy) Thomas, who was general secretary of the National Union of Railwaymen from 1918 to 1931 and Labour MP for Derby from 1910, was the foremost exemplar of the workers' tribune who managed to be both militant and conciliatory. He managed more or less to maintain his members' confidence while convincing successive governments that he was doing all he could to bring peace. Clever, ambitious, calculating, a minister in Lloyd George's wartime Coalition, in 1919 he even made a film for the new cinema audiences to explain the NUR's demands as it threatened a national rail strike. Thomas's career ended in humiliation in the 1930s. He was one of only three Labour MPs who agreed to serve in Ramsay MacDonald's National Government, but was found guilty of leaking budget secrets for financial gain and forced to leave the Commons in disgrace. In a similar mould, Frank Hodges, the secretary of the Miners' Federation from 1918 to 1924, served on the first of the postwar inquiries into the coal industry, and became a Labour MP and minister in the first Labour government, after which he abandoned trade union politics altogether. Like Thomas, he was more interested in power than in standing on political principle, and he believed power was better exercised through Parliament than through industrial strength.

Other trade unionists, like Ernest Bevin, had less faith in the Labour movement's political leaders. Born in 1881 in the Exmoor village of Winsford, the illegitimate son of a widow with five older children, Bevin was only eight when his mother died; at eleven he went to work in Bristol and over the next twenty years was slowly drawn into trade union activity as a way of securing better pay and a little more security in the uncertain world of casual dock labour. Within a year of joining the dockers' union, this bull-like man with a sharp brain and a hard-headed negotiator's skill had become a union organizer; he made his name nationally in 1920 as the 'dockers' KC', arguing his members' case before a wages inquiry. His advocacy won their biggest pay rise for thirty years. 'The great struggle of my own people has been my university,' he told the triumphant dockers at the end of the inquiry. 'I do not decry education. I lament the lack of it and I curse the other class for monopolising it.'[9] In 1922, from a disparate assortment of dockers' unions and other, local, unions, Bevin created the mighty Transport and General Workers' Union.

Trade union mergers were encouraged by, and often followed, a similar trend of rationalization and mergers in industry. The exception was coal. Underinvestment, inefficiency and industrial militancy resulted in an industry that was once the powerhouse of the Industrial Revolution being unable to meet the challenge from the rest of the world. In a series of government inquiries triggered by industrial disputes, its ills were well analysed. But there were no leaders, whether among the employers, the workers or the politicians, who combined a willingness to think afresh about the industry's future with the power to change its direction. As a result it became the focus for many of the country's discontents, a reservoir of bitterness and poverty on one side and of intransigence and ultimate extinction on the other, the cockpit of the nation's political extremes.

Nearly a million men worked in the country's three thousand pits. The danger and discomfort of life underground and the meagre rates of pay earned by some, although not all, miners were a national embarrassment; the terraced houses that mining families rented, often from the company that employed them, were, one inquiry declared, 'a reproach to our civilisation'.[10] Many years later one miner, Max Goldberg, remembered the detail with painful clarity:

> You had a tap behind the door which you put a bucket underneath, you had the so-called pantry with one stone slab only, you walked out of the street in to the room which was paving ... which you put sand down over; a small room at the side and then you had a spiral staircase, and when you went up you went from one large bedroom into a small one, and there was no banister, nothing. It was just like a hole in the floor. And then if you wanted to use the conveniences, so called, you had to go out the back, go up the steps and walk about fifteen or twenty yards and carry a bucket of water with you to the toilet as well.[11]

The squalid houses were packed into confined spaces and narrow valleys, in a dark monoculture that offered few other employment possibilities and no cushion in times of hardship. Geographically, another miner, Jim Evans, recalled, it was just as barren:

The valley we were living in, the mountains were rising very, very sharply, it was the top end of the valley. Trees were unknown in the top end of the Rhymney valley, the river was black carrying the coal dust and the sewerage down the river, fish were unknown in the river. The houses were infested with blackpads, beetles, you just couldn't get rid of them, you could put your gin traps down and powders and you would be doing it every day of the year, but if you'd get up in the middle of the night and go downstairs, switch a light on, the floor would be covered.[12]

In each district there would usually be only one employer. When the coal ran out or became too expensive to mine, the only alternative was to move to find new work. In the early years of the twentieth century, men came from all over Europe to work in South Wales. Within thirty years, many were forced to move again to the new coalfields in the Midlands, sometimes leaving their families behind. The industry was without shelter from the vagaries of rival foreign trade, and the owners lacked the vision, and often the resources, to make the investment that might have lifted productivity to the level that would enable it to compete on the world market. The importance of solidarity for survival in the pits, the shared danger at work and hardship at home, the stark division between labour and capital, and the lack of anything else to do made God and Socialism popular and often overlapping sources of solace.

Unusually, in the newly centralized trade union world, the Miners' Federation was still controlled by powerful district or county federations which, although strengthening the weakest against the strongest in their national negotiations, also hampered efficient decision-making at the top. On the employers' side, the only recent concession to rational reorganization in the industry was the formation of a Mine Owners' Association, which was dominated by the least profitable and most conservative of the owners. Nonetheless they also negotiated on behalf of the large-scale owners and industrialists such as Lord Londonderry and Sir Alfred Mond, later Lord Melchett, who was already restructuring the chemical industry to create the great conglomerate, ICI. These relics of a tired industry, hard-faced owners with shrinking dividends and callused miners whose only weapon was collective action in defence of a decent rate for a terrible job, rocked back and forth on a narrow see-saw of wages versus profits that demanded frequent government intervention.

Under emergency regulations during the war, the government had taken control of the coal industry and pooled both the output and the income from all the pits; nationalization, a specific objective in the new Labour Party programme, appeared a logical next step. In 1919, the miners put state ownership of the pits at the top of a list of demands that also included a six-hour working day and a 30 per cent pay rise. Lloyd George, whose Coalition was dominated by Conservatives, successfully batted the proposal to a Royal Commission into the industry's future. It was to be chaired by a judge, Sir John Sankey. Although the Sankey Commission, which took evidence in a lofty red and gilt hall in the House of Lords, was billed as 'capitalism on trial', the jury reached no verdict. The Commission was equally balanced between miners and pit owners, with three economists, Sidney Webb, R. H. Tawney and the exotic and appropriately named Sir Leo Chiozza Money, all sympathetic to the miners' cause, balanced by three industrialists who were not. Unsurprisingly, they were unable to agree on the industry's future. Three different reports were produced, and that was only on the question of miners' pay and hours; after a ballot, the miners supported Sankey's personal, intermediate, position: a seven-hour day to be cut to six hours in July 1921 if economically possible, a wage increase of two shillings a day and a levy of a penny a ton to improve the housing and amenities of the mining districts. (In many areas, pithead baths and miners' welfare halls dated from this era.)

In its most controversial aspect, the nature of future ownership of the coal industry, a narrow majority made up of the miners, economists and Sankey himself supported nationalization: but the

owners and the industrialists found it 'detrimental to the development of the industry and to the economic life of the country' and
refused to sanction it. This was Lloyd George's excuse to condemn
the Commission's report to a dusty corner of Whitehall. The miners
got their pay rise, there was no strike, but despite a 'mines for the
nation' campaign launched by Labour and the TUC, nothing more
was done to promote nationalization; for the miners, it came to
be regarded as the only solution to the industry's problems.

Although many of the miners' county leaders were as solid and
unromantic as any TUC bureaucrat, South Wales had thrown up
radical and Marxist leaders since the turn of the century. The
mining community of Maerdy in the Rhondda Valley was so
famous as the centre of Communist activity that it was known as
Little Moscow. Pay rates here were marginally higher than elsewhere, allowing activists to take home a living wage for four days'
work, leaving three days for campaigning. Maerdy became a centre
for a Communist front organization, the new National Minority
Movement. In the 1970s, Max Goldberg recorded his memories for
the South Wales coalfield community oral history project: 'We
were young and romantic about the situation, we thought the
revolution was coming and we used to be on the mountainside
learning to speak, learning to address meetings, we were actually
fitted up with field telephones, we were going to help the Red
Army and our own Red Army.'

Syndicalist ideas were gradually giving way to Communist
influence, which it is now clear was liberally sustained by cash from
Moscow; but *The Miners' Next Step*, co-written in 1912 by Noah
Ablett, one of the leading figures of the South Wales coalfield, and
a young miner called Arthur Cook, remained an influential blueprint for the syndicalist objective of the capture of an industry by
its workers. Cook, the son of a soldier from Somerset, had been a
'Sunday boy', a part-time Baptist preacher, and his long and
emotional political speeches never lost the rhythms of the evangelist. After a course at the Central Labour College, the Socialist
alternative to trade-union-dominated Ruskin College in Oxford,

Cook became what the Home Office later described as 'an agitator of the worst sort'.[13] Although never a Communist himself, in 1924 he was to unseat the moderate Frank Hodges as secretary of the Miners' Federation, on the casting vote of the Communist leader of the Welsh miners, Arthur Horner.

The confusion of industrial with political objectives in these years of instability was taken as further evidence of the revolutionary intentions of some at least of Britain's Labour leaders. Early in 1920, for example, with a national rail strike threatening in Britain, the cabinet secretary Sir Maurice Hankey wrote from the peace talks in Paris to his deputy Tom Jones in London that there was 'red revolution and blood and war at home and abroad!'.[14]

Jones, the son of a Welsh shopkeeper who grew up among miners and steelworkers, plays a Boswellian role in the story of government and workers in these revolutionary years. He was to serve three prime ministers, from Lloyd George to Ramsay Mac-Donald, on the closest of terms. He brought to them a wide range of contacts in political and academic circles, an intuitive sympathy for the aspirations and demands of the industrial working classes (he became, discreetly, a Labour sympathizer), and a robust independence of mind. Throughout his time at No. 10, he kept a diary filled with gossip and sharp observation, a fluent commentary in which, not unnaturally, he is the god in the machine – writer of speeches, deviser of compromises, the ultimate Jeeves to every prime minister's bungling Wooster.

It was typical of his range of acquaintance that among his friends Jones included the earnest godparents of the Labour Party and founders of the Fabians, Beatrice and Sidney Webb, whose long married partnership was devoted to reducing working-class grievances to statistics that could be turned into programmes for reform. Sidney, short and neat with a pedant's goatee beard, wrote Labour's 1918 programme, 'Labour and the New Social Order'. Beatrice, in her exhaustive diaries, described Jones at about this time: 'He is undistinguished-looking, short and stumpy, with badly fitting clothes, homely manners and speech, the very antithesis of the model civil servant.'[15] But she liked his refusal to join in the circus of protocol, the presentation to the King and the annual invitations to the Buckingham Palace garden party.

Jones was impatient with Lloyd George's Conservative ministers, few of whom had any idea of a graduated response to industrial disputes and who talked wildly of military preparations. 'How many airmen are there available for the revolution?' Lloyd George, not entirely tongue-in-cheek, asked the Chief of Air Staff, Sir Hugh Trenchard in 1921.[16] Parliament approved a new Emergency Powers Act under which the government could deploy the military and imprison without trial. If wages had not been rising ahead of the cost of living, unrest might have been a great deal worse. When the postwar boom gave way to slump early in 1921, the reversal in wage increases that followed was calculated by the *Economist* to have eroded the earlier gains by three-quarters. Unemployment rose above a million at the end of 1920, and did not fall below that figure for the next twenty years. For those out of work, unemployment benefit – recently extended by Lloyd George – was still available only to the insured and only for short periods, and was paid at half the average wage. Dependants received just five shillings a week for a wife and a shilling for each child. After that, only locally funded and means-tested Poor Law relief was available, at varying but always inadequate rates. Behind trade unionism's battle for job security and a living wage lay more often desperation than a thirst for revolution.

From their disappointed demands for nationalization in 1919 until their final defeat at the end of 1926, miners in particular saw themselves not only as victims of an unjust system of ownership that produced poverty wages and intolerable living conditions, but in the vanguard of a class struggle that with courage, determination and solidarity might transform Britain's politics. They were not only pioneers; they were also the most powerful of the legions of the dispossessed, and therefore entitled to demand support from other trade unions. Even the miners, alone, could not overthrow the system: but if, through concerted action by other workers, it became impossible to import or transport coal at the same time as domestic production was stopped, then the economic threat would force the government to concede the workers' demands. The Triple Alliance of miners, dockers and railwaymen was first instigated in 1914 but fell into abeyance during the war years. In 1920, the threat of united action was revived.

At first, however, postwar prosperity and government influence staved off confrontation. The export price for British coal was at an unprecedented height. The government, still controlling the industry, could sanction the 1919 wages claim approved by the Sankey Commission. The next year a second claim went in, this time supported by the dockers and the railwaymen in the first postwar invocation of the Triple Alliance. The government intervened and secured a temporary settlement. By the time this expired in March 1921, profitability in the mines had collapsed and the government declared it was time to divest itself of its wartime responsibilities for coal as it already had for railways. The coal owners, faced with self-reliance, resorted as always to a simple formula: cut the cost of production – lower wages, longer hours. The miners refused to accept the new terms, and on 1 April 1921, the day after government control ended, a lockout began. The miners were fighting not only against pay cuts of up to 50 per cent in areas where profitability was in sharp decline, like South Wales, but also in support of what was in effect the substructure of nationalization: a national pay scale, which would require a national profits pool that would support unprofitable pits, and a national wages board.[17]

For the second time, the Triple Alliance was invoked. The miners called on the dockers and the railwaymen to bring Britain to a standstill: a strike of all three was called for 12 April. The government responded by declaring a state of emergency; but it also offered a subsidy to support the price of coal for a limited period, and reopened negotiations. The strike was delayed; and at the last moment the conciliatory Frank Hodges, the miners' secretary, appeared to hint at an opening for negotiation on the contentious issue of district wages, leaving the question of a national profits pool for subsequent settlement. But his executive refused Lloyd George's invitation to a meeting. When the dockers and railmen called on them to reconsider, the miners demanded that their allies call out their own members, to 'get on t'field', if they wanted the right to intervene. The allies said there would be no strike unless the miners would negotiate, and the 'general' strike was called off in bitter acrimony. Black Friday, 15 April 1921, was branded on the souls of all good trade unionists as the moment when a timid leadership sacrificed the miners and, with them, the supreme virtue of solidarity. 'It has been a crucifixion,' Bevin was to say four years later. 'We cannot go through it again.'[18]

The miners stayed out until June. When they returned, their pay was reduced, in many districts halved. Unskilled workers in the pits at the bottom of the pay league, like Bristol and Durham, were left with less than 7 shillings a shift, with an average five shifts worked a week, which meant weekly earnings well below the average wage of £2 16s (about £60 in today's money). Even cabinet ministers were shaken. 'A drop from 80s to 44s is a bit thick,' commented Dr Macnamara, the Minister for Labour, of the worst of the rates. Later that year there were more pay cuts in engineering and in the shipyards. Trade union strength was being sapped by recession. Industrial action was dramatically curtailed. In 1921, eighty-five million days were lost; by 1924 only eight million.

In 1921, Black Friday averted a general strike; but the episode was a defining moment for the politicians, for the trade unions and for the government machine.

INITIALLY, Lloyd George's attitude had been relaxed. According to Tom Jones, he was confident that the railmen's leader Jimmy Thomas, at least, wanted no revolution – 'He wants to be prime minister.'[19] Lloyd George also enjoyed teasing his Conservative coalition colleagues. But in the final days before the collapse of the strike threat, talk of machine-gunning strikers from the air no longer seemed such a good joke. Preparations were made to bring battalions back from the nearer corners of the Empire: Egypt and

Malta. Decisions were taken about troop dispositions. Reservists were to be called up; intelligence reports from the Scottish coalfields indicated a collapse in law and order. 'We need 18 battalions to hold London,' the War Minister Sir Laming Worthington-Evans said gloomily. Hyde Park and Regent's Park were turned into vehicle depots, and soldiers camped in Kensington Gardens. At the behest of the Chief of the Imperial General Staff, a defence force was created which was said, improbably, to have attracted seventy-five thousand volunteers. It was to be the haves against the have-nots, the 'masters' against the 'hands'. Stockbrokers were referred to so often as a loyal and fighting class by one minister in Cabinet that Tom Jones fancied battalions of them poised, sword in one hand, furled umbrella in the other, in every town. The tension was reflected in popular culture. A character in *Middle of the Road*, a novel by the former official war journalist Sir Philip Gibbs published in 1922 (and in its fourth edition by 1923), declared: 'This clash has got to come. We must get the working classes back to their kennels. Back to cheap labour. Back to discipline. Otherwise we're done.'[20]

Twice, the threat of united trade union action had brought the government to the negotiating table; but however anxious government ministers felt about imminent revolution, the trade unions were uncomfortably aware that when the Triple Alliance had finally been tested, solidarity had evaporated like mist on a summer morning. Union leaders began to search for ways of strengthening their powers of cooperation and coordination. Theories ran along two paths: either the unions must find more formal ways of working together, through a strengthened TUC in the first instance; or – in a revival of syndicalist optimism – they must simply merge into One Big Union, a great weight of workers to swing like a wrecking ball against the employers.

In Moscow, Lenin and his propagandists, although more dubious than the popular press in Britain about the revolutionary instincts of the current generation of trade union leaders, nonetheless remained convinced that in organized labour lay Britain's revolutionary potential. But they would not begin at the top. Communist strength in industry, where it existed at all, existed on the shop floor; from there it must work upwards until it captured the leadership. The workers would 'thrust aside ... the old reactionary bureaucrats'[21] through two new organizations that cut across existing union structures. First came the Unemployed Workers' Movement and then, at the end of 1923, in respectful echo of its Bolshevik model, the National Minority Movement. 'We stand for the formation of a real General Council [of the TUC] that shall have the power to direct, unite and co-ordinate all struggles and activities of the trade unions,' the Minority Movement's secretary Harry Pollitt explained. For the right, this synchronicity of strategic thinking between Communists and the industrial arm of the Labour movement only confirmed their fears of revolutionary intent among the workers.

The idea of a General Council for the TUC had first come from Ernest Bevin, partly because he still believed industrial action offered better prospects of success than the work of the movement's largely undistinguished political leaders. But he was also aware that his members were more vulnerable than fellow workers on the railways and particularly in the mining industry, where it was all but impossible to bring in blacklegs to replace a striking workforce. In the docks, it was the work of moments to fire one man and replace him with another willing to take lower pay.

After Black Friday, it became received wisdom that a final clash between capital and labour would come. Bevin was looking for alternatives: he was already raising the possibility of cooperation rather than confrontation with management. But he felt progress would be slow.

The struggle for economic possession is bound to come. How shall it come? Will public opinion welcome an expansion of possession and with it the extension of responsibility among the workers in industry? Or will public opinion, especially among the employing classes, be negative at best, at worst retrogressive and obstinate ... Experience has driven me to the conclusion that we shall be drifting in the next five years towards a great upheaval.[22]

Only an elected Labour government could be expected to shift the power of the state from support for the employer to support for the worker. Industrial failure and economic depression strengthened the appeal of politics. But trade union votes were not enough to win a majority in the House of Commons. For that, it needed a broader, less class-based appeal. Labour's weakest link was its inability to distance itself in the public perception from Communism. In vain did it, in 1920, report after a visit to Moscow that the Bolshevik regime was a dictatorship, in 1921 reject applications from the Communist Party to affiliate, in 1924 proscribe dual membership of the Communist and Labour Parties and request trade unions not to send Communist delegates to Labour Party conferences. For against all that, one Labour candidate, John Maclean, had been Moscow's consul in Glasgow, and in 1922 two Communist MPs, Shapurji Saklatvala and J. T. Walton Newbold, were elected with Labour support and sat on the Labour benches. It was thus all too easy to imply a shared outlook between Communism and Socialism. Newspapers, particularly the ultra-Tory *Morning Post*, referred to Labour MPs as Socialists; few newspapers attempted a distinction between Socialism and Communism.

James Ramsay MacDonald, who in 1922 became for the second time Labour's parliamentary leader, was bitterly aware that the fear of Bolshevism which coloured all political life was restricting the prospects for the development of Labour. Born in 1866, the illegitimate son of a Scottish crofter, MacDonald became first a clerk and then a journalist and political activist. Elected for Leicester in 1906, he came to national prominence as chairman of the Labour Party in 1911. But as a leading opponent of the war, he like many others lost his seat in the surge of postwar patriotism that gave Lloyd George's Coalition a landslide in 1918. Not until 1922 was he re-elected, this time for Aberavon, in the year when Labour became the second-largest party in the House of Commons and the official Opposition. This election marked another significant milestone in the party's development, for it ceased to be the near-exclusive preserve of MPs sponsored by trade unions. MacDonald was one of thirty-two Labour members out of one hundred and forty-two who had entered Parliament not from a background of trade union activity, but through the Independent Labour Party. Many of them, like Sidney Webb, came from professional backgrounds. Their influence was to turn the party away from a party of class preoccupied with industrial matters; but in so doing, it exposed deep divisions about its wider objectives.

Neither in the public mind, nor in its own, had the Labour Party reconciled its search for democratic legitimacy with the way it had grown from the body of the industrial trade unions. The 1920s established it, a party founded to promote the interests of the organized working class, as a political force committed to nationalization at home and internationalism abroad, strictly within the confines of the constitution. But in a party almost equally divided at Westminster between the radical left and a pragmatic trade union wing, the debate about whether its first loyalty was to the nation or to the trade unions, and whether working-class interests were served better by defeating capitalism or by managing it, had barely begun.

MacDonald was already fifty-six when he became leader of the Opposition again in 1922. He was widowed, often lonely and prone to gloomy introspection. But he was also incomparably the best parliamentarian in the Labour Party, charismatic and fluent, a powerful speaker in the radical cause on foreign affairs. On domestic policy, however, he was notably cautious. He was orthodox on the economy, a convinced gradualist about wider reform. Change was coming for the working classes, but only by inches. His party, he believed, must extend its appeal in order to win power. He became Labour's self-appointed emissary to the new middle classes.

*

THE FIRST WORLD WAR had changed everything – and nothing. The distribution of income and opportunity remained grotesquely disproportionate. A quarter of the population owned almost three-quarters of the capital; one-tenth took 42 per cent of the national income and of those, just 1.5 per cent took more than a fifth of it. Only one child in ten at elementary school went on to secondary education. Less than one in a hundred children from elementary school went on to a university.

Yet even though between the censuses of 1911 and 1921 there had been only the most marginal shift in the ownership of Britain's wealth, a new, elastic middle class was becoming an influential political constituency. It stretched from clerks to clerics, drapers and bank managers to professors and lawyers. Many lived in a new suburbia, deserting the Victorian terraces of the inner cities for modern, comfortable houses built on green-field sites. From there, they commuted back into the city centre on newly electrified train lines and motor-buses. Christened 'By-Pass variegated' by the cartoonist Osbert Lancaster, these new housing developments drained the population from the centres of Britain's cities. Inner London declined by around two hundred thousand, while Greater London grew by a million between 1921 and 1931. The new suburbanites were soon isolated and ignorant of the conditions of their old working-class neighbours, who were still a decade away from large-scale attempts by local government to improve their living conditions.[23] Stanley Baldwin was serving his second term as Prime Minister when, in Dundee in 1925, he saw slums for the first time. 'We first visited some slum houses. I never saw such a sight. Oddly enough I have never been in real slum houses, and I as near as two pins sat down and howled: the whole thing came to me with such force. Five and six in one room. Think of the children!'[24]

The new suburban classes, not rich, not poor, but careful of correct behaviour, were ambitious for self-improvement. Pelmanism was the rage, offering mental training for the go-ahead by teaching focus and concentration. A new kind of newspaper sprang into existence to meet their interests. The *Daily Mail* was the first of these, founded in 1896. Then came the *Daily Express* in 1900 and the *Daily Mirror* in 1903, each distinguished by banner headlines and, in a revolutionary development pioneered at the *Daily Mirror*, by the extensive use of photographs, often informal. The royal family was established as a favourite subject matter; there were features for women and columns about cooking. They were partisan papers of the right – the *Mirror* only moved to the left in the 1930s – often critical of the Conservative government, alarmist as an act of policy, and interested in the nooks and crannies, the kitchens and motor-cars, of people leading ordinary lives. These were newspapers, one High Tory observed in horror, 'produced by office boys for office boys'. Another described them as 'an attempt to ensure that all discussion was low'. They were also, as the *Mail*'s founders proclaimed, the 'Voice of Empire in London Journalism'. By the mid-1920s, the *Mail* and the *Express* were the two highest-circulation national newspapers; in 1930 the *Mail* was selling nearly two million copies a day.

For a rapidly growing number, there was also the infant British Broadcasting Company. The new medium of wireless, promoted by the manufacturers of radio receivers, was launched under the aegis of the Postmaster General at the start of 1923 and funded by licence fees paid by the owners of the new wireless sets. Its success was immediate, but its future was uncertain. The initial licence was for three years only. Progressive thinkers wanted to capture for the public good this bewildering technological miracle. (When the Archbishop of Canterbury, Randall Davidson, and his wife first heard it, Lady Davidson inquired whether it was necessary to leave a window open; and when the Archbishop asked to hear a piano solo, John Reith, the Company's managing director, simply rang the office and asked them to play Schubert's 'Marche Militaire'.)

Reith, not yet forty, a driven, chippy, difficult Scot with an arrogant confidence in his own judgement, was in the midst of his extraordinary single-handed effort to shape the BBC's future. He believed strongly in the inherent possibilities of the Company as a vehicle for 'giving people what we think they need', and defended its monopoly on the grounds that without it, commercial pressure would only force the broadcasters to give people what they thought they wanted. By the start of 1926, not only was the BBC's future at stake, Reith too was already angling for 'the next big job' – Viceroy of India, perhaps, or ambassador in Washington – and for that he needed political supporters at the very top. Many Conservatives, as well as the newspaper proprietors, thought the BBC should develop in the commercial sector. The debate hung in the balance, an unspoken consideration in the tense negotiations during the General Strike, unresolved until the end of 1926. In the meantime, the Company presented itself as the guardian of the public interest, struggling against a hostile newspaper industry that feared free news, instantly transmitted, would destroy their own product. Only after prolonged negotiation had the BBC contracted to broadcast nightly bulletins from material supplied by news agencies. These, together with a mix of music and drama, were the staple of its broadcasts.

TECHNOLOGICAL ADVANCE, industrial decline and economic change, set against a background of continental regicide and revolution: in this unsettled world, many Britons wanted something safe to hold on to. The modest figure of Stanley Baldwin turned out to be it. Baldwin was leader of the Conservative Party from 1923 until 1937, served as Prime Minister for eight of those years, and was deputy prime minister in a National Government for four more.

The manner in which this prosperous businessman, already in his fifties but with only fifteen years' experience as an MP, became party leader and Prime Minister, was a powerful indication of a new world, a world where the party of the right was the party of capitalism, 'full of hard-faced men', as Baldwin himself remarked disparagingly, 'who look as if they've done very well out of the war'. Opposing them, Labour MPs were perceptibly smaller and less well fed.

Baldwin had played a leading part in the collapse of the Lloyd George Coalition in 1922. Andrew Bonar Law became Prime Minister, but after less than six months in office was forced by ill-health to resign as both Prime Minister and Conservative Party leader. Baldwin had just two years' experience as a cabinet minister, and was undoubtedly the junior of the two candidates for the succession. He had a reputation for silence in Cabinet, and when he did speak he did so with a curious, disengaged style unkindly caught by Tom Jones in the early days. 'After a very friendly greeting, his face started twitching, he rolled his tongue about, and looking away into space he began...'[25] Although his admirers thought he had the essential qualities of honesty, simplicity and balance, the more flamboyant politicians thought he lacked greatness. To Churchill, he was simply 'a great turnip'.

The man who expected to succeed, the grandest old man of Conservative politics, was the Marquess Curzon of Kedleston, the Foreign Secretary. Baldwin, who had once described Curzon as 'giving him the kind of greeting a corpse would give an undertaker', had told a friend he would rather have a one-way ticket to Siberia than be prime minister. Curzon certainly assumed he would succeed, with Baldwin acting as his deputy in the Commons. But the final choice lay with the King, and he thought otherwise. Perhaps the decisive factor was a memorandum that might have been interpreted as the unofficial advice of the dying Bonar Law. In a note written by J. C. C. Davidson, a Conservative MP close to both Bonar Law and Baldwin and sent to George V at Aldershot where he was holidaying in the wooden bungalow described as the Royal Pavilion, the King was told:

> The prospect of [Lord Curzon] receiving deputations as Prime Minister from the Miners' Federation or the Triple Alliance, for example, is capable of causing alarm for the future relations between the Government and Labour − between moderate and less moderate opinions ... Lord Curzon is regarded in the public eye as representing that section of privileged Conser-

vatism which has its value but which in this democratic age cannot be too assiduously exploited.[26]

The monarch, who after the 1912 miners' strike had anonymously sent 1,000 guineas to alleviate hardship among the strikers' families, chose the man who would become the apostle of consensus over the voice of tradition.

The recognition that an unelected politician could no longer lead Britain was reached only reluctantly, a forced acknowledgement, by the party of tradition, of irresistible change. But Davidson's memorandum illustrates that the impossibility of having a prime minister in the House of Lords was only one of several considerations. Baldwin, the Midlands businessman who had always taken a paternal interest in the affairs of his employees, had already begun to establish himself as a communicator, a politician who could reach out to the new electorate. Curzon, a former Viceroy of India who had not fought an election for twenty-five years, imperious even to his colleagues, lacked every necessary quality for the coming battle to shape and control a mass democracy. He was, one obituarist was to note, a man who failed to triumph over his own anachronisms.

The King, intensely conservative and alarmed by the republicanism of the trade unions and elements in the Labour Party, took a close and often active interest in the politics of his people. He surveyed with anxiety the 'chaotic and indeed dangerous'[27] state of most countries in Europe. The unhappy fate of his Russian cousins was a salutary lesson that had left him with an acute appreciation of the need to appear in touch with the daily concerns of the people, while being careful always to maintain the mysterious aura of inherited position. Nor was he unaware of the paradox that he, the monarch, was determining the political leadership of his democratic country. His private secretary, Lord Stamfordham, told the editor of the *Times*, Geoffrey Dawson, that 'the King was so far convinced that his responsibility to the country made it almost imperative that he should appoint a Prime Minister from the House of Commons. For were he not to do so ... the country would blame the King for an act which was entirely his own and which proved that [he] was ignorant of, and out of touch with the public.'[28] Curzon remonstrated with the King, angrily dismissing his rival: 'Not even a public figure. A man of no experience. And of the utmost insignificance.'[29] Baldwin's genius was to make insignificance a political asset.

George V had succeeded his father Edward VII in 1910, when he was a comparatively youthful forty-five. In the first fifteen years of his reign he had established himself, in contrast to his father, as a modest, unflashy monarch. He and the Queen disliked large houses, entertaining, and all forms of profligacy (by royal standards) except perhaps racehorses. He cherished an emotional attachment to 'good old England', a recurring theme in his copious diaries. 'Dogmatic and boisterous', Asquith once said of him, George disliked change of all sorts, nearly provoking a constitutional crisis when Baldwin wrote a mildly frivolous account of a parliamentary session suggesting the Commons in the early hours of the morning looked like 'St James's Park at midday. Members were lying about the benches in recumbent position.' This the King thought unacceptable (particularly, he said, since some Members of Parliament were ladies). In a dramatic breach of constitutional etiquette, which dictates that the monarch be excluded from every aspect of Commons proceedings, he instructed the Speaker to keep better order. Baldwin refused to pass on the instruction, and the King backed down. Although more flexible than his fallen European cousins, he shared Baldwin's perception that the first battle in which to engage was the perennial campaign to keep up standards, whether of parliamentary behaviour, court dress or even in the new medium of film. He once personally remonstrated with the headmaster of Eton for showing *The Battleship Potemkin* to the boys. The head's protestations that it was good for them to see new film techniques, even from Soviet Russia, was brusquely dismissed. 'Nonsense,' said the King, himself a former naval officer. 'It is certainly not good for the boys to witness mutinies, especially not naval mutinies!'[30]

In George V, Baldwin was to find an unconscious but important echo. George, the accidental king who became heir apparent only in adulthood, and Baldwin, the unexpected prime minister, shared a modesty of outlook and a commitment to tradition and service. When Baldwin said, in his broadcast on the King's death in 1936 (a broadcast that became a best-selling gramophone record), that in his dedication to duty and to the public interest he had embodied the finest qualities of the nation, he was describing the attributes he most valued in a public figure; and in the peroration, his statement that through the King's example 'men had led better lives in the accomplishment of their daily duties' reflected his own purpose in public life.

If Baldwin trusted the King's moderation in style and thought as 'the bulwark against revolution and tyranny', other more febrile forces wanted to claim him as the figurehead of overt resistance to the threat of Communism. Society grandees muttered disapprovingly of George's lack of charisma. The millionaire Conservative MP and diarist Henry 'Chips' Channon reported gossip about the 'feeling of disappointment and almost resentment' that 'a certain class' felt. 'He is so uninspiring and does nothing to stem the swelling Socialist tide.'[31]

It was in order to stem this 'swelling Socialist tide' that the first British Fascist organization dedicated to 'unswerving loyalty to the King' had recently opened its doors in the London borough of Chelsea. The man who was to become Britain's most notorious Fascist, Oswald Mosley, was still in the Labour Party on his progress across the political spectrum, when on 5 October 1923 the new organization's founder, the twenty-six-year-old Miss Rotha Lintorn-Orman, daughter and granddaughter of army officers, was pictured in the *Daily Sketch* 'watching a new member sign on' to Britain's own Fascisti, 'pledged to oppose all Communistic movements'.

The Fascisti admired Mussolini's fight against Communism, but insisted they borrowed no more than the name from Italy. They claimed to be neither a response to crisis nor a provocation, but a movement to pre-empt disaster by the simple device of upholding the constitution. Their literature, however, framed a choice that exploited the idea of the Left as an alien force whose containment required active intervention: 'The Union Jack or The Red Flag – Which will YOU serve?', issue number 4 of British Fascisti demanded. 'Apathy ... must be overcome NOW before it is too late ... it is not enough to ENCOURAGE patriotism, we must FORCE it on our people ... Bolshevism MUST be smashed. British Fascisti are intolerant of SHAM in affairs of Politics and Government.'[32] Aliens, whether represented by Communists, international finance or just themselves, were the most serious menace to stability. The organization's president was another military man, Brigadier-General R. B. D. Blakeney, whose principal qualification appeared to be the experience of commanding the 3rd Balloon Section in the Boer War. He envisaged Fascism as a kind of scouting movement for grown-ups, helping the whole country prepare to resist 'the swarms from the slums' who were being corrupted by Communism.

There was always an element of overlap between extreme right-wing organizations and parts of the Conservative Party, and critics often alleged even closer involvement, especially among the aristocracy. The relationship between moderate and extreme was a matter of constant dispute on both left and right. The Left energetically portrayed Fascism as a dangerous outcrop of Conservatism, while the British Fascists' staple message alleged that Communism was spreading like dry rot into the heart of Labour. 'Steadily the Communist grip is closing round the body of the Labour movement in Great Britain,' one bulletin of 1924 reported. A rally in Trafalgar Square at the end of that year attracted, according to MI5, about eighteen hundred existing members; MI5 thought it might have recruited as many as three thousand more on that occasion alone, mainly from London, although the organization also boasted twenty county branches. A conflicting report suggests that the organizer of the Trafalgar Square rally, Ormond Winter, a colourful figure who claimed to have been a Soviet agent, recruited just four people, including 'two typists, one of whom he has taken out to dinner'. Winter, however, soon retired to take up training at a racing stable near Newbury. Violently anti-Semitic and xenophobic, the remaining British Fascisti found themselves uncomfortably compromised by the apparent link with Italian Fascism with its implications of foreign control – one of their main complaints about the Communists. Despite dropping the 'i' to become 'Fascists', by the end of 1924 they were crumbling, and a breakaway organization, the National Fascists, had been set up.

The main Fascist activity was to picket, disrupt and if possible prevent Communist meetings and demonstrations. In particular K branch in Hampstead, north London, had attracted the support of members of the disbanded Ulster Volunteers who had opposed Irish home rule and threatened resistance to the British government. These were men with military training, many of whom still had access to arms and a taste for violence and who, according to the MI5 file, thought there was too much talk and not enough action. One of its leading figures – and also the district officer for Chelsea – was William Joyce. It was on a British Fascist mission to disrupt an election meeting held by Shapurji Saklatvala, Communist candidate in Battersea, that Joyce, later the infamous Nazi propagandist Lord Haw Haw, was attacked by a man with a razor and permanently scarred. A fellow Fascist felled his assailant with a blow from a twelve-inch spanner. MI5 monitored this eruption of extremism with distaste. 'This seems a rotten show,' Sir Vernon Kell, secretary of MI5 noted on the file. '[It] has possibilities for harm more than good. We must keep in touch on this.'

THE CONSERVATIVE PARTY that Bonar Law and Baldwin led out of the ruins of the post-First World War coalition was a coalition itself – of enemies of Socialism. The threat was agreed; the question that divided them was the nature of the response to it. Baldwin, in his only budget as Bonar Law's Chancellor of the Exchequer in 1923, had already spelt out his: 'It is no good trying to cure the world by repeating the pentasyllabic French derivative "proletariat".

The English language is in thought the richest in the world. The English language is the richest language in the world in monosyllables. Four words of one syllable each are words which contain salvation for this country and for the whole world. They are, "Faith, Hope, Love and Work".[33] The need to lead and to educate 'a new democracy in a new world' was a constant refrain in Baldwin's speeches of this period. He spoke vividly of democracy approaching 'at a gallop', of being in a race to educate the electorate in the responsibilities of power before it succumbed to the politics of utopia.

Almost unknown beyond Westminster, Baldwin's first move after he became Prime Minister was to establish a public image of himself as a plain man concerned only with straight dealing, motivated not by personal glory but by a sense of service that he had inherited along with his Worcestershire parliamentary seat from his father, a long-serving backbencher. In June 1923, less than a month after his appointment, he told an Oxford audience that to be described as 'honest to the verge of simplicity' would be for him a matter of pride, not insult. He was photographed in tweeds and soft hat in rural surroundings, often with the pipe that was to become such an important prop. Colleagues were scandalized at his ubiquity in the new picture-hungry newspapers; he surely rehearsed poses in front of the mirror, they sneered. But he made a genuine appeal to a vision of England that was particularly alive in the imaginations of the new suburban middle classes in the world the grandees called 'villadom'. He announced that he would rather keep pigs than be prime minister, and, as much by his style as by substance, that he really was thinking what they were thinking: 'The times are new and strange and extraordinarily difficult,' he confessed in November that year.

Baldwin was the first politician to exploit the BBC's potential. He saw in this essentially middle-class tool, where radio receivers were disguised as pieces of furniture, sometimes even rose bowls, and the broadcasts sought to be uplifting, a way of reinforcing the shared identity of citizenship that was the basis of his vision of one nation. In the 1924 general election, in which Ramsay MacDonald was recorded on the platform at a public meeting shouting political slogans, Baldwin made the first studio election broadcast, speaking in intimate tones into people's living-rooms.

Baldwin stressed his honesty and his simplicity in part to distinguish himself from Lloyd George, in whose Cabinet he had briefly served before the Coalition broke up in 1922. However, as well as his well-documented and near-obsessive distaste for everything represented by the man to whom he always referred as the Welsh Goat, there was a strategic consideration. With a Conservative Party on the right of the political spectrum and a Labour Party most of whose membership, if not leadership, was well to the left, there was an opportunity at the centre that Baldwin suspected Lloyd George, more or less divorced from his old Liberal allegiances, was angling to grab. Baldwin was determined to step in first with a 'one nation' Conservative Party to which Disraeli's sense of social purpose had been restored.

In his first conversation with the man who was to become his indispensable deputy cabinet secretary, Tom Jones, Baldwin declared his objectives: the need to achieve stability in Europe in order to reopen Britain's export markets, to maintain trade with Communist Russia despite evidence of Soviet attempts to destabilize the Empire in the Middle and Far East, and finally the need to attend to the welfare of the people, the so-called 'third canon' of Disraeli, inventor of one-nation Toryism. In a speech soon afterwards, Baldwin told his audience: 'I want [the people of this country] to realise that we in the Unionist Party are as anxious as anyone who speaks in the name of Socialism to do all in our power for the betterment of our people ... if there are those who want to fight the class war we will take up the challenge, and will beat them by the hardness of our heads and the largeness of our hearts.'[34]

'Is honesty enough?' pondered Tom Jones in his diary a few months later, after a quiet weekend at Chequers dominated by Mrs Baldwin's conversation about the curtains at Downing Street which had been Gladstone's, and were too short, Mrs Baldwin complained, while the bath – Disraeli's – was too deep. With his quick, lively mind, Jones complemented Baldwin's deliberate and silent ponderings ('Is he thinking, or just wool-gathering?' he wrote impatiently on another occasion). They became an intimate and effective partnership, united by a shared appreciation of the nature and seriousness of the situation that faced the country after more than ten years of industrial unrest, four years of world war, and now economic depression and mass unemployment in the country's Victorian industrial core of coal and iron.

Baldwin was profoundly concerned by the idea of moral crisis, 'a sense of cultural fragility', that he felt had been provoked by the terrible revelations of war. Now that the civilization that had seemed 'to our fathers so secure and permanent' had 'rotted and cracked',[35] he detected a revolutionary climate comparable to that evoked by the French Revolution. He had grown up in a tradition of benevolent paternalism – one of his first gestures as prime minister was to invite employees of the family firm of Baldwin & Sons to Downing Street – and working-class Conservatism, and saw the materialism of Marxian class war and Socialism as forces that could 'destroy the moral standards [of] our people'; by which he meant the working classes. He articulated a widespread anxiety about mass culture and the speed of change, about the elevation of material improvement over moral purposefulness, in language that curiously echoed the Fabians and William Morrisites of his father's generation.

One of Baldwin's objects was to reunite the Conservative Party after the years of coalition with Lloyd George. Baldwin believed himself the antithesis of the unprincipled and immoral Liberal leader – sometimes above party politics altogether. He had once considered ordination, and each morning he and his wife knelt and commended their day to God;[36] and God, he felt, would not have approved the compromises and petty deceits of coalition government. He was determined that his Conservative Party should offer the country the non-Socialist alternative. That meant first bringing together its disparate factions, and then enunciating principles that would draw to it all those 'men of goodwill' of whom he saw himself the spokesman.

Many of his colleagues, like Curzon, thought their new leader merely an empty space in the political firmament. Reconciling them to his leadership was made much harder by the slender achievements of his first government and was almost destroyed as an objective when, at the end of 1923, Baldwin recklessly squandered the handsome parliamentary majority he had inherited from Bonar Law by calling an election in order to secure a popular mandate to reintroduce trade tariffs to protect British industry. It was a policy that united the great majority of his party and distinguished them from the free-trade Liberals. But it did not quite work out as he had intended. Baldwin was left without an overall majority; and although Labour had won only 3 per cent more of the vote than the Liberals, that had secured them comfortably more MPs – 191 to 159, with 258 Conservatives.

Suddenly and quite unexpectedly, the Conservatives had precipitated the very event the party had been most determined to prevent: a Labour government. Churchill, not a politician to underplay a drama, declared it would be 'a serious national misfortune such as has usually befallen great States only on the morrow of defeat in war'. At the Travellers Club, as Tory seats toppled, Tom Jones observed one soon to be ex-MP's wife 'almost beside herself with panic for the fate of [the] country'. The only alternative to allowing Labour to form a minority government would be a coalition with the Liberals, an alliance that Baldwin, destroyer of the last coalition, could hardly seek, and which anyway Asquith, despite 'appeals, threats, prayers from all parts, and from all sort and conditions of men, women and lunatics',[37] rejected. With Beaverbrook's encouragement, Whitehall swirled with intrigue whose sole objective was to replace the leader – last seen, colleagues complained bitterly, sitting in the Commons smoking-room reading the *Strand Magazine* – who had thus so casually endangered the safety of the realm. Plotters in Parliament and Fleet Street even considered approaching the King to appeal for support for an

anti-Labour coalition that would force Baldwin's resignation. Only
the reception of a series of speeches he made in the next few
months, showing his potential as the spokesman for a new and
humane side of the businessman's party, shored up the otherwise
uncertain position of the 'little dud', the man caricatured as 'the
chief patient in the convalescent home'.[38] Instead of resigning,
Baldwin's friends persuaded him, it would be wiser to form a
government and await defeat; in effect, to let Labour into power.

But on the other side of the House, the Opposition was equally
uncertain whether to take this tainted chalice. Labour had been the
official Opposition since 1922, a role that gave the party position
and status. If it now let this opportunity to form a government pass,
it would risk forfeiting its claim to be the alternative political
power. Government, even minority government, was its right and
also its duty. Ramsay MacDonald decided to accept the challenge.
Labour's programme, rather than immediately testing the limits of
what Parliament would take, should be limited to 'moderation and
honesty'. The workers' party would slip its puny body into the
rigid confines of a parliamentary democracy that had been shaped
by generations of use to fit the well-fed shoulders of the capitalist
parties.

Labour's 191 MPs were united by a faith in democracy and
progressive reform, the minimum wage and democratic control of
industry that had been set out in 'Labour and the New Social
Order' in 1918. But these were objectives that could not be achieved
at once. Even if a programme acceptable to all shades of opinion
could be agreed, a minority government could achieve little that
was controversial, particularly when it had no experience of power
beyond the few ageing trade unionists who had served in coalition
with Lloyd George.

MacDonald and his supporters on the centrist wing of his party
appreciated that this was the safe way of introducing Labour to
power, a way to silence what Sidney Webb called 'even the wildest
shouters'. If democracy was seen to be working for the left as well
as the right, a faith in parliamentary institutions would be estab-

lished in the minds of the new electorate. In particular, the wild men in the movement would lose support for revolution; direct action and syndicalism, ideas that had been popular when political power still seemed a mirage, would wither away with the other enthusiasms that undermined Labour's electoral appeal and stoked the extreme right.

For if MacDonald greeted the first Russian revolution in the spring of 1917 with delight, he took a grim warning from subsequent events in Europe, when infant social democracy in Georgia and Hungary, Italy and Germany was violently extinguished either by Communists or the extreme right. He rued Europe's 'furious violence of hate' and tended to equate 'strikes in Yorkshire' with revolution in Portugal. In his first nine months in office he would take no risks. Stability, not revolution, would be his theme.

2

THE INEVITABILITY OF GRADUALNESS

First let me insist on what our opponents habitually ignore, indeed what they seem intellectually incapable of understanding, namely the inevitable gradualness of our scheme for change.

Sidney Webb, Labour Party Conference, 1923

[A Labour government] will not depend on the Fabian Society for their power, they will depend on the men in the mine, the mill and the shipyard, and that is where the bulk of the Communist Party happens to be.

Harry Pollitt, future Communist Party general secretary,
Labour Party Conference, 1921

PREDICTIONS OF ENGLAND's 'final eclipse' were, after all, exaggerated. When, in January 1924, the country's first Labour government took office, the sun still rose, and by its light it could be seen that, far from planning revolution, Labour's new Cabinet was no more radical than the Liberals', from where many of their middle-class recruits had come. The Webbs hosted a 'jolly party – all laughing at the joke of Labour in Office'; the amply endowed former Liberal Lord Haldane – a man who, it was said, could enter a room 'like a whole procession'[1] – persuaded by MacDonald to be Labour's Lord Chancellor, took an even larger trade union cabinet colleague home to try to find a frock-coat to fit him. The rail union leader Jimmy Thomas was said to have told the officials at the Colonial Office where he was to be secretary of state that he was there 'to see there was no mucking about with the British Empire'. And while Mrs Webb, a woman of independent means, formidable brain and tireless industry, busied herself finding a housekeeper, cook and butler for another member of the Cabinet, Ramsay MacDonald, Labour leader for barely a year, was at the palace getting to know the King.

Like the more moderate politicians, George V had been persuaded, not least by his powerful private secretary, a parson's son from Norfolk now created Lord Stamfordham, that it was more dangerous to try to subvert the constitution than to have Labour take office in the constrained circumstances of a minority government. It was the twenty-third anniversary of Queen Victoria's death, the King noted in melancholy reminiscence. 'I wonder what she would have thought of a Labour government.'[2] On his first meeting with his new Prime Minister, he restricted himself to a complaint about the singing of 'The Red Flag' and 'The Marseillaise' at a victory rally. MacDonald, almost as hostile to revolutionary emotions as the King, apologized. 'They had got into the way of singing ['The Red Flag'] . . . by degrees he hoped to break down this habit.'[3] In his diary, MacDonald recorded that the King was 'most friendly' and talked 'most steadily'. At the swearing-in and receiving of the seals of office, it was observed that John Wheatley, the Clydeside MP with the most radical reputation of the new government, went down on *both* knees *and* kissed his monarch's hand.

However, almost immediately a row broke out over the proper attitude to be taken by a radical government to the pomp and circumstance of office. The 'gold lace affair' appeared trivial, but it went to the heart of what Labour was trying to achieve and raised the question of whether the methods it adopted would limit its success. Lord Stamfordham wrote tactfully to point out that the King insisted court dress be worn at official palace functions, recommending Moss Bros as a good place from which to hire it. Lord Haldane later told Beatrice Webb that the King himself had paid for the appropriate court uniforms for the government whips who had become, in the arcane procedure of the Commons, officers of the royal household. Except for Sidney Webb, President of the Board of Trade, whose principles would not allow him to attend any royal function, most of the new ministers happily complied with these sartorial exigencies, and their wives and daughters joined the small social elite of those who had been presented at Court.

The radicals were scandalized that their leaders were playing the establishment game, and in a way that suggested not compromise but capitulation to the mores of a hostile regime. MacDonald was unrepentant. The green and gold court uniform was 'but a part of official pageantry and as my conscience is not on my back, a gold coat means nothing to me but a form of dress'. To one of the 'anti-gold lace people' who demanded why he went to Buckingham Palace functions he retorted: 'Because its allurements are so great that I cannot trust *you* to go.' The waspish Chips Channon, observed in his diary: 'Ramsay MacDonald was very distinguished in his privy councillor's full dress uniform ... giving his arm to the Duchess of Buccleuch to whom, I hear, he made himself most affable.' MacDonald argued that most Labour supporters, since they were treated as inferiors in their own everyday lives, would welcome evidence that their leaders dealt on equal terms with the highest in the land. It was also a matter of good manners. He thought the King had behaved well to him, and he should return the courtesy. 'The King has never seen me as a Minister without making me feel that he was also seeing me as a friend,' he wrote. His delight in the company of duchesses, his defenders said, owed as much to reverence for the historic associations of an ancient name as it did to snobbery, and he luxuriated in being a guest at Britain's grandest houses at least partly for the same reason.

There was also a strategic justification. If MacDonald's immediate concern was to establish Labour as a party fit to govern, the trappings of high society could just about be described as the natural corollary of power – what his biographer David Marquand described as 'the role of convention as the invisible thread binding society together'.[4] Binding society together, squeezing out the extremists, was part of what MacDonald was about. However, Beatrice Webb's acerbic commentary noted: 'It may be right to be wisely moderate, alike in action and in words; it cannot be right to be worldly.'[5]

On domestic affairs the new government seemed not so much moderate as timorous and uncertain. Only under goading from the Opposition was a desperately needed programme of works for the unemployed developed, including the creation of a national electricity grid that was immediately branded Leninist by the Conservatives, although they would adopt it unaltered when they returned to government. This unexpected lack of revolutionary zeal reassured the nervous suburbs; but it did nothing to satisfy those outside Parliament who had looked to the first Labour government for a transformation of their prospects. It also proved the embarrassing truth of Neville Chamberlain's remark that a minority Labour government would be 'too weak to do much harm, but not too weak to get discredited'.[6]

THE NEW ADMINISTRATION was still being fitted for its court uniforms when in February Ernest Bevin threatened to close every port in the country with a national dock strike. The nation held its breath: how would a Labour government handle its brothers-in-arms? MacDonald had to decide whether to support the strikers, or behave like a Conservative and be prepared to break their strike. There was really a choice only in the eyes of his most radical colleagues. MacDonald finessed it. Privately, he informed the Transport and General Workers' Union that he was prepared to seek emergency powers, while at the same time setting up a court of inquiry that, conveniently, found in favour of the dockers.

A month later, Bevin called out all London's bus and tram drivers in protest at the lack of progress in implementing an agreed standardization of wage rates. This was a strike with political undertones, for Bevin wanted a London-wide traffic authority to end the unregulated competition that was driving down pay – something that would require legislation. The Transport Minister when this long-running saga came to a head was the TGWU's own president,

Harry Gosling. But although the union conceded a delay for further negotiation, on 21 March 1924 they struck.

Another court of inquiry was invoked. It accepted the need for the rationalization of London transport services, but also the employers' case that they could not afford a pay rise. To a private appeal from MacDonald, Bevin brusquely responded that the Prime Minister could come and see him if he wanted, but it was none of his business. When he announced that London Underground drivers were going to come out too, the government 'rushed down to Windsor', Bevin later complained, to ask the King to proclaim a state of emergency. Finally, a London Transport bill was rushed into the Commons, enabling a temporary deal to be struck. Bevin was accused of holding the public to ransom, sabotaging the national economy and of being a dictator; behind his back, even his colleagues called him 'Napoleon'. In fact, the disputes owed less to a truculent desire to prove that the use of industrial power could succeed where politics failed than to his struggle to stanch the loss of members from his new Transport and General Workers' Union caused by recession. Much as the Commonwealth regiments' experience of battle in the First World War had given their countries a sense of nationhood, Bevin's battles helped consolidate the disparate parts of his union.

For Labour in power, the readiness to use emergency powers was a chance to show they too could be tough on the unions, if not on the causes of unions. But the party was perplexed about the proper relationship between a Labour government and its founding fathers; politicians and theorists argued whether, when a Labour government was in power, all sides of the movement owed it a duty of loyalty. Bevin, backed by Citrine at the TUC and reflecting the views of a membership that had yet to see any personal advantage from a Labour government, asserted that if they saw an opportunity they must take it. To impose industrial peace would be 'too big a price to pay,' Bevin said, 'we must therefore go on with the economic war, waging it the whole time and utilising every opportunity on behalf of the class we represent'.[7] If a Labour government made the employers more timid in confrontation with trade unionists, here would be a chance to claw back some of the losses endured when employers had been supported and emboldened by a Conservative administration.

In September 1924 at the annual TUC Congress, the unions, far from preparing to hang up their rule books out of respect for their Labour government, decided to strengthen the General Council so that it could coordinate sympathetic strike activity between its member unions when one of them was involved in a dispute. Much of this was the work of Citrine, less a revolutionary than a bureaucrat who wanted to build an effective organization. Nonetheless, the move appeared to indicate a lurch to the left. Well known left-wingers took over key posts on the Council. The new president was the MP for Coventry, Alf Purcell, a furniture polisher by trade, who was in no doubt about whether the political or the industrial wing of the party dominated. 'Even the Labour Party having a sufficient majority and in power leaves us still confronting capitalism on the field ... a well disciplined industrial organisation is the principal weapon of the workers – a weapon to strike with if need be.' An investigation into union mergers with a view to achieving more powerful industrial unions was launched. A Russian fraternal delegate was received enthusiastically, and moves began to reunite the Social Democrats' international trade union structure with the Moscow-dominated Red International of Labour Unions.

The government clung to power from January until November. Although MacDonald, acting as his own Foreign Secretary, achieved progress abroad, at home his government did little that distinguished it from its predecessor. Philip Snowden, Chancellor of the Exchequer, established a committee that set in motion the process of returning Britain to the Gold Standard after the wartime decision to float the pound. The Gold Standard, icon of economic rectitude, would restore Britain to world pre-eminence. But that was for the future: it would be another seven years before gold brought down a MacDonald government. On unemployment, neither Snowden nor Sidney Webb, who chaired a committee responsible for developing policy, had anything to say beyond anticipating an upturn in trade. Predominantly in Britain's traditional industries of coal, shipbuilding, steel and cotton, the number of jobless remained constant at around one and a quarter million. The standard of living of working men and women continued to fall. As an attempt to convince its supporters outside that democracy could be made to work to redress their ills, Labour's first time in government largely failed. As a gesture of reassurance to the suburbs, it was only a very partial success, and the reasons for its fall did much to undo such progress as it had made.

One of MacDonald's early decisions in foreign affairs was to open negotiations with Soviet Russia with a view to extending trade and normalizing diplomatic relations. The Left believed that bringing the Soviet Union back into the world economy would provide the market for British goods that would reinvigorate the British economy. But such was the fear of the Soviet Union and so deep the hatred of all it stood for, that Liberals as well as Conservatives rejected MacDonald's plans. By the end of the summer session of Parliament, it seemed quite possible that his government would be brought down on the issue, which had also triggered another wave of negative press about Soviet Russia and Labour's relations with Moscow.

Labour's relations with the security services were tense from the start. In an act of bravado countermanded by some of his ministers, MacDonald claimed to be so confident that Communists were not burrowing their way into Britain's society and institutions that he suggested to the head of Special Branch, Sir Wyndham Childs, that rather than draw up a weekly report containing information readily available to anyone who read the Communists *Daily Worker*, he would be better occupied – and his weekly report 'more exhilarating' to read – if instead it reported on Fascist organizations and found out who funded the *Morning Post* (well known to be the Duke of Northumberland). Sir Wyndham retorted that the *Morning Post* did not advocate revolution.

None of this was common knowledge when a cack-handed

decision on a political prosecution was taken in the summer of 1924. Labour's first Attorney General was Sir Patrick Hastings, a celebrated criminal barrister whose conversion to Socialism was attributed by the uncharitable to personal ambition and a need for some public salvation to redress the memory of the conviction of his father, a solicitor, for embezzlement – an event by which Sir Patrick had been scarred as a schoolboy. He knew little of Labour's more tender sensitivities and apparently anticipated no difficulty when, on the recommendation of the Director of Public Prosecutions, he authorized the prosecution of a Communist called John Campbell for incitement to mutiny. Campbell had been the stand-in editor of a small-circulation Communist publication, one issue of which had carried an article calling on soldiers and sailors to refuse to fire on their working-class comrades in any circumstances. Incitement to mutiny was one of the Communist Party's most energetic but – according to MI5 files – unproductive of activities. But many Labour sympathizers shared the view that soldiers were their working-class comrades who should not have to obey capitalist orders in the event of a class war. In addition, Campbell himself was a war hero, invalided out of the army after the amputation of all his toes (although not, as was generally believed, the result of enemy action, but of a nasty case of frostbite).

Once the news of Campbell's arrest was out, Labour MPs erupted. MacDonald had known in vague terms that prosecution was being considered, but not that it was to go ahead. At Cabinet, ministers agonized: to initiate the prosecution had been a mistake, to back out now would be a disaster. But there appeared to be an escape route. Campbell was only temporary editor, and was said to be willing to write a letter that would amount to apology. Such was the relief at this apparent way out that only the wily old rail leader Jimmy Thomas (often spoken of as the best politician in the Labour Party) warned that they would pay later. MPs went on holiday for two months, and while they were away the case was formally dropped, even though Campbell's letter of expiation had not arrived. In court when the proceedings were being wrapped up, it was intimated that the government had intervened. When MPs returned in October, the Opposition demanded to know what had happened. At that point, MacDonald denied that he had been involved in the decision to drop the prosecution. But the Opposition had somehow acquired the cabinet minutes, which recorded quite the opposite. MacDonald, who had long since approved the minutes whose accuracy he now disputed, claimed they were wrong. As ever, his attempt to cover up for what was almost certainly a genuine mistake made when he was in the midst of complex international negotiations, was far more damaging than the mistake itself. He was humiliatingly exposed – if not convicted – as a liar; the Liberals abandoned him and an election was called, with Labour's alleged submission to Communism the central issue in a very dirty campaign.

Posters appeared in which Socialist candidates were portrayed with long hair, bulging eyes, squat noses, bristling moustaches and scrubbing-brush beards. It was the image of a 'stage Cossack'. Conservative Party literature warned that health visitors might be Communist spies; that children might be lured by the promise of Sunday School into a Communist sect where they would be taught street fighting and warfare; and that Communism destroyed marriage.[8] One jingle went: 'Bolshevik Bolshevik, where have you been? – Over to England where the grass is still green.' In vain did Labour's annual conference, a few weeks later, declare membership of the Communist Party incompatible with membership of the Labour Party. Grigori Zinoviev, president of the Communist International, an organization devoted to spreading revolution, and thus chief propagator of international revolution and the principal conduit of subversion, was the Opposition's favourite target. Even the normally scrupulous Baldwin devoted much of his annual party conference speech to attacking 'Labour's extremists': 'It makes my blood boil to read of the way in which Mr Zinoviev is speaking of the Prime Minister today. [Labour politicians were commonly denounced as capitalist lackeys.] Though one time there went up a cry, "Hands off Russia", I think it's time somebody said to Monsieur Zinoviev, "Hands off England." [9] Baldwin, it has been suggested, was seeking to force Labour to shed all connections with the Communists so that it could become the Tories' respectable partner in power. However, he may equally have been aiming at winning the election and restoring his reputation with his own, still critical, party.

Certainly, voters were well prepared when, only four days before polling day, the *Daily Mail* published a letter purporting to be from Zinoviev to British Communists, with whom he was in frequent contact. The letter declared that MacDonald's controversial Russian treaties normalizing diplomatic relations were intended to 'assist the revolution'. Furthermore, the letter apparently instructed the British Communist Party to organize in the armed forces with the purpose of provoking mutiny. MacDonald, out on the road electioneering and hampered by an overloaded schedule and poor communications, fumbled his response, which at first was inaudible, and subsequently failed to point out that the letter's authenticity was in doubt.

Labour's defeat was assured. It was forty years before the letter was proved categorically to have been a forgery, the work of White Russians, or perhaps Poles, anxious to destroy Britain's developing relationship with the Soviet Union. But it should have been clear to anyone who took MacDonald's advice and read the *Daily Worker* that Moscow had long since written off Labour's political leadership, captured as it was 'in the leading strings of the bourgeoisie'.

A close colleague of Baldwin's said much later that they had had secret information proving that cells had already been formed within the forces, and that they genuinely believed the letter – which they had seen in advance of its publication in the *Mail* – to be authentic.[10] That leaves unexplained Conservative Central Office's involvement in its over-hasty publication, and its later payment of what was then the vast sum of £5,000 to a man called Donald im Thurn, allegedly to pay to the source who first gave him the letter. 'If you look at the history of the Conservative Party,'

J. C. C. Davidson, a future party chairman, reflected later, 'you will always find that it is when the country is scared of wild-cat schemes and wants safety that it turns to the Conservative Party.'[11]

After 1918, Conservative Central Office and MI5 had established close links; some intelligence agents went to work for the party. At least one Conservative MP implicated in the Zinoviev affair, Sir Richard Hall, was a former agent. Three years after it, in 1927, a former MI5 officer, Sir Joseph Ball, became the party's first director of publicity. Superficially at least, it almost appears that Conservative headquarters had become a front organization for British intelligence. But perhaps it would be safer merely to assume a natural synergy between MI5 and Conservative fears and the capacity of a strong Conservative government to confront and overwhelm the Left.

Baldwin won the 1924 general election by a landslide: Conservatives won 419 seats to Labour's 159. Labour's only comfort was that in its heartlands its vote had gone up. Elsewhere, ex-Liberals had rushed headlong into the arms of the Conservatives, leaving their old party reduced to a rump. The right was triumphant, and the left was in crisis, with a political leadership found wanting, unemployment mounting and wages cut.

It was a crisis that Baldwin intended to use, to replace class war with his own brand of benevolent paternalism. He declared that his mission was to heal the nation's divisions. At Stourport in January 1925, he said: 'There is only one thing which I feel is worth giving one's whole strength to, and that is the binding together of all classes of our people in an effort to make life in this country better in every sense of the word.' In March he put substance to the sentiments of that speech. Agitation in the Conservative Party to rescind trade union privileges had been strong at the previous autumn's conference, and a backbench MP, F. A. Macquisten, brought in a bill to end their right to levy from members a contribution to their political fund without specific consent. This attack on the Labour movement – for it would almost certainly have led to a dramatic cut in the funds available for the Labour Party – was popular in the

Tory Party, and in Cabinet as well. But in a speech that epitomized the lingering whiff of Victorian paternalism that clung to his political persona, Baldwin faced down his 'extremists' and made a powerful appeal for conciliation in preference to confrontation. It was on this appeal, he said, that he had won the votes of thousands of non-Conservatives at the last election. Now was the time to drop the bill and refrain from pushing political advantage. 'We stand for peace ... we want to create an atmosphere, a new atmosphere in a new Parliament for a new age, in which the people can come together ... I know that there are those who work for different ends from most of us in this House, yet there are many in all ranks and all parties who will re-echo my prayer: "Give peace in our time, O Lord."'

The bill – which might have revived unity among the Left – was dead. Yet within weeks, Baldwin's Chancellor of the Exchequer was to take a decision that, by its deflationary pressures, would undermine every attempt to improve relations between employers and employees. A return to the Gold Standard had been at the core of Treasury orthodoxy since the end of the war; in effect it would fix the pound's value, and the intention was to do so at the pre-war level. The government would no longer be able to inflate the currency. The pound would be 'kept honest'. Of course, government spending would have to be tightly restricted, but like the battle to remove government controls from the coal industry, it was all part of regaining pre-war status, in particular for the City, and asserting Britain's continued position as the world's greatest power. Somewhat unrealistically, given the relative strengths of the two economies, it was also imagined to be a way of preventing the dollar replacing the pound as the world's most trusted currency – of letting 'the pound look the dollar in the face'.

THIS APPEAL to empire and glory was almost guaranteed to succeed with Baldwin's new Chancellor, for he was the former Liberal (and 're-ratting' Conservative) Winston Churchill. Churchill was the scourge of the Bolsheviks, a man who thought consensus was for the common people, and probably the most controversial politician in the House of Commons. Having lost his Dundee seat in 1922, he had fought a flamboyant by-election in Westminster as the anti-Socialist candidate, a point he underlined by driving around his putative constituency in a coach and four, before finally finding a permanent and secure seat in Epping Forest in time for the 1924 general election.

Churchill was in the unenviable position of having to make a decision about the Gold Standard within a few months of taking office, in a climate of anticipation created by a great weight of established opinion that formed a short but mighty bastion from the Treasury to the City. Influenced by a powerful attack from John Maynard Keynes in the columns of his newspaper the *Nation*, however, Churchill paused; and in a savage memo written from his bed one Sunday morning, he demanded of the Governor of the Bank of England why he 'allows himself to be perfectly happy in the spectacle of Britain possessing the finest credit in the world simultaneously with a million and a quarter unemployed'. He ended famously: 'I would rather see Finance less proud and Industry more content.'[12] He arranged a dinner party to hear the arguments on both sides. Keynes underperformed and Churchill decided to take the advice of his officials. In his first budget, on 28 April 1925, he announced that the pound would return to the Gold Standard at its pre-war level of $4.86.

This overvalued it – according to Keynes – by as much as 10 per cent; either the cost of exports would have to rise, or industrialists' costs would have to be cut. 'Mr Churchill's policy of improving the exchange by 10 per cent is, sooner or later, a policy of reducing everyone's wages by 2s in the £,' Keynes wrote a little later in his celebrated pamphlet, *The Economic Consequences of Mr Churchill*. Keynes, a Liberal with a passionate concern for social justice, dwelt at some length on the impact of the decision on the miners in particular:

> If miners were free to transfer themselves to other industries,
> if a collier out of work ... could offer himself as a baker, a

bricklayer, or a railway porter at a lower wage ... it would be
another matter. But notoriously they are not so free. Like
other victims of economic transition in past times, the miners
are to be offered a choice between starvation and submission,
the fruits of their submission to accrue to the benefit of other
classes ... Why should coalminers suffer a lower standard of
life than other classes of labour? ... They are victims of the
economic juggernaut ... the 'moderate sacrifice' still necessary
to ensure the stability of the gold standard.[13]

The impact of Churchill's decision remains a matter of dispute;
Keynes may have overstated the deflationary impact as much as the
Treasury and the Bank of England underestimated it. But among
Liberals in the summer of 1925 the perception was established
that workers in general, and the miners in particular, had been sold
out for the benefit of financiers and the City. Although the return
to gold was generally applauded, there was widespread sympathy
for the victims it would create. Even Conservative newspapers like
The Times acknowledged the miners' cause was deserving. In June,
the mine owners announced a new round of pay cuts. Once again,
the interests of capital and labour appeared irreconcilable.

The coal industry had enjoyed a fleeting recovery when, two
years earlier, the French had occupied the German coalfields on
the Ruhr. Taking German coal off the market had led to higher
prices for British coal, and the miners took the opportunity to claw
back some of the pay cut imposed in 1921. Early in 1924 the
owners agreed readjustments that amounted to the restoration of
the wartime national minimum wage. Unfortunately, just as the
new terms came in, the prospects for coal were dramatically
reversed by the resumption of German exports – the result of
MacDonald's diplomacy – which reduced both prices and demand
simultaneously. As profitability slumped in the first half of 1925,
the employers once again looked to pay cuts to restore their
margins. When the effect of the stronger pound cut in, the slump
became a crisis.

On 30 June the employers announced that at the end of July they would end the previous year's agreement in favour of one that paid only the standard wage, with no minimum profit-related addition (although profits for the owners continued to be regarded as part of the industry's proceeds): once again, this meant a pay cut – in some cases, of 50 per cent. However, terms could be improved if the miners were prepared to abandon the seven-hour day, won only in 1919, and return to working eight-hour shifts. On 3 July they rejected the terms and made no alternative proposals that could be a prelude to negotiation. They were ready to fight. The mine owners said their losses were now running at £1 million a month. Their profits in the four years between 1921 and March 1925, the miners retorted, had been £58.4 million, while the average shift worker was earning between 9s 4d and 12s 8d (45–60p) a day.

Baldwin had sought to avert confrontation. Instead, he created the circumstances that seemed to make it unavoidable. The newly strengthened TUC General Council invoked its right to intervene on its members' behalf. On 12 July, the miners welcomed their involvement. An Industrial Committee was set up, and less than a fortnight later it was decided that if there was a strike the unions would impose a blockade on the movement of coal. At the same time, the old Triple Alliance, now expanded to include the engineering, electrical, shipyard and iron and steel workers and renamed the Industrial Alliance, was in the final stages of approving a constitution that would also ensure unified action. But, as Bevin warned the first conference of his newly merged Transport and General Workers' Union, it would involve sacrifice: 'You cannot have autonomy and unity at the same time.' The conference voted for unity, even at the expense of being called out on strike without a ballot.

The plan was overtaken by events, but this gesture of earnest intent impressed both the rest of the trade union movement and the government. It also opened up the constitutional question. What was this Industrial Alliance intended to achieve? newspapers and politicians asked themselves. Surely it was revolution? Bevin tried to argue that the complexion of the government was an entirely unrelated matter. 'The constitutional issue ... won't be raised by those of us who have to lead the strike. The question of the form of Government in this country will not come within the purview at all.'[14] All major achievements won by the working classes had required both strikes and legislation: they were not attacks on the constitution, he went on. But this was an argument that had been undermined by the use of strikes for revolutionary ends.

On 23 July the miners met the TUC General Council and left their union colleagues with the clear impression that they too were prepared to sacrifice autonomy for unity. Plans for the embargo on coal movements were prepared; and the TUC became a player in the dispute. On the 27th its representatives met the Prime Minister and pressed the need for further talks. Two days later, both miners and mine owners were invited to Downing Street.

The miners now stuck fast on what became their slogan: 'Not a minute on the day, not a penny off the pay.' No changes that meant lower wages, and no reversion to the eight-hour day. 'We have nowt to give,' the miners' president Herbert Smith said, when pressed to negotiate. The Prime Minister warned there would be no government subsidy. 'All the workers of this country have got to take reductions in wages to help put industry on its feet,' Baldwin was reported to have told them.[15] The following day, the General Council triggered a national embargo on coal movements. On the 31st, the government capitulated. It announced an inquiry into the scope and methods of reorganization of the industry, and Baldwin offered a subsidy that would meet the difference between the owners' and the miners' positions on pay until the new Commission reported; the subsidy would end on 1 May 1926. The lockout notices and the strike were suspended.

This was Red Friday, hailed by the entire union movement as a triumph mighty enough to blot out the bitter memory of Black Friday, four years earlier. 'It's a good job it's over,' Churchill said to the miners. 'You have done it over my blood-stained corpse. I have got to find the money for it now.'[16] Churchill was a leader of the faction that the cabinet secretary Maurice Hankey described to the palace in a frank assessment: 'Many members of the Cabinet think that the struggle is inevitable and must come sooner or later. The PM does not share this view. The majority of the Cabinet regard the present moment as badly chosen for the fight ... public opinion is to a considerable extent on the miners' side.'[17] The Home Secretary William Joynson-Hicks voiced the prevailing opinion in Cabinet: 'The danger is not over. Sooner or later this question has got to be fought out by the people of the land.'[18]

The popular press were outraged at what they saw as Baldwin's capitulation. 'Victory for Violence,' the *Daily Mail* thought, while the *Express*, echoing the mine owners, called the subsidy 'Danegeld'. The Labour right was almost as scared. Ramsay MacDonald was particularly angry, accusing Baldwin in an astonishing outburst – even if intended only for the ears of an ILP audience – of 'siding with the wildest Bolsheviks' and 'handing over the appearance of victory to the very forces that sane, well-considered, thoroughly well-examined Socialism feels to be probably its greatest enemy'.[19]

Baldwin's decision to back away from confrontation shocked and bewildered his own party as much as the popular press. All the rumour and gossip about his fitness for office, which had died out with his landslide election victory less than a year earlier, resurfaced in the bars and corridors of Westminster and the salons of political London. Lord Salisbury sent Baldwin a memorandum in which he accused him of destroying the government's credibility. 'The moral basis of the Government seems to me to have dropped out,' he concluded. As with Baldwin's sudden decision at the end of 1923 to ask for a mandate to introduce protectionist trade barriers, elegant explanations were later given for this seeming capitulation. In conferences and in Parliament that autumn it was said that neither the state's emergency transport and supply machinery, nor popular opinion, were ready: both needed careful preparation for what was to be the final showdown. Only the latter part of the argument was true. And the angry reaction to the subsidy pinioned the government: it could not be repeated. The TUC was equally trapped by the emotional baggage of Black Friday. It could not withdraw support from the miners again.

After it was all over, Baldwin explained to his friend Edward Wood (later Lord Halifax, Viceroy of India) that he believed it had been right to 'buy off the strike ... though it proved once more the cost of teaching democracy. Democracy has arrived at a gallop in England and I feel all the time it is a race for life. Can we educate them before the crash comes?'

3

SCARE STRATEGIES

Armed warfare must be preceded by a struggle against the inclinations to compromise which are embedded among the majority of British workmen, against the ideas of evolution and peaceful extermination of capitalism. Only then will it be possible to count upon the complete success of an armed insurrection.

Letter from Grigori Zinoviev to the Central Committee of the
Communist Party of Great Britain[1]

Old ladies are frightened in order that young Tories may be elected.

Ramsay MacDonald, *Hansard*, 1 December 1925

The revolutionary worker has not yet come to the realisation of the necessity of creating and developing a strike strategy . . . They should remember that an army marching into battle without a plan, without central-ised leadership, without the direction of its various sections by a single will, is doomed to defeat.

'Strike Strategy in Britain'[2]

AFTER RED FRIDAY, the Strike Strategy document intercepted by the Post Office earlier in 1925 assumed a new significance. Baldwin might portray his election victory as a triumph of one nation over the propagandists for class war, but there was no expectation that these revolutionary evangelists would retreat quietly back to Moscow; even if the coal dispute were settled and a strike averted, it had to be assumed another confrontation would develop elsewhere.

Special Branch undertook a detailed analysis of the source and origins of the document, which appeared to confirm its importance; its thirty-five pages were typed on very thin, apparently foreign paper, similar in texture and shape to that used by the 'Moscow Executives'[3] and the Mid-European Bureau of the Red International of Labour Unions. It was written in the sloganese of the Moscow-trained revolutionary. Although the document was undated, from references it contained it must have been written shortly before the fall of the Labour government in the autumn of 1924.

In July of that year, delegates to the 3rd Congress of the Red International of Labour Unions, Moscow's instrument for spreading revolution among the workers, had been harangued on the need to prepare such a strike strategy. Its author was thought to be one of the British delegates to the conference, Tom Quelch, whose father, Harry, had entertained Lenin in London in 1902. Tom had been a founding member of the Communist Party of Great Britain in 1920; he was a frequent visitor to Moscow, important enough to have talked there to his father's old friend (he had explained to Lenin that English workers would regard anything weakening the British Empire as 'treachery').[4] Quelch could be taken to be a senior figure whose ideas would be regarded seriously. MI5, and the government, now had in their hands what could be a blueprint for turning a general strike into insurrection. At the end of May 1925, it was decided to circulate the Strike Strategy document around government departments. The decision was taken by Sir Ernley Blackwell, the legal adviser to the Home Office, who had been involved during his twenty-year career in many of the department's more contentious decisions, including the Black Diaries that revealed the Irish nationalist Roger Casement as a homosexual shortly before his execution for his part in the Easter uprising in 1916, and the introduction of firearms control in 1918 to prevent guns falling into the hands of 'anarchists and half-savage tribesmen'.

To add authenticity to the document, several aspects of its plan described events that had in fact taken place since it had been written: the TUC's Labour Research Department had recently been re-ordered, and Robin Page Arnot, a Communist, had been appointed to conduct precisely the kind of investigation into British industry that it recommended. The TUC General Council was assuming greater powers and the Triple Alliance unions were building a common organization. The TUC had agreed to investigate industrial unions. All of these were recommendations in the Strike Strategy document, part of the instructions to create a centre capable of the unified leadership of a general strike. The document elaborated at length on the need to broaden grievances, in particular the issue of pay cuts in industries like the miners', into 'general class actions': every worker's wages were threatened by the return to the Gold Standard, the TUC asserted. The 'numerous bodies and institutions created by the astute capitalist class of Britain for attacking, influencing and corrupting the Trade Union bureaucracy' must be overcome; so must the dead weight of most TUC leaders, 'whose mental calibre', the document lamented, 'is not particularly brilliant, though many of them are members of parliament'. They would be replaced by the National Minority Movement, the new Communist front organization that ignored traditional union boundaries and sought to forge a radical vanguard. 'All is fair in War,' it argued; the element of surprise was vital. 'Agreements are only truces in the class war.'

But the section of the document that seemed most alarming concerned what might happen once a general strike had been called. 'Great mass strikes have more and more the tendency to develop into actual civil war ... the strike leaders of the future ... *must assume actual military war* [original emphasis] to be the ultimate result of a prolonged struggle' whose objective would be 'bringing about such actions as will lead *to the final conflict and the overthrow of capitalism* [emphasis added in pencil in 1925]'. 'The national unions [must] force the General Council of the Trades Union Congress to assume the leadership of the strike' and turn it into a strike against the state. 'The strike, as it spread, would necessarily become more *political* in its character ... [and could become] a general struggle for power [making] actual revolutionary demands'. The Co-operative Movement (the democratically governed profit-sharing organiz-ation that ran shops in many working-class communities) must be 'captured' so that it could operate as a supply system to the strikers and, even more importantly, to their wives and children; seats on local government must also be won so that the meagre benefit that it administered to the poor and unemployed could be used to support the strikers.

The strike must open with the greatest possible force; one early aim should be to cut off the bourgeoisie from food and other supplies. In the vanguard would be the left wing of the South Wales miners (where Tom Quelch often spoke), which was 'very strong ... Already as far as the miners of Britain are concerned, the organisational ground-work has been laid for the development of a revolutionary policy.' (The secretary of the Miners' Federation was Arthur Cook, briefly a Communist, who owed his election to the votes of the National Minority Movement.) Finally, the document concluded, a general strike could mobilize the working classes; for although economic conditions were ripe for such action, currently the capitalists had almost complete control over the minds of the masses: 'The souls of the workers are in the enemy's keeping.'

The security services watched carefully to see whether this document appeared in print in any of the Communist-funded publications; but although much of its substance became familiar over the coming months in propaganda sheets and resolutions from the Minority Movement, the document itself was never reproduced. Much of the strategy is common sense. It bore a close resemblance to the plans Walter Citrine was drawing up in private at about the same time, and to the ideas Bevin would have when the General Strike finally came. Yet it would have been curious if the govern-ment had not found in it precisely the evidence that it both sought and feared – that there were forces at large intent on making a general strike the precursor of revolution.

This was the message that the government needed time to

promote. The strike should be seen as a constitutional outrage, a threat to the state. This was a marked change of approach from the official response to the challenge of industrial over political authority in 1920, when the Labour movement threatened to prevent Britain arming Poland against Russia and Lloyd George backed down. After Red Friday, building to a crescendo in the autumn of 1925 and mounting to a second peak after the final collapse of negotiations in the spring of 1926, the anticipated general strike was referred to everywhere in precisely the terms the Communists wanted: it would be a strike against the state. Depicting it as that kind of threat, however, heightened tension and sharpened the perceptions of those who wished to maintain the existing order, as well as of those who intended to upset it.

The *Yorkshire Press* was merely echoing much public opinion when it said that 'Socialism, Communism and Trade Unionism appear to be inseparable.' But the industrial wing of the Labour movement needed no prompting from Communists to see Red Friday as triumphant proof that whereas a minority Labour government could only don the archaic dress of court lackeys and prop up the status quo even to the point of threatening to take emergency powers, industrial muscle could accomplish real change.

High summer and autumn of 1925 were dominated by fevered talk of insurrection. While the former Liberal Home Secretary, Sir Herbert Samuel, aided by two industrialists from outside the coal industry and Sir William Beveridge, Director of the London School of Economics and a former official at the ministry of Labour, inquired once more into a future for the coal industry acceptable to both sides, the undemocratic activists of both left and right were becoming noisily active, adding to the anxiety of ordinary citizens. The Home Secretary William Joynson-Hicks – 'Jix' – was already branded by his more moderate colleagues as the government's 'Mussolini Minor'; he was one of the diehards, a Conservative of the deepest hue with a well earned reputation as a reactionary, who had imposed crackdowns on unlicensed drinking and drug-dealing at nightclubs, and prosecuted D. H. Lawrence not for his writing but for his paintings. Later, 'Jix' led a campaign of the utmost reaction against the revised Book of Common Prayer. In the eyes of history, perhaps his most redeeming action was to commit the Conservatives to giving women the vote at twenty-one, a pledge honoured in time for the 1929 general election.

'I sincerely believe his enthusiasm almost exceeded my own,' wrote Sir Wyndham Childs of Special Branch in his memoirs. 'Had he had his way, there would be no Communist Party in Britain today.'[5] His opposite number at MI5, Sir Vernon Kell, continued to keep the Communists under close surveillance.

They also took an interest in the Fascists, whose activists were largely young middle-class men given to propaganda stunts; they appeared to enjoy suspiciously lenient treatment in court. In March 1925 a Fascist gang kidnapped Harry Pollitt from a train taking him to Liverpool. Both sides appear to have regarded the exercise more as a publicity stunt than as a serious threat, and for that reason Pollitt did not immediately go to the police. When he did press charges, five of the Fascists, on trial for unlawful imprisonment, defended themselves with the claim that they had been going to take Pollitt away for a pleasant weekend. They also alleged he had taken £5 for expenses, which may or may not have been true, but which appeared to sway the jurors; the Fascists were acquitted.[6] In October that year, a gang of National Fascisti, the breakaways from the British Fascists, stole a van belonging to the Labour-sponsored *Daily Herald* and drove it into some church railings. When they came up before the magistrate, the public prosecutor reduced the original charge from larceny to committing a breach of the peace. The charge would have been dropped entirely, but 'however meritorious it might have been from one point of view', it was still improper behaviour. Even the magistrate thought this extremely lenient.[7] In some areas, chief constables were warning that Fascism was a serious force. In Wolverhampton in August 1925, the chief constable reported that he had expressly requested the Fascists, whom he numbered at 'about 1,200 strong', not to break up a meeting addressed by the man whom Labour had failed to prosecute for sedition, J. R. Campbell, now a Communist hero.

To the Left, the Fascists seemed a good deal more than perpetrators of jolly undergraduate japes. At the Independent Labour Party's annual conference in Gloucester, a stranger bearing an invitation to discuss land policy on a nearby farm approached the ILP MP James Maxton. When he went outside, he found twenty men with black ties and a large motor vehicle, seemingly planning another high-profile kidnap.[8] He reported the episode to Glasgow journalists, but without explaining how he escaped, which remains a mystery. Fascists trying to break up Communist meetings used low-level aggravation and violence. They took part in public parades and drills, and wore membership badges at all times; vigilantes were ready to nip the merest signs of Communism in the bud. All this in turn was used by Communist activists to agitate for workers' defence corps, echoing an instruction heard often from Moscow. The corps would be the foundation of a Red Army; until the revolution arrived, it would protect Communists from attack by Fascists, police or the military. By early September, Cardiff's chief constable claimed six branches of the workers' defence corps were in the process of being raised in his city alone.

Moscow, meanwhile, appeared to be pumping money into revolutionary activity. In April 1925, MI5 were in possession of documents suggesting that the Communist Party was funded to the extraordinary (and curiously specific) extent of £98,764 a year, perhaps £100 million at today's prices. Almost all of this Red Gold was apparently intended for 'underground propaganda', especially amongst the military. If that was how it was actually spent, then British troops must have been awash with seditious literature. In August, fly posters were even found stuck to a sentry box at Buckingham Palace.[9] The documents also showed that in the previous election more than £2,000 had been spent supporting Communist or Communist-sympathizing candidates, including William Gallacher who stood against Churchill in Dundee, where

£500 was spent. (Twenty years later, when the Soviet Union was a vital wartime ally and Gallacher a Communist MP, Churchill treated him as a good friend.) They also included among recipients of generous handouts Ernest Bevin, who as an avowed enemy of Communism was unlikely to have received any cash unless via some front organization.

However, if only some of the amounts mentioned in the documents were genuine – and there was other evidence that the *Daily Herald*, which had certainly once relied on subventions from the Soviets, was still being offered cash despite now receiving funding from the trade unions – then it was one more reason for taking the Communist threat with the utmost seriousness. But such was the climate of fear, and the appetite for information, that the security services' files are full of reports of dubious authenticity. Self-appointed agents, often Fascists, reported 'undesirable aliens' being landed by night along the east coast. Informants accused newspaper boys of sedition, seamen fell under suspicion simply for getting drunk in foreign ports. John Lang, a sailor suspected of 'excessive fraternisation' during trips to Russia, had 'imbibed more drink than doctrine', a bored wit inscribed on the file.[10]

Joynson-Hicks authorized intensive surveillance of everyone connected with the politics of the Left, but Scotland Yard and MI5 were particularly interested in the activities of the National Minority Movement. It was at the NMM's annual conference at the beginning of September, where 610 delegates claiming to represent 650,000 workers had gathered, that the first appeal was made for workers' defence corps. Inflammatory, possibly even seditious, speeches where made by Tom Mann, a prominent member of the Communist Party, and by the only Communist MP to hold his seat in 1924, Shapurji Saklatvala.

Joynson-Hicks wrote anxiously to Baldwin, away on holiday, on 4 September: 'There is a very strong feeling in the country that I should move.' But it was barely a year since the previous Labour government had embarrassed themselves by interfering in the processes of justice over the Campbell case. The *Mail* and the

Express, cheerleaders for the rigorous application of law and order, bayed for the courts to act: privately, officials pointed out that 'a second Campbell case would finish any government', and that 'the prosecution of an MP (even a coloured one) for seditious libel or some such offence raises ... serious considerations'. Finally, it was admitted that the only record the authorities had of seditious speeches came from the press reports. There had been MI5 men present at the meeting, but since they were under instructions to be discreet, they had not liked to take notes. (This practice soon changed: before the end of the month, Mr W. T. Collyer from Holborn Labour Party complained bitterly to the Labour annual conference that not only did all his letters arrive at least two deliveries later than they should have, but that at one meeting he had attended inexplicable scuffling noises had been tracked down to a pair of spies under the platform writing down every word spoken by the people above. Another speaker at the conference chipped in to reveal that at a respectable dinner of MPs, the waiters 'were carefully disguised members of the Secret Service'.[11]) 'It seems to me inconceivable,' stormed another memorandum in the MI5 file,[12] 'that a criminal charge should be based on the words attributed to Mr Saklatvala in the press reports' – Saklatvala had stated that he was an inveterate enemy of the Union Jack and of British Imperialism – '... such proceedings rarely have any other result than a strengthening of the position of the person proceeded against'.

In parallel with these excitements, between 7 and 12 September the Trades Union Congress met in Scarborough under the lively chairmanship of the Communist-sympathizing Alonzo Swales, who hailed the revolt against the state symbolized by Red Friday, spoke warmly of the 'new order of society ... inevitable before we can remedy the existing evils',[13] and pledged to prepare 'to struggle for the overthrow of Capitalism'. A resolution demanding that the TUC itself prepare for revolution was carried by two to one (although a more substantive attempt to achieve organizational unity was lost by the same margin). Scarborough came to be seen as the high-water mark of revolutionary fervour. Indeed, the delegates had talked left but voted right, and on the new General Council the men who had made the revolutionary running were now replaced by the soothing presence of Margaret Bondfield (a sensible woman partial to brogues and later the first woman in Cabinet), the railmen's leader Jimmy Thomas and, for the first time, the mighty figure of Ernest Bevin. But at the time, the turn that events were taking was not so clear. 'The Mole of Revolution is digging,' trumpeted the Soviet journal *Rabochaya Moscva*. Even the death a few weeks later of the TUC general secretary Fred Bramley, a leading supporter of closer ties with Communist Russia, and his replacement by the bank-clerkly figure of Walter Citrine, failed to quell the scaremongering.

In Whitehall, and in letters and telegrams that winged up and down between departments of state and the larger country houses of the north where Conservative politicians were enjoying the fruits of the season on the grouse moors and in the deer forests, the search for grounds for a prosecution for sedition continued, propelled by a storm of ever shriller newspaper reports of alleged Communist activities of dubious authenticity, which ministers did not trouble to correct. On 9 September the *Mail* claimed to have 'another Zinoviev letter' calling for the creation of illegal military organizations to be ready at the decisive moment 'to lead the army against the bourgeoisie', while the *Daily Chronicle* reported that 'a Red plan' had been 'foiled by detectives'. A reassuring telegram was sent by the Director of Public Prosecutions to Dunrobin Castle in Sutherland, where the Home Secretary Joynson-Hicks was taking a break. The stories were 'a triumph of imaginative journalism,' he wrote, but '*we are not issuing any contradiction* [author's italics]'.

Where were the newspapers getting the stories? One source was probably their deliberate placing from within MI5 and Special Branch. Later evidence suggests this. The following May, as the General Strike was beginning, a document on 'new instructions for military espionage' detailing measures for recruiting 'clerks, journalists, translators, typists, servants etc.' in garrison towns, included this note: 'You are at liberty to show the document to the [War Office] and if the present situation at home takes a serious turn, extracts might usefully be issued to Intelligence officers.' The note was addressed to 'Ball'; Joseph Ball, the future publicity director of Conservative Central Office, was at that time working for MI5.[14]

Over the next ten days, as Labour prepared for its annual conference, the hysteria mounted. The Chief Constable of Sunderland reported the discovery of notes apportioning to certain revolutionaries the responsibilities to be assumed on the arrival of the red dawn. Tom Mann was to cut railway communications and blow up bridges. Another well known Communist, Arthur McManus, was to be in charge of machine-gunning and bombing in Manchester. Sympathetic MPs (most of the Clydesiders were named) were to capture both Houses of Parliament and set up a soviet. To this excited report was drily appended the comment: 'I suggest the time has come to warn Chief Constables in the North not to deal with "B".' It is not clear who 'B' was, but the nation was in the grips of a terror. At Scotland Yard, Wyndham Childs was visited by an old friend of normally sound judgement who was convinced of a plot to chloroform the guard at Buckingham Palace. Obliquely, Childs hints that the Conservative Party was to blame for exacerbating anxieties.

The Communists too encouraged this dramatic portrayal of a strength they did not possess. The *Workers' Weekly* took the credit for an unofficial seamen's strike in August in which the men were refusing to accept a £1 pay cut negotiated by their union, even though the men denied there was any political motive. 'There is no Red propaganda behind this dispute, which is a legitimate protest against the reduction of wages,' protested the strikers. However, the Home Office was convinced that the strike had been provoked by clever tactics on the part of the National Minority Movement, who had instructed district organizers to foment unrest on the grounds of a lack of consultation.

On 17 September, the MI5 files suggest, grounds for sedition had finally been established against Harry Pollitt, John Campbell and ten other well known Communists. Within days, the *Daily Mail* declared: 'Fifty Reds to Be Deported'. Autumn manoeuvres were now taking place on Salisbury Plain; if the incitement to mutiny that so frightened Fleet Street was indeed stirring the troops, plainly this was a time of grave danger. Somehow it had become known to certain journalists that 'a large force of selected men of the Special Branch ... have been drafted into the armies. They wear full Army equipment and are indistinguishable from the soldiers.'[15] The same day, the *Daily Sketch* had an even better story: 'Red agents in vans loaded with seditious propaganda ... drove away from the neighbourhood of Soho and Southwark yesterday. But they did not go unseen.' That night the *Evening Standard* revealed that Joynson-Hicks was to ask the Commons for further powers 'to facilitate mass deportations'. The *Daily Graphic* reported that 'seditionists' were receiving as much as £4,000 a year in subventions from Moscow. On this point Joynson-Hicks wrote privately: 'I don't believe [the report] is genuine.' But again there is no evidence of an official denial.

In rural Hampshire for the summer, Beatrice Webb watched anxiously as 'the *expression* [original emphasis] of revolutionary Socialism becomes every day more conspicuous among the communistic Trade Unionists on the one hand and the ILP on the other ... they really have convinced themselves that the capitalist citadel is falling.'[16] Webb despaired of MacDonald's leadership in Parliament, his shunning of the radical Left and his evident enjoyment of the company of aristocrats and intellectuals, which left him out of tune with the Labour movement and unable to provide it with effective leadership. Her husband Sidney joined her at the start of the summer recess, full of reports of a plot to replace MacDonald with someone who dallied less in fine houses and spent more time listening to his supporters. The Webbs foresaw a reaction from the right that would lead to the kind of repression that had held back the development of democracy after every radical upsurge of the nineteenth century. 'If I had to prophesy I should forecast some such catastrophe to the Labour Movement as the price of a return ticket to sanity,' wrote Webb, high priestess of reformism, on 17 August.

MacDonald feared a general strike as much as the Webbs did. Trapped by his desire to position the party at the centre of parliamentary politics, he was powerless to redirect the energies of the Left. Now fifty-eight, lonely, gloomy and increasingly idiosyncratic in his politics, he had never been in sympathy with the industrial wing of the Labour movement. He feared the public impact of the bitter attacks of some trade union leaders like the miners' secretary Arthur Cook, who talked wildly of 'beating the strongest government of modern times';[17] and similarly of Ernest Bevin, 'a swine' in MacDonald's view, who was leading the attempt to commit Labour never again to take office without a majority. But MacDonald was more vulnerable, personally as well as politically, to the attacks of the Independent Labour Party, of which he was still a member, and which was now strongly influenced by the most radical group of MPs, the Clydesiders. In the aftermath of the experience of minority government and impatient with gradualism, these men were starting to develop their own programme for Socialism – unfortunately, precisely the sort of activity MacDonald regarded as disruptive, if not dangerous.

The ILP had expressly rejected Communism, but their approach to the expected general strike closely echoed the sentiments of the Strike Strategy document now circulating in Whitehall. Where MacDonald saw a threat, the Clydesiders saw an opportunity. After the disappointments of office, here was the prospect of a great leap forward. John Wheatley, who had been MacDonald's Housing Minister, predicted that a general strike would be 'the greatest struggle in our history'; where MacDonald feared it could bring capitalism to its knees, James Maxton sincerely hoped that it might. Furthermore, the ILP MP asserted, 'the strike weapon was the most moral weapon that could be used'. Out of office and out of sympathy even with his party at Westminster, MacDonald offered no leadership worth the name as, riding high on a surge of emotionalism, the Labour movement plunged towards the potentially disastrous General Strike.

In vain, MacDonald accused the Conservatives of the 'wanton use of Communism for purely party purposes', a charge supported by the liberal *Manchester Guardian*. The *Guardian* described not the Communists but Joynson-Hicks as 'the gravest of existing menaces to law and order. For many months the rather scrubby little cause of British Communism has had no such public crier to advertise it as he.'[18]

But such protests went unheeded. Government and newspaper editors alike not only believed there was a Communist threat; they also saw its political value. In such circumstances, they did not always trouble to be scrupulous. The Labour Party struggled to distance itself from the charge of infiltration within its ranks. At its conference in Liverpool at the end of September, watched by the Communists who had taken a larger hall close by, the movement voted to make individual membership of the Communist Party incompatible with Labour Party membership. The resolution was carried overwhelmingly, although it turned out to be extremely hard to enforce on party activists in a handful of constituencies. In the short term, it provided a platform for a succession of speakers to condemn Communism in terms that ought to have reassured those who had believed that Labour was on the verge of being reduced to a front organization. Frank Hodges, the former secretary of the Miners' Federation who after his defeat by Cook and the Minority Movement was particularly hostile to the Communists. He denounced them, in terms of which Churchill himself would have been proud, as 'the intellectual slaves of Moscow, unthinking, unheeding, accepting decrees and decisions without criticism or comment, taking orders from the Asiatic mind'. In addition, trade unions were asked to stop sending Communist delegates to Labour Party conferences. Liverpool was, for MacDonald, a personal triumph. For the moment, even the threat of a general strike appeared to recede. But the routing of Communist-inspired resolutions did little to stifle the press onslaught.

Having fomented nationwide anti-Communist paranoia, editorials next began to doubt the government's readiness to meet the challenge of a strike that was to 'paralyse national life'. The letter pages of *The Times* began to fill with demands for the formation of some sort of organization – but on a larger scale than had been tried in previous transport strikes – that would channel the volunteers who would be taking over the strikers' jobs. On 25 September Joynson-Hicks, suggesting disingenuously that the best preparations were sometimes secret preparations, used the same letter pages to announce that there would indeed be such a volunteer organization – the Organization for the Maintenance of Supply. It would, however, be quite separate from the government's own preparations. It would register, rather than enrol, men and women who in the event of a general strike would 'fulfil the very humane tasks of seeing that the people of the country were not starved of the necessities of life'. There were to be independent branches in every city, organized along identical lines and under the supervision of a council headed by the former Viceroy of India, Lord Hardinge. Walter Seton, an academic and ex-wartime agent with experience in the Balkans, was on the council; other members had had periods of undefined War Office service during their careers, which often indicated work for military intelligence. Recruits to this new service were to be registered in five classes ranging from 'A', fit younger men to serve as special constables, down to 'unclassified' for women, who were 'in no circumstances to be employed in places where there is any danger of rough handling'.

The Communists branded it legal Fascism. In fact, the OMS was much less successful than its founders had hoped and the Left had feared. Joynson-Hicks got some of the headlines he wanted. 'Defence against the Reds,' cheered the *Mail*. Improbably large numbers of volunteers were reported to be deluging local recruiting offices. But other newspapers, including the *Daily Express*, were anxious that the Communists might be right and that it could look like a kind of Fascism – reminiscent, even, of the Klu Klux Klan: 'To movements of this character, the *Daily Express* is equally hostile, and to Black Shirt and Red Flag alike it says: A plague on both your houses!' Joynson-Hicks insisted that it was only to avoid the charge of provocation that no earlier announcement had been made. Ramsay MacDonald called the OMS not only provocative but 'irresponsible'. The BBC refused to broadcast a speech by an OMS representative. 'We feel it would prejudice our reputation for being non-political,' Reith wrote.[19]

Government officials seemed to agree. In November a representative of the OMS, General Sir Robert McCalmont, an Anglo-Irishman with a distinguished war record, made an appointment in Whitehall in order to complain that no one in government was interested in their activities and that recruiting was not going very well. The Commissioner of the Metropolitan Police had already told the OMS that he wanted nothing to do with them, for their recruits might have political objectives. McCalmont made no progress. In December, another OMS representative was brusquely informed that the most useful thing the organization could do was to provide lorry drivers when the time came. There were to be no further official meetings; moreover, if it became known that any had taken place, it would be explained that they were only to clarify that in an emergency, the OMS would be suspended; its registers of volunteers would be taken over by government.[20] In the public mind, the OMS continued to be associated with Fascism.

Chief constables' attitudes varied. At their annual conference in Harrogate it was agreed, somewhat obscurely, that there were 'various ways' in which the Fascist movement could be used: 'The Home Office saw no objection to Members of the Fascisti Movement being enrolled individually in the Special Constabulary providing the Chief Constable was satisfied that the applicants were suitable persons to be enrolled.'[21] In some areas the OMS was closely linked to the Conservative Party too. Its York branch, founded in 1926, was actually based at the Thirsk and Malton Conservative Association. Its first recruitment poster was unequivocal in its evocation of the threat that lay ahead: a general strike, it asserted, would overthrow the government and substitute it with a 'government chosen by a revolutionary element largely composed of aliens!'[22]

COMMUNISM, associated as it was with civil war, brutality and the wanton expropriation of private property, was in many quarters still beyond the bounds of the politically acceptable. In contrast to the 1930s, the occasional middle-class recruit to Communism became at once a social outcast. The sculptor Claire Sheridan, cried Robert Graves and Alan Hodge in *The Long Week-end*, a social history of the years between the wars, was 'socially ruined' by her series of 'Russian Portraits', while a Balliol undergraduate was asked to leave his college, despite its reputation for Socialist leanings, for visiting Moscow, and two others were rusticated merely for espousing the cause. 'According to the Conservative Press,' *The Long Week-end* reported from the sunlit peaks of the moral high ground at the end of the 1930s, 'the Bolshevists were not only murderers and ruffians and enemies of private property: they were also active atheists and had "nationalized women for sexual purposes".'[23]

On 12 October, the existence of the Strike Strategy document was revealed by Joynson-Hicks in order to bolster the government case that a general strike risked developing into civil war. On the 14, Communist Party headquarters in King Street, Covent Garden, were raided in the fishing expedition discussed in Chapter 1, and the twelve leading members were arrested. At this the Home Secretary, according to *The Times*, was heard to emit a 'most improper whoop'. Less than a month later, Harry Pollitt and the eleven others were convicted of sedition. All were sentenced to between six and twelve months' imprisonment; seven of them, despite the Communist Party being a legal organization, were told by the judge that if they agreed to rescind their membership they could go free. Other members of the Communists' Executive went into hiding.

It was an awkward moment for Labour, too vivid a reminder of the embarrassing Campbell prosecution, too close to the heart of Labour supporters who believed that in the war with capitalism, no ally should be rejected. Parallels were drawn with Conservatives who had survived unscathed their open support for the equally seditious, and considerably more threatening, Curragh Mutiny in 1914. In the current trial, Sir Henry Slesser, the former Labour Solicitor General, led the defence. In the Commons, Ramsay Mac-Donald boldly moved a vote of censure, condemning 'a political trial inspired by political motives'.[24] He warned: 'The newspapers tomorrow morning will say we are a seditious and unconstitutional party', but, he argued, attacking free speech could only strengthen Communism. To say so was not to suggest Labour sympathized in any way with Communist objectives. 'We are not only not Communists, we are actively opposed to Communism.' Churchill, in a speech in Battersea soon afterwards, made just the association MacDonald had predicted: 'Behind Socialism stands Communism. Behind Communism, Moscow, that dark sinister evil power,' he thundered, 'a band of cosmopolitan conspirators.'[25]

The Communist Party was decapitated. If there was to be a general strike, there would now be no Communist leadership. Harry Pollitt, the secretary and prime mover of the National Minority Movement, was sentenced to a year's imprisonment. Robin Page Arnot, who ran the Labour Research Department at the TUC in Eccleston Square in London and was the most permanent link between it and Communism, was sentenced to six months.

PUBLIC OPINION was well prepared; so too were the logistics. Whatever might come of the OMS, the arrangements for supplies in the event of a general strike had been under review since 1923, when Baldwin became prime minister for the first time and invited his close confidant J. C. C. Davidson to be Chancellor of the Duchy of Lancaster. Davidson was appointed Chief Civil Commissioner with instructions to prepare to meet the revolutionary threat that even he, a Tory moderate, regarded as imminent. 'The Government had the duty to protect the people against any attempt at direct action by revolutionary methods to put in an anti-democratic body to control the country ... An attempt to substitute an oligarchy with no claim to represent the majority of the people had to be resisted at all costs.'[26]

Davidson set to work. He divided the country into twelve districts and appointed a deputy civil commissioner to run each. In the event of a strike, the Commissioner would have the powers to do all that was necessary to maintain public services; freight and passenger transport, food distribution, light and power would all be under his direct control. Each district would have, in addition, a volunteer service committee to recruit local people to help maintain services. When details of the plan emerged, critics observed that in effect this established a centrally controlled structure that bypassed the independent local authorities, which in most industrial areas were Labour-controlled. Consideration was also given to taking over the BBC and setting up a government newspaper.

Baldwin's unexpected decision to call an election at the end of 1923 had, embarrassingly, meant the handover of Davidson's plans to the incoming Labour administration, which would include some of those regarded as subversives. His political adviser Lancelot Storr appears to have recommended, improperly, that rather than hand on the papers they should be kept secret. Davidson instead took his successor, Josh Wedgwood, into his confidence. Wedgwood agreed to keep the papers secret, and handed them back when the Labour government fell. 'I haven't destroyed any of your plans,' he told Davidson. 'In fact, I haven't done a bloody thing about them.'[27] By then the system already had a life of its own: Whitehall officials continued exploring solutions to likely difficulties, without ministerial intervention or instruction.

In November 1925, to allay the continued fears raised by the relentless warnings of the dangers of the anticipated strike, Baldwin released the outline of Davidson's plans in a Ministry of Health circular. The deputy civil commissioners were named and were observed to be largely men of military rank and experience. Each had the power to undertake detailed organization and recruitment, so that when the strike finally came there would be in every district a fully operational strike-breaking force staffed by private transport operators and their employees. Stocks of essential supplies such as flour, yeast and coal were to be built up. The commissioners and their teams would spring to their posts on receipt of a telegram bearing the single word, 'Action!' Chief constables were given permission to recruit up to full strength, and to exceed that by up to 50 per cent in areas in or near coalfields.[28] In December, Churchill publicly attributed July's decision to pay a subsidy to the miners to the need to inform the country 'about the character and immense consequences' of a general strike. It had been decided to postpone the crisis, he said, partly in the hope that trade would improve – a consequence of the return to the Gold Standard that was still awaited – and partly in the hope 'of coping with [the strike] effectually when the time came'. The energy the government expended in both planning and propaganda was quite unmatched by anything heard or seen from Labour or the TUC.

4

JUDGEMENT DAY

It is a tragedy to think that this inspired idiot [Arthur Cook], coupled with poor old Herbert Smith, with his senile obstinacy, are the dominant figures in so great and powerful an organisation as the Miners' Federation.

Beatrice Webb's Diaries 1924–1932, 10 September 1926

Evan Williams [mine owners' spokesman] . . . has not made a single constructive contribution towards the solution of the problem. One would feel inclined to dissociate oneself officially and in every other way from the vapourings of these people [the Mine Owners' Association].

David Davies, mine owner and Liberal MP, to Tom Jones; *Thomas Jones: Whitehall Diary*, ed. K. Middlemas, vol. 2, 21 January 1926

ON THE LEFT, planning for the strike was becoming inescapably associated with Communism. As the year turned and the Communist leaders settled to sewing mailbags in Wandsworth Prison, Communist journals began to publish demands that echoed the recommendations of the Strike Strategy document first drafted more than a year earlier. On 15 January 1926 the *Workers' Weekly*, one of several of the Communist organs generously sponsored by Moscow, called for a stronger TUC General Council and the enlistment of the Co-operative Movement as the 'victuallers of the revolution'. (The 'co-ops' were often generous with credit to their customers, but in mining areas many still had large debts accumulated during the 1921 strike and were reluctant to incur more.) The Communist programme demanded a minimum wage, one hundred per cent trade unionism and more support for the unemployed to prevent them undercutting wages, as well as the now familiar demand for workers' defence corps.

Efforts to excite workers about the notion of setting up defence corps were making little progress. At the end of 1925 the London organizer, Thomas Coules, wrote to all London comrades, calling them to a meeting in Lavender Hill, south London; but despite the prospect of learning ju-jitzu, boxing, wrestling and hand-signalling, only three people turned up. The Communists' organizations seemed to have about the same degree of popular appeal as the Fascists' and the OMS; and as with the meetings of the latter two, discussion was dominated by matters of form – to wear sashes or not to wear sashes? or sashes under a coat? secrecy or openness? were they to flaunt their power, or try to avoid confrontation?

In an editorial in February's issue of another Moscow-backed publication, the *Communist Review*, there was a new call to arms: 'The time is rapidly approaching when the courage and revolutionary fervour of every Party member will be tested … in the period of the decline of British capitalist production, the most backward trade union becomes potentially a revolutionary battalion and every demand for higher wages, or even the maintenance of present standards, poor as they are, becomes a revolutionary demand.'

Walter Citrine also began to consider the implications of a general strike, although he found little encouragement in the four-storey house in Eccleston Square where the TUC's growing empire was uncomfortably based. Nonetheless, he drafted a long memorandum trying to anticipate the course of events and the proper response to any proposals the government might make in the remaining months before the coal subsidy expired at the end of April. His conclusions were sensible, but his style was dense and his audience unenthusiastic. The TUC's Special Industrial Committee, which had been set up to handle negotiations with the government over the mining dispute, firmly believed that strikes were not planned, they were spontaneous eruptions of anger and

frustration. Citrine disagreed. 'Walter, you are too logical,' he had
been told by an old trade unionist soon after he became acting
general secretary of the TUC the previous autumn. 'Trade unions
are never logical. You look too far ahead. Don't worry. Let things
develop.'[1] But before he had even come to London, Citrine had
decided that the Labour movement must be centralized; now he
had the chance to show what *should* be done. In his assessment, the
coal industry needed reorganization to survive and interim financial
support while reorganizing. But he saw that Red Friday had made
it politically difficult, if not impossible, for the government to
intervene again, as he laboriously explained: 'The outbreak of
political opposition which succeeded the granting of the subsidy in
July last, makes one reflect on the possibility of the Government's
being stimulated to decline further assistance at the end of the
present subsidy period.'[2] Rather more tersely, and acknowledging
another of the fears of the TUC conservatives – the danger of
making a self-fulfilling prophecy – he warned that without a
subsidy, 'another crisis in the industry is inevitable'.

At its first presentation before the Special Industrial Committee,
the idea of making preparations for a general strike seems to have
been treated roughly. Citrine's final draft continued: 'I know it is
the opinion of several experienced leaders that there is a danger of
over-anxiety in the matter of preparation. There is a feeling that
when the moment of crisis comes, the British Labour movement
will be aroused spontaneously to an attitude of determined resistance; that unless resistance is spontaneous it cannot be really
effective.' However, the government had a vast majority, the
political climate was hostile, and allegations of Communist infiltration into the movement were widespread. The diehards were
determined to revive anti-union legislation; there could be no
solution without government intervention, and there was little
likelihood that it would come. The government had revealed the
extent of its own planning by publishing the official circular from
the Ministry of Health giving powers to the civil commissioners.
Law and order was threatened by 'the Fascisti Movement ...

1. Tsar Nicholas II of Russia with his first cousin the Prince of Wales, soon to be George V, in 1909. After the Revolution in 1917, George refused to allow Nicholas and his family asylum in Britain and the following year they were murdered by the Bolsheviks, a fate that haunted the king for the rest of his life.

THE SUBSIDISED MINEOWNER—POOR BEGGAR!

2. Popular view of a mine owner. Even Baldwin thought the Conservative party had too many 'hard-faced men, who look as if they've done very well out of the war.'

3. Rudyard Kipling, the most famous poet of his generation, with Stanley Baldwin, his first cousin, in the background. A line from Kipling's *A Song of the English* was used to underline the government's controversial instruction to soldiers to do all that was necessary to maintain order during the strike: 'By the peace among Our Peoples let men know we serve the Lord.'

4. The Baldwins at Chequers. Lucy Baldwin was Stanley's emotional bedrock. 'Every morning when we rise we kneel together before God and commend our day to Him.'

5. Winston Churchill playing polo in a
Lords v Commons match, *c*. 1925. Baldwin
had wooed 'the most dangerous man in politics'
back to the Conservative party and made
him Chancellor of the Exchequer.

6. Major-General Sir Wyndham Childs,
head of Scotland Yard's Special Branch.
'Communism was the burning problem . . .
I [was] full of confidence that I should
be able to deal with the problem and
smash the organization.'

THE GREAT COMMUNIST TRIAL, 1925.

(*Back Row*) J. T. Murphy, W. Gallacher, W. Hannington; (*Middle Row*) H. Pollitt, E. Cant, T. H. Wintringham, A. Inkpin; (*Front Row*) J. R. Campbell, A. McManus, W. Rust, R. P. Arnot, T. Bell.

7. The twelve Communists sentenced to between six and twelve months in prison in the sedition trial of October 1925. Harry Pollitt is on the extreme left of the middle row. J. R. Campbell, whose non-prosecution in 1924 contributed to the fall of the first Labour government, is on the extreme left of the front row. Robin Page Arnot who ran the Labour Research Department is second from the right in the front row.

8. Celebrating the seventh anniversary of the Bolshevik Revolution in 1924. The poster depicts the political death of Ramsay MacDonald who despite restoring diplomatic relations with Russia was deemed a traitor of the revolution by Moscow. It reads 'MacDonald: Death to the lackey of the king and traitor to the workers.'

9. Miners' president Herbert Smith in flat cap with other miners' leaders during the strike. 'Three hours of an argument . . . left Herbert Smith's attitude on every point precisely what it had been at the beginning . . .'

10. The Communist-sympathizing miners' secretary Arthur Cook, 'This inspired idiot . . .',

11. The rail leader Jimmy Thomas. 'He doesn't want a revolution. He wants to be prime minister.'

12. Walter Citrine, the general secretary of the TUC, 'Loquacious, naively vain and very disputatious'.

13. Ernest Bevin, founder of the Transport and General Workers' Union, 'swarthy of countenance and square of jaw, with the shoulders and chest of a heavy-weight all-in wrestler'.

14. Sydney and Beatrice Webb, godparents of the Labour party. Beatrice wrote: 'The failure of the General Strike of 1926 will be one of the most significant landmarks in the history of the British working class.'

15. Margaret Bondfield, trade unionist, with the Labour leader Ramsay MacDonald who made her the first woman Cabinet minister.

16. Baldwin exploited technological innovation to present himself as the representative of England's unchanging values.

17. Baldwin was a dominant international figure despite the continued disdain felt for 'the little dud' by some of his more flamboyant Cabinet colleagues.

18. Strikers playing cards. The TUC's first strike instruction was to keep everyone smiling. 'Let none be disturbed by rumours or be driven by panic to betray the cause.'

19. Unions where most members had been called out struggled to raise the cash for strike pay. Children were sent out to scrounge coal from railway lines.

drilling and organizing its forces'. The movement must prepare for a strike.

The Special Industrial Committee could not be roused. They were unhappy with the idea of consultation with the government. 'It is no doubt a disadvantage to spread the area of consultation too widely,' allowed Citrine. They were also indifferent at this point to Citrine's demand for clarity about who was conducting the dispute – the miners or the TUC. He struggled to engage them with the constitutional issues. The Parliamentary Labour Party must be brought in to put pressure on the government to continue with its financial support to the miners, so that the trade union movement did not appear to be acting in a political capacity. He implored the committee to consider the proper role of the trade unions in the maintenance of supplies. Should they cooperate with the government, try to set up their own network, or guarantee to safeguard essential services? 'It was clear to me that the meeting did not want to face the issues raised in my memorandum and would do anything to put off a decision,' the notoriously thin-skinned Citrine wrote many years later. But he was right. At heart, the trade union movement remained convinced that its real strength lay not in negotiation and compromise, but in ambush and surprise, death or victory. The gap between the ambitions of the author of 'Strike Strategy in Britain' and those of the strike organizers on the TUC could hardly have been wider.

At the end of January, the government prepared for a new session of Parliament. The King had been following developments closely. At the height of the crisis the previous summer, he had invited the miners' leader Arthur Cook to the palace. Cook, scenting another ruse by the wily capitalists, or at least an appeal that would be difficult even for a revolutionary to reject, refused to go. George remained concerned to placate wherever possible. He was anxious that a passage in the King's Speech referring to the danger of a miners' strike was insufficiently conciliatory. His private secretary rang Tom Jones, Baldwin's deputy cabinet secretary, to ask for 'a more direct personal and stirring appeal to his people'.[3]

In the end, from the throne in the House of Lords the King called for 'all parties to face the future in a spirit of conciliation and fellowship and to avoid action which would again postpone the return of good trade and prosperity for which we have so long hoped'.[4] It did not entirely work: in the debate that followed, Labour MPs heralded the collapse of capitalism. The Durham coalfield had been 'devastated not by the march of enemy armies, nor by any Socialist follies ... but by the breakdown of the Capitalist system,'[5] said the future Labour Chancellor of the Exchequer Hugh Dalton.

Yet in that dead time before Sir Herbert Samuel and his small team on the Coal Commission reported, there was a perceptible lowering of the temperature. The trade unions still believed the government could not just end the subsidy without agreement. 'Nobody wants a row,' Ernest Bevin told the executive committee of the TGWU in February, speculating aloud for the first time about what gains could be made by a general strike. Nonetheless the TUC remained committed to the miners' cause, and the miners' leaders still optimistically waited for Samuel to reprieve them. Only a close textual analysis revealed a slight weakening of the TUC's position after their meeting with the Miners' Federation in February, and the note of anxiety about Communist activity that had crept into its final statement: 'The Committee particularly desire to urge the Trade Union Movement not to allow itself to be influenced by unauthorised and unofficial suggestions which are being made in many quarters regarding the Mining problem.'[6] The Yorkshireman Herbert Smith, the Miners' Federation president 'in his blue suit and soft collar, with his little moustache turning grey and his high balding forehead with his spectacles resting on the end of his nose,'[7] reiterated the miners' determination to make no concession on hours or on pay. Arthur Cook, the 'raving, tearing Communist' whose election as secretary of the Federation had terrified the TUC two years earlier, said the same thing more colourfully: the employers would 'never stampede the miners into slavery'. On 19 February, miners and TUC agreed to do nothing until Samuel reported.

All hopes now rested on the Samuel Commission somehow identifying a route through the labyrinth of competing interests: a way of preserving the gains the miners had made in 1921 – national pay rates and the seven-hour day – and the mine owners' profits after the government's subsidy ended. It is a measure of the desperation of those involved that they allowed themselves to believe that there was a ready solution. 'A peculiar atmosphere had been created round about the report of the Coal Commission,' Robin Page Arnot observed when he reviewed matters the following year for the Labour Research Department, 'an atmosphere almost of religious reverence, of worshipfulness.' And, he added scathingly (in a slim volume designed to prove that only the Communists had stood by the miners), he perceived 'an air that was extremely enervating to Trade Union leaders susceptible to that kind of influence'.[8] Yet, when it came to negotiation, Samuel had the right pedigree. A former Liberal Home Secretary, he had long experience as a conciliator; his most recent job had been as High Commissioner in Palestine. There he had been so taken by the inability of religions to coexist that he had resolved to retire quietly to the southern shores of Lake Garda in Italy and write a philosophical synthesis that would provide the foundations of world peace. Sadly, he was interrupted almost before he had begun by Baldwin's pressing invitation to reconcile not God with God but capital and labour. And on 6 March, before retiring again to his library in Italy – which now included two volumes of Pliny's *Letters* given to him by his colleagues on the Commission – he presented the results of his inquiry. There were seven weeks left before the subsidy expired.

The Samuel recommendations were eminently reasonable but, without active government support, entirely unworkable. The report disapproved of the subsidy: the government was found to have spent on it not £10 million as it had at first predicted, but

£23 million. Nearly three-quarters of the coal produced in the last
quarter of 1925 had cost more to get out of the ground than it was
worth on the market. The overall tone was politely sympathetic to
the miners: there was no point extending the day to eight hours
when there was already an oversupply of coal; reorganization, pit
closures and amalgamations were essential and should be under-
written by the government; the principle of a national minimum
wage was conceded, although in an ambiguous form that allowed
the mine owners to interpret it as permission to reimpose district
pay rates; and profit-sharing, together with investment, when conditions allowed, in non-pay benefits such as more pithead baths and
better welfare, were all recommended. Selling arrangements should
be modernized, and local conglomerates linking coal with gas and
electricity production and oil and chemical plants might be established to maximize consumption. None of this was palatable to the
bulk of small pit owners that made up the Mine Owners' Association. There was insufficient inducement to make the inevitable
costs of reorganization palatable. But the miners' demands were
not met, either. In the immediate future, they would have to take
a pay cut. It was unavoidable. But it should be for the short term
only, until reorganization had returned the industry to profitability.
And nationalization, which the miners were convinced would solve
the industry's difficulties, was rejected. It offered no 'clear social
gain'.

Thus Samuel's Commission offered only uncertain benefits in
return for immediate pain.

It was a sign of the national sympathy for the miners and
concern about the danger of a general strike that the report was a
popular triumph: a cheap 3d edition had to be produced to meet
demand, and over ten thousand copies were sold (no similar report
sold as well until Sir William Beveridge's wartime work on the
Welfare State).

If neither of the groups at whom the Commission report was
aimed could find enough in it to persuade them to accept its less

congenial aspects, then government intervention would be essential to avoid a relapse into deadlock. Indeed, had the government stepped in immediately with the intention of knocking heads together, then perhaps the report might have held the key to a settlement. But Baldwin was profoundly opposed to the 'bad habit' of state intervention encouraged by Lloyd George. He thought it sapped the spirit of self-reliance and the entrepreneurial instinct, and he had seen too many crises in the mining industry where both sides leant on government for a solution that allowed each to escape their responsibilities. He was also reluctant to allow higher wages to force the closure of uneconomic pits, throwing perhaps thousands of miners out of work; he regarded the Federation as 'ruthless' in its insistence that every miner should be paid a decent wage, even at the cost of many of their members' jobs. Equally, he felt that a subsidy raised from taxes on lower-paid workers in other industries that would go to the highest paid as well as the lowest in the mining industry was unjust.

When the report was published, Baldwin made a short state-ment assuring the parties of his support in their efforts to reach agreement, then sat back to let them get on with it. There were no meetings with the parties for a fortnight, and when he finally brought them together, he had little to offer beyond a promise that, if both groups accepted the Commission's findings, the government would help to fund the cost of reorganization and to soften the blow of pay cuts with a very short-term, tapering subsidy applicable only in the worst-hit areas. He promised legislation that would facilitate reorganization, but he would not be able to lay it before them until the end of the month. The miners, men with long memories who still smarted from having nationalization denied them by Lloyd George in 1919, were unwilling to commit them-selves to accepting the report without something tangible on the table in return. 'Give us a lead, Prime Minister,' Herbert Smith begged. But Baldwin was determined that the assumption by both sides of the industry that the government would come to the rescue should be disproved. By then the original subsidy had just five weeks to run.

There now existed two parallel universes. In one, hard-headed negotiations had to take place between cash-poor mine owners, once again demanding steep pay cuts agreed at district not national level, and intransigent miners determined to defend what in many places were already inadequate wages through a national standard. At the margins, more liberal (and more prosperous) coal owners tried to persuade the government to put more pressure on the hardliners in the Mine Owners' Association, and Labour leaders tried to press it to intervene to help the miners. Closer at hand, Tom Jones reminded Baldwin that if he saw the owners privately, but not the miners, he was giving the former a political advantage; the government must use the situation to strengthen its own position and fight down the owners' opposition to reorganization.

Meanwhile, in the other universe, in the newspaper headlines and, consequently, in the public mind, the threat of national crisis and of Communist insurgency – indeed, the threat to England herself – were duly conflated into one alarming story. Linking the two was a prime minister held in scant respect by the most powerful and bellicose members of his Cabinet, a pacifist with an instinctive distaste for the intervention that, bar a miraculous transformation in attitudes within the industry, was the only route to a peaceful settlement.

One of Samuel's principal ideas for reorganization entailed nationalizing not all of coal production but the mineral rights of the pits, a familiar proposal that had been found too controversial in the past. Royalties entitled owners of the land on which coal was mined to claim a levy, payable regardless of the profitability of the pit. (The Duke of Northumberland earned at this time £73,000 a year from his royalties; Churchill described it as like having an allotment.) To abolish royalties would remove a burden from the mine owners but would be a step politically so contentious for a Conservative government as to seem virtually impossible; to abolish them without compensation was clearly out of the question. Nonetheless, Samuel recommended it, and Baldwin was forced to consider a response. This time, the cabinet committee he chaired to review the possibilities stalled on the vital question of government finances. All Chancellor Churchill's calculations following the return to the Gold Standard depended on converting expensive war debt into a cheaper form of loan. Far from being able to borrow more, the government was struggling to reduce debt, and to do that it had to grip public spending in a fist of iron. The Commission's proposals, Churchill wrote, 'hit our finances in the most delicate place and at the most inopportune moment'. Nonetheless, in the interests of a settlement, nationalization of the mineral rights was reluctantly conceded, but only as part of the complete acceptance by both sides of every aspect of the Samuel Commission report.

In vain, Tom Jones pressed Baldwin to offer funding for reorganization, to run in parallel with the initial pay cuts. Baldwin was determined that the miners must make their sacrifice first. As Citrine had foreseen, with an angry party at his back, Baldwin's room for movement was restricted. He told the TUC that they should not mistake Red Friday for weakness on the part of the government; it had been a desire for peace. He could be pushed too far. More liberal industrialists like Sir Alfred Mond, the future Lord Melchett and founder of ICI who had considerable coal interests, pressed Baldwin to get involved, to impose a settlement. 'If the responsibility was taken off the shoulders of the two contending parties they would be pleased,'[9] Mond wrote to him.

At the start of the second week of April, with three weeks until the government subsidy expired, miners and the TUC held separate delegate conferences. From behind the scenes encouraging noises about negotiation were heard. But in public the miners' leaders were as obdurate as ever. At their delegate conference they promised there would be no wage cuts without seeking delegates' approval at a further conference. However, the TUC Special Industrial Committee, it was observed, did not repeat to its delegate conference quite the orginal guarantee it had given to the miners.

Arthur Pugh, the chairman of the TUC General Council who was also chairing the Industrial Committee that was conducting negotiations, believed tactics required the miners to throw the ball to the employers by offering to accept the Commission's report 'in substance', but subject to 'subsequent negotiations on any point of reasonable modification'. He believed the Commission report offered some possibilities – more, perhaps, than any threat of a general strike – and that it was 70 per cent in the miners' favour. He did not see how they could call out the whole movement in order to secure a subsidy for one industry. The two most outspoken left-wingers, Alonzo Swales and George Hicks, who had led the TUC in 1924, argued for throwing the movement's whole weight behind the miners; the majority preferred caution. The Committee's final resolution called for further negotiations. There was no mention of a general strike; but nor was there any renewal of the threat of one. To retreat, to desert the miners as they had in 1921, remained the unmentionable elephant at the back of the room.

From the mine owners emerged rumours of swingeing pay cuts – over 25 per cent in some areas – as well as a demand for longer hours, which the owners believed the miners would prefer to cuts. On 14 April, at a meeting with the mine owners, the Minister of Labour Sir Arthur Steel-Maitland ('a tall, athletic-looking, dark man who came into the House with a tremendous reputation and promise, which he never really fulfilled'[10]) irritated Tom Jones by his muddled thinking. 'The total impression is one of weakness and cloudiness,' Jones wrote.[11] But Steel-Maitland did better than the Mine Owners' Association, whose main spokesman was Evan Williams, 'an insignificant little man' who was usually seconded and amplified by Sir Adam Nimmo, a lay preacher and chairman of the Fife Coal Company, who Jones thought 'one of the greatest stumbling-blocks in the path of peace'. Unwilling or uninterested in searching for ways of improving the offer (Mond, for instance, wanted to look at unified selling agencies), a development of one of Samuel's proposals, or in finding ground for compromise, Nimmo and Williams left the meeting in no doubt that their actions would provoke a strike, news Jones carried immediately to Baldwin; but Baldwin preferred to discuss cricket. That evening the TUC Special Industrial Committee was introduced to the Prime Minister, who made clear the government's determination not to extend the subsidy. The burden of the history of the negotiations seemed to have made peaceful resolution almost impossible: neither miners nor mine owners would look beyond the immediate issues of pay and profitability. Outside the industry, the right suspected the workers of intransigence motivated not by a just cause but by revolutionary feeling; the workers assumed the employers had Fascist leanings; and Baldwin feared both sides regarded him as weak because he had granted a subsidy the previous July.

The political leaders tried discreetly to exert influence. Jimmy Thomas, the leader of the National Union of Railwaymen, Labour MP and former Labour minister, a man of sinuous politics viewed with deep suspicion by almost everyone on his own side, spent an evening closeted with Baldwin. The Prime Minister warned that a general strike would make it impossible to resist pressure from within the Conservative Party for legislation to rescind trade union privileges; Thomas pleaded with Baldwin to bring both sides together and chair the meetings himself. Elsewhere, MacDonald also appealed for solidarity, trying to convince the miners' leaders of the damage that anything other than the most calm and rational conduct would inflict on the Labour Party's prospects for power.

On 15 April, Baldwin, 'sympathetic and teachable', met the Miners' Federation executive. They explained their anxieties about pay; the mine owners now formally posted the rates they would pay from 1 May when the subsidy ceased, terms not only applicable district by district rather than nationally, but so savage in their effect in some places, particularly South Wales, that it became inconceivable that the TUC could desert the miners. Privately, even the radical Arthur Cook begged Baldwin to chair negotiating sessions. The public was becoming anxious. On the 16th the Roman Catholic controversialist and joker, Father Ronald Knox, presented a BBC programme that purported to be live coverage of a riot of

the unemployed in central London. Even though it included
eye-widening accounts of the public spit-roasting of a well-known
philanthropist, more than two thousand alarmed listeners contacted
the BBC to find out whether it was safe to go outside.[12]

A whole week later, on 21 April, with just nine days of the
subsidy left to run, Baldwin met the mine owners. On the 23rd, he
chaired for the first time a joint meeting of miners and owners.
Jones's lucid brain was appalled by the incoherence of the miners'
president Herbert Smith, struggling with the vast obscurity of
district pay rates (Jones had made sure Baldwin was briefed with a
'Child's Guide'). Unhappily, the mine owners' determination not to
improve their offer was delivered with uncompromising clarity.
That afternoon, Baldwin met the miners, now reduced to a small
negotiating committee, on their own. They discussed the impact on
the industry of allowing pay to continue at the existing rates: two
hundred thousand men out of work, an end to mining in Northumberland, Durham and South Wales. The choice appeared stark:
either a few efficient, money-making pits with a small, well paid
workforce that left thousands on the dole, or a large but under-
paid workforce in an industry where unprofitable pits were kept
afloat by the profitable and by frequent recourse to government
subsidy. The miners pointed to the thousands already out of work;
but the logic of their position was that, forced to choose, the former
option was preferable to the latter.

The miners were followed into Downing Street later in the
afternoon of the 23rd, by the mine owners' negotiating committee.
Jones, son of the valleys, could not disguise his indignation at the
difference in atmosphere. 'They are friends jointly exploring a
situation. There was hardly any indication of opposition or censure.
It was rather a joint discussion of whether it were better to
precipitate a strike or the unemployment, which would result from
continuing the present terms. The majority clearly wanted a
strike.'[13] Afterwards, as Baldwin and Jones walked in St James's
Park, Jones tried to stiffen the Prime Minister. The key to unlock-
ing the deadlock appeared to be to find a way of linking short-term

pay cuts to an irrevocable commitment to reorganization. The owners must be told that they were misinterpreting a crucial part of the Commission's report relating to a national wages board, and underplaying the powers of a central pay body to adjudicate on district pay rates. The miners, for their part, must be made to realize there was nothing else on offer. Compromise was the only way out. Did Baldwin have the nerve to push them hard enough to get that point across? Jones doubted it.

That evening, the TUC sent out notices for a conference of union executives to meet on Thursday 29 April: it would be invited to approve the decision to call a general strike.

5

FOR KING AND COUNTRY

A general strike is not an industrial dispute. It is a revolutionary movement intended to inflict suffering upon the great mass of innocent persons in the community and thereby to put forcible constraint upon the Government. It is a movement which can only succeed by destroying the Government and subverting the rights and liberties of the people. This being the case, it cannot be tolerated by any civilized Government and it must be dealt with by every resource at the disposal of the community . . . we call upon all law-abiding men and women to hold themselves at the service of King and country.

Daily Mail leader, 3 May 1926

BALDWIN'S APPROACH to the final days of negotiation was at marked variance with the anxiety whipped up by press leaks, arrests and court cases over the preceding nine months. Now the talk was of drift, and of last-ditch solutions. 'Hungry dogs eat dirty pudding,' the *Star*, a London evening paper, remarked graphically. The cabinet secretary Maurice Hankey was aghast at the casual way Baldwin failed to keep Cabinet informed. There was, it is true, no progress to report from the meetings with the two sides to the dispute; there is evidence that Baldwin, who was tense and nervous in front of the joint meeting of all the parties on 23 April, found the egos on his own side, particularly in his Cabinet, trying to deal with. He also knew that he would come under pressure from the faction that was more interested in taking a stand than finding a compromise. His options were tightly constrained; that he remained uncertain in his own mind about how to circumvent the deadline was clear from his frequent conversations with the one man in Downing Street who was familiar with the miners and had unofficial contacts with their advisers, Tom Jones.

As assistant cabinet secretary, Jones had been working closely with Baldwin for more than two years. But the Welshman had yet to be entirely convinced by Baldwin's long pauses for reflection and his unwillingness to take a lead, and he was frequently irked by his rudeness about Lloyd George. Where Baldwin saw sophistry and deceit in the former Prime Minister, Jones remembered brilliance and creativity. But over the next two weeks, Jones was first to be Baldwin's closest confidant and then to emerge, and remain, one of his most convinced admirers. From his position as prime-ministerial gatekeeper, he used his power to bring together men who might influence both sides in the mining dispute; he kept the Prime Minister informed with news from the TUC, and he struggled to steer him away from the demands for confrontation from the more powerful personalities in his Cabinet.

The day after his bilateral meetings with miners and owners, 24 April, Baldwin invited Jones to Chequers for the weekend. Baldwin, facing the greatest challenge of his political career, was showing himself a committed herbivore. He preferred rumination, the slow and sporadic discussion of a problem, to incisive intervention; and he was acutely vulnerable to ambush by his meat-eating cabinet colleagues.

On the Sunday morning he and Jones set off together on a long walk through the bluebell woods of the Chilterns. Baldwin, Jones felt, had been unduly swayed by a dinner on Thursday night with the leaders of the Mine Owners' Association, who had convinced him that the miners' executive, not the miners themselves, were the only barrier to an agreement; the men would accept longer hours if it meant maintaining rates of pay. At Jones's suggestion, Arthur Pugh, the TUC chairman, was secretly driven down to Chequers for tea. Pugh was a countryman from Herefordshire who had become a steelworker; a steady, shrewd negotiator. As Jones had anticipated, he made a coherent case for trying to lift the miners' eyes from the immediate issue of pay to the scope and potential of reorganization as a way of keeping the maximum number of miners in reasonably rewarded work. Talks, Pugh proposed, should start by searching for areas of agreement on restructuring, thus narrowing the areas of disagreement to the utmost. In this he may have been over-optimistic. Reorganization, the closing of uneconomic pits and the grouping of others to allow more efficient work, would mean huge dislocation for miners as well as unacceptable losses for some owners.

On Monday morning, Baldwin and Jones caught the train back to London. (Baldwin bought his own ticket, Jones noticed, where Lloyd George would have sent a secretary. But on this occasion the Prime Minister refrained from consulting the stationmaster for his opinion on world affairs.) Baldwin spent the journey absorbed in the *Daily Telegraph* crossword. To Jones's frustration, he was showing no interest in trying to understand the miners' outlook.

Just four days remained in which to find a settlement, or face a general strike that could provoke civil unrest, even civil war. Yet the climate of fear, created with the complicity of the government, made public and political acceptance of any deal hard to achieve. Nor were the employers a homogenous group. The majority, the smaller owners, were set on ignoring the Samuel Commission's finding in favour of national pay awards. They could only survive with district pay agreements that reflected local conditions. They wanted the men to work longer hours. They were extremely cool about reorganization. A little influence could be exerted through some of the larger owners, but it was the government alone that could insist on reorganization, perhaps with the blandishment of legislating to repeal or suspend the seven-hour day.

In London, Baldwin summoned the TUC Special Industrial Committee to sound out the scope for negotiation. A further, inconclusive, encounter with the mine owners followed. They refused to trade concessions on pay in return for the restoration of the eight-hour day. The TUC committee, meanwhile, met the miners again; again the miners refused to negotiate on pay without a guarantee of restructuring. That night, Conservative Central Office gave an indication of government thinking when it put out a briefing document stressing the uneconomic nature of the pits and the advantage of a longer working day.

On Tuesday the 27th, Baldwin confided to Jones that he was planning to wait until almost beyond the eleventh hour – only three days away – and then to offer himself as arbitrator. Politically unable either to extend the subsidy or to underwrite reorganization without some concession from the miners, yet still instinctively pacifist, he would present a package of measures that would retain existing wages but extend the working day. He would also agree to look at measures for cooperative selling and to offer assistance to men displaced by pit closures. Jones warned that by so doing he risked making the government party to the dispute; he also pointed out an apparent overture from Cook in the trade union paper the *Daily Herald*, which could be construed as acceptance of a pay cut. Baldwin dismissed the newspaper as a 'rag' and ignored Cook's signal.

At its monthly meeting in Eccleston Square, the TUC General Council was for the first time fully briefed. The news of the apparent deadlock in negotiations was a shock as unpleasant as it was unexpected, for all but the handful of members of the Special Industrial Committee. No one else had been kept up to date with the negotiations, although Bevin had approached the miners privately, asking to be updated on progress; and, warning Cook of the dangers of 'drifting to war on slogans', he had pressed him to find a way to talk about money. Even as experienced a negotiator as the Transport and General Workers' leader found the quantums, minimums and percentages of the miners' labyrinthine pay structure impenetrable. He had asked Cook to set out the minimum acceptable figure for pay in every district, and sketched out a plan for the implementation of the Samuel Commission report. He also resolved to make sure that the miners were prepared to hand over authority

to a negotiating committee before his union committed itself to a
general strike. Bevin's document would remain under consideration
until negotiations finally broke down.

The TUC at last had to accept that they must be ready for
negotiations to fail; preparations had to be made for that eventuality.
'As usual,' Bevin wrote in the strike's aftermath a month later, 'there
was a lot of talk on the General Council by people who thought
they were not going to be involved.'[1] Anxious about transport
workers' vulnerability to strike-breaking, Bevin was determined
that his members would not be left bearing the brunt of a coal
embargo that would threaten their own jobs, with little chance of
achieving the strike's objectives. In a move that improved its
effectiveness but did nothing to dampen Fleet Street excitement,
Bevin, the man with the reputation of being the most intransigent
of union leaders, became the driving force behind the Ways and
Means Committee at last established to prepare for the strike. It
was chaired by the left-wing French polisher Alf Purcell, whose
revolutionary demagoguery had set the radical tone for the 1924
TUC conference. Later, it became the Strike Organization Committee, while the Special Industrial Committee, which had been
struggling with mediation, evolved into a negotiating committee.
On Wednesday the 28th, miners' delegates met again; and, again,
bound their executive to bring any pay cuts back to the table for
their approval.

The next day, TUC executives from across the country gathered in London. On the platform of the Memorial Hall, Farringdon
Street, the birthplace twenty-six years earlier of the political wing
of the Labour movement, nearly a thousand members of its industrial wing prepared for a show of power that could succeed only
by undermining representative democracy. The platform speakers
observed the heavy sense of duty that hung over the solid citizens
below. 'The hall was packed to suffocation,' wrote Citrine in his
memoirs, adding as a ponderous afterthought, 'I have many times
noted that a crowded hall adds to the excitement.' But not this
time. Arthur Pugh, the TUC chairman, whispered to him, 'Don't

you think this conference realises its responsibility?' Journalists commented on the lack of revolutionary fervour; Arthur Cook's impassioned appeal failed to rouse the usual response. It was Bevin, determined the conference should grasp what it was being asked to do, who was cheered when he declared: 'Twenty-four hours from now ... you will have to become one union with no autonomy. The miners will have to throw in their lot and come into the course of the general movement and the general movement will have to take the responsibility for seeing it through ... you are to be our parliament.'[2] The conference was adjourned for further nego- tiations; delegates sang hymns and music-hall songs and told jokes. The movement's foremost woman, Margaret Bondfield, sat quietly in a corner playing patience.

At the end of the afternoon, the Industrial Committee met Baldwin at the House of Commons; he had not abandoned hope, he said. Later still, the miners joined them. Baldwin spoke of the need to accept longer hours. A long silence ensued, broken finally by Herbert Smith, the miners' president. 'Are you waiting for us to speak, Mr Prime Minister?' Citrine remembered him saying. 'Do you think our people are likely to go back to longer hours? Ah don't think you can expect us to do it, and we're not going to.'[3]

The meeting ended, but the miners and the TUC, expect- ing the mine owners to join them for further talks, waited in a committee room overlooking the Thames, where the lights of a ship at anchor reflected across the water. Walter Citrine took notes. The railway leader Jimmy Thomas repeated Baldwin's warning of a few days earlier. 'He talks to me like a pal ... [the government] have made up their minds that there will be trouble. They are going to smash it.' He looked round the room, where some of the miners' delegates were wrestling with one another. Others threw a paper ball around. 'A few of these people will get shot, of course,' Thomas went on. 'More of them will get arrested. The government will arrest the remainder and say it is a case of putting them away for their own safety. Of course the shooting won't be done by them direct, it will be done by those damn Fascists.' Thomas had been a

minister during a train drivers' dispute in 1924, and he had seen
the intelligence operation at first hand, he told them, the copies of
letters and details of speeches on his desk each morning. Swales,
the left-winger, claimed arrests would be useful. 'It will be just the
thing to rouse our movement.'[4]

The mine owners, a disparate mix of the super-rich, the
paternalistic and the diehard, were divided among themselves.
Closeted in internal negotiations, they failed to meet the TUC
committee that night, or until 1 p.m. the following day – Friday
30 April, the final day of subsidy. At midnight, the notices setting
out the rates individual employers were willing to pay at each pit
would be formally activated. From then on, no miner need turn up
for work who would not accept the pay cuts. Baldwin had secured
one small victory: a national pay scale was once again to be offered.
But it was entirely dependent on longer hours. The terms, to run
for the next five years, were of a national minimum of 20 per cent
over the standard which had been set twelve years earlier, in 1914,
and an eight-hour day. This represented a 13 per cent cut on the
1921 rates. Baldwin, who must have known it would be unacceptable, added a proposal for a committee to include representatives
of both sides, to advise on reorganization, and promised that the
seven-hour day legislation would be suspended, not annulled.

This was the first formal proposal for negotiation to come from
either side. But it was not enough for the TUC to feel able to order
a retreat. In particular, the 'lockout' notices of the individual pit
pay rates, now due to come into effect in only a few hours' time,
remained. And there was no government-backed guarantee of
reorganization, only the definite prospect of a pay cut and longer
hours.

As with the Schlieffen Plan and the timetable for the outbreak of
the First World War, from 30 April preparations for a general strike
suddenly started to assume a momentum independent of the
negotiations. The mood turned from the expectation of a settlement

to anxious anticipation of a breakdown. The King, a concerned observer of developments, was distracting himself at the One Thousand Guineas at Newmarket, where his filly Aloysia finished a good fourth. But on Friday evening, at the request of the government, instead of going home to Windsor Castle he immediately drove to Buckingham Palace where he held a Privy Council meeting to approve the final preparations for the declaration of a state of emergency, ready for publication in Saturday's papers.

The signal, 'Action!', was sent out to the deputy civil commissioners and to the military. A young midshipman, John Howson, aboard HMS *Sovereign*, was ordered to the ship's safe to remove the secret orders marked 'U, C'. The letters, Howson discovered, stood for 'Unrest, Civil';[5] his ship sailed immediately to lie off the naval dockyard at Rosyth. Others steamed towards Liverpool, to Plymouth, up the Clyde. Leave was cancelled. No risks were to be run with possible mutiny. Troops were despatched to South Wales, Lancashire and Scotland.

The Ministry of Health issued a circular to local authorities, reminding them of their commitments in the event of a general strike. The names of the individual commissioners were published again. The Great Western Railway received orders to run two special trains from Devonport to Lancashire to transport naval ratings, six hundred men 'plus horses and vehicles'; a further train was ordered to take men from Plymouth to London.[6] At Westminster, the TUC negotiators were deliberating on the mine owners' offer when a sympathizer brought them the printers' proofs of a poster inviting volunteers to join the Organization for the Maintenance of Supply which, with the declaration of the emergency, became an official government organization. Apparently surprised by the government's preparations, the TUC men challenged Baldwin with it. He admitted they were about to proclaim a state of emergency. The union side declared they had been betrayed; Thomas spoke emotionally of being dragged into a whirlpool. 'The State must win on an issue like this ... I feel it is a desperate state

... Our love of our country and our anxiety for the future of our country, not our politics, is the driving force, the impelling motive, that makes us plead.'

More talks followed, as the TUC negotiators tried to harden a government guarantee of reorganization against the miners' willingness to accept pay cuts until reorganization had restored profitability. 'I want to see the horse I am going to mount,' Herbert Smith insisted. At 9.45 on Friday evening, the Industrial Committee had a last meeting with Baldwin and an inner Cabinet. Churchill bumped into Thomas outside Baldwin's room. 'It's over as far as we're concerned,' he said. 'I have given you twenty-four millions [in subsidy] and that is all you are going to get. You can't have another bob.'

The negotiations narrowed to phrases, forms of words, that would allow pay cuts to be included. The TUC committee was prepared to 'review the suggestions made in the [Samuel] Report as a whole and arrive at an arrangement, one element of which might be a reduction in wages, but they could not consent to begin negotiations with this one element having been fixed as a certainty'. This was amended, with the miners' agreement, to giving 'full consideration to all the difficulties concerned with the industry when the schemes for such reorganisation will have been initiated by the government'.

But at midnight, when the lockout notices came into force, there had been no agreement. The government would not undertake to impose reorganization. The miners would not accept a pay cut without knowing what the return would be.

In the Memorial Hall, where for the second day trade union executives had idled away long hours waiting for news, hundreds were still gathered at midnight when the negotiating committee finally arrived. Negotiations had broken down on a phrase, they were told. There was still hope; the conference was only adjourned, not dismissed, and still no resolution for a general strike had been made. The delegates left for the night with Jimmy Thomas's words still ringing in the air: 'We have striven, we have pleaded, we have begged for peace, because we want peace. We still want peace. The nation wants peace. Those who want war must take the responsibility.'[7] But on their way out, trade union general secretaries were invited to stay behind to hear from Bevin and Purcell's Strike Organization Committee what would be required of them if it came to a general strike.

On Saturday morning, 1 May, traditional May Day parades passed by newspaper placards prematurely declaring 'General Strike Ordered'. The newspapers reported the proclamation of a state of emergency. Citrine mistook the band at the head of the London procession for a Guards regiment marching through the City in a deliberate show of strength. Along Park Lane, dustcarts from Labour councils, decked in scarlet bunting, bore children singing 'The Red Flag'. Behind them walked the men, carrying a forest of trade union banners. A carload of Fascists drove back and forth alongside, jeering provocatively. The hero of the hour in Hyde Park was Battersea's Communist MP, Shapurji Saklatvala, whose anti-imperialist invective would land him in Bow Street magistrates' court early the following week.

A few miles to the south-west of Hyde Park, in his cell in Wandsworth Prison, Harry Pollitt wrote to his wife Marjorie, whom he had married only a week before his arrest. His normally light-hearted style was sombre. 'Today has been the worst day we have spent in prison, May Day has so many memories in connection with the movement ... This morning on the exercise ground it was drizzling with rain when a lark rose up from the Common over the wall, and it poured out its lovely song, as merrily as if it were a glorious morning. I said to myself says I, "By the shades of Lenin, that's a sign." '[8] But there was also a warning: 'Now that the coal trouble has started, it's a certainty that [emergency powers] will be introduced. My love of loves, watch your step – and your tongue. Don't let the excitement carry you away and make you forget your judgement. It would be rather funny to commence a correspondence between Holloway and Wandsworth, but please wait till I've been out some time.'

Early on Saturday afternoon, the last, decisive meeting of the TUC executives' conference began. The individual unions had first to meet in their own delegations to approve Bevin's plan of action, and it was after midday when they gathered for the final session. From the chair, Arthur Pugh asked for individual declarations of support for the effective creation of a single union for the duration of the strike. 'The scheme requires,' Pugh emphasized, 'that the Miners' Federation hand over to the General Council the conduct of this dispute ... that condition of this document *is accepted by the Miners' Federation* [author's emphasis].'[9] The proposal was over-whelmingly accepted; unions representing 3.6 million people were in favour. The only refusal came from the National Sailors' and Fireman's Union, a decision that was to play a significant part in the strike's denouement.

'We are not declaring war on the people. War has been declared by the Government, pushed on by sordid capitalism,' Bevin announced to cheers. Bevin and Purcell planned the largest strike ever seen; it would start big, but it would retain the capacity to grow even bigger. A first tranche involving all transport workers, printers, electrical workers and most building workers would come out at once. Power, 'useful' building work and sanitary services would initially be exempt. A volunteer system for the distribution of essential supplies was envisaged. Trade unionists would offer to cooperate with the government to distribute food and milk. Bevin held open the door to 'enthrone reason' and pursue last-minute negotiations. 'The best brains of this movement are available to help to find a solution for this country of this great problem.' He concluded: 'I rely, in the name of the General Council, on every man and every woman ... to fight for the soul of Labour and the salvation of the miners.'[10]

But when the miners' president Herbert Smith followed Bevin to the platform, he made no mention of further negotiations. He was leaving London, he announced, sure that everything that could have been done, had been done. He explained that the pre-1921 rates, to which a return was now envisaged, had driven a quarter of a million men on to outdoor relief, and he talked of the catastrophic underinvestment that drove down productivity. Far from conceding the right of the TUC to reach a deal, he spoke of 'sharing in the negotiations', confident that no trade unionist would expect them to accept either longer hours or less money. He did not reject Samuel's report, he would go through it, and 'accept the findings when we had gone through it'. But, as he had said all along, he was not going to agree to a pay cut before he knew what he was going to be given in return.

Finally Ramsay MacDonald, avowed opponent of the idea of a general strike, spoke. That night, he wrote dispiritedly in his diary: 'No definite idea of what they are to consider as satisfactory to enable them to finish & go back to work. Position wonderfully like 1914. Strike cannot settle purely economic problem of bankruptcy of industry.'[11] But before the trade unionists, he was a soldier in their cause, a champion on the barricades, as he described in emotive terms the miner's wife unable to feed her child, the toiling masses denied the chance of living honourable and magnificent individual lives. He blamed the government for breaking off negotiations, and accused it of flaunting the sword of war in the face of the British people.

It was left to a colleague, J. R. Clynes, to warn in a May Day speech elsewhere that no stoppage or lockout would resolve the problems of the coal industry. In the Memorial Hall, carried away by their own cheers, delegates approved unanimously the General Strike, to start at the end of shifts on the evening of Monday 3 May. But as the delegates streamed out into the drizzling afternoon on the dying chords of 'The Red Flag' – in which, it was noted, even Ramsay MacDonald had joined – journalists observed not revolutionary fervour but the mood of an army of martyrs. More ominously, at the last minute Herbert Smith returned to the platform. He said he wanted to clarify the miners' position; he left it obscured in ambiguity. 'I did not mean to say in my speech that

I agreed to accept the [Samuel] report. What I did intend to imply was that I am prepared to examine the Report from page one to the last page and to stand by the result of the inquiry.'

In Manchester, May Day marchers paraded through the rain to the hall in Belle Vue Gardens. When the news came that a general strike had been declared, the cold and subdued crowd erupted into life. 'A wild burst of cheering broke out,' reported the *Manchester Guardian*. 'The Communists waved red streamers and hats were thrown into the air. Thereafter every reference from the platform to "the coming fight" and every appeal to "stand by the miners" was received with cheers and applause. The solidarity of the meeting was incontestable.'[12] Similar scenes were being repeated at May Day celebrations across the country. A few voices were raised in warning, but they sounded either treacherous or eccentric. The Labour candidate for West Stirlingshire, George Smith, an evangelist for Socialism as an aspect of Christian principle, asked: 'Who is going to suffer? You know deep down in your hearts that the people going to suffer most are the people who least deserve to suffer. It is a horrible jungle struggle.'[13]

Still it was not all over. As TUC general secretary, Citrine's first move after the ending of the conference, was to report to Downing Street that the TUC was now in charge of negotiations, although formally these could not be resumed until the lockout notices were withdrawn. 'Talks about talks' began at once, this time between two small groups. The trade union side, at one remove from the miners, was dominated by Arthur Pugh and Jimmy Thomas. With Baldwin on the government side were the declining but still powerful figure of Lord Birkenhead, Secretary of State for India, and the clever but ineffectual Minister of Labour Sir Arthur Steel-Maitland. Lord Birkenhead, the sharpest lawyer of his generation but too fond of both wine and women for those who took their politics seriously, called the railmen's leader 'Jimmy', and Thomas called Birkenhead 'Frederick'. No notes were to be taken and nothing that was said that night was to prejudice any final agreement. A long evening's discussion resulted in agreement that details of wages should be set aside and heads of agreement on the nature and scope of reorganization should be drawn up. What had to be achieved was a delay in imposing pay cuts while the full details of restructuring were negotiated; a subsidy would be required.

By the early hours of Sunday morning, it seemed a breakthrough was possible. A form of words had been arrived at that might permit negotiations to restart: the TUC side was 'confident' a settlement could be reached 'along the lines of the [Samuel] report within a fortnight'. By implication, the government would continue the subsidy during these final negotiations and, also by implication, the miners were understood to have accepted the report, including its recommendation for pay cuts. Not for the first time, the negotiators were glossing over contradictions that neither of the principal parties to the dispute were likely to accept. At 1.15 a.m., the trade union men retired, intending to consult the miners for their agreement to harden up the statement before returning in the morning. Although Birkenhead, who had drafted the form of words, said later that agreement had never been possible, at that point both sides apparently felt they were on the brink of a deal. But already there were doubts. Steel-Maitland scribbled a note of martyrdom to Lord Birkenhead: 'A taper has been lit this day in England.' Birkenhead scribbled back: 'If it's a taper without a wages agreement not even God's help will enable it to be put out.'[14]

None of this was known outside, where public opinion was being prepared for disaster. On Saturday evening, the BBC had broadcast a 'message from the Prime Minister': an anonymous voice came on the air. 'Be steady. Remember that peace on earth comes from men of good will.' It was repeated three times, 'each time with louder and more pompous emphasis'. It was the voice of John Reith, the company's ambitious managing director. 'The one note of hysteria,' Beatrice Webb noted. 'Perhaps if Baldwin himself, in his kindly and commonsense accent, had spoken his own words the effect would have been different. But in the emissary's melodramatic shout it sounded not a little absurd ... bathos is easily detected in the silence of your own sitting room.'[15] Reith's diaries reveal the background to the alarming announcement: 'Davidson [now Deputy Chief Civil Commissioner] phoned to say that the TUC were meeting the PM at 8.30 and that the PM wanted to suggest this message to me – "Keep steady; remember that peace on earth comes to men of goodwill." I gave this myself at 9.40.'[16]

But still for most people, even those close to the negotiations, life's measured tread continued. Hamilton Fyfe was the editor of the *Daily Herald*, the newspaper that the trade unions had taken over in 1922. Fyfe had launched a brilliant editing career when in 1903, at the age of only thirty-four, he had transformed the fortunes of the *Daily Mirror* and introduced an entirely new breed of newspaper for the new breed of commuters. 'Packed in tram, train, or omnibus, standing up perhaps and holding on to a strap with one hand, they required in the other, not a journal to stir thought or supply serious information, but one to entertain them . . . occupy their minds pleasantly, prevent them from thinking. It was easier to look at pictures than to read print. Everything in the *Daily Mirror* was calculated to be easy of absorption by the most ordinary intelligence.' That May Day, Fyfe, whose politics had shifted sharply to the left and who now aspired to be a Labour MP, took up his invitation to attend the private viewing of the Summer Exhibition at the Royal Academy before going to his office to prepare the final pre-strike edition of the *Herald*. At a banquet at the Academy that night, the Home Secretary Sir William Joynson-Hicks, a late substitute for Baldwin, told his fellow diners that men who had given so unselfishly in the Great War would surely 'obey the call of their country to sacrifice on both sides of what they deem to be their rights in order to preserve peace in our land'.[17]

In official circles, however, the gloom deepened. The Communists had issued a call to arms. The *Sunday Worker* launched a manifesto attacking the TUC for failing to make preparations, and pressing for the immediate formation of workers' defence corps, councils of action and a 'commissariat department jointly with the local Co-operative to demand that the General Council shall immediately summon an International Conference'. Tom Jones, as he walked through Horse Guards on his way to work, wondered gloomily whether the next time he saw soldiers they would be quelling riots. In Downing Street, he found the previous evening's agreement with the TUC negotiators being unpicked. Ministers, even those directly involved, thought they had gone too far in trying to find a formula for reopening negotiations. Not for the first time, there were rumours of a coup attempt against Baldwin by what in later, similar circumstances were referred to as 'the usual suspects'. Former coalitionists allied with the clever and the merely carnivorous in a loose grouping most often headed by Birkenhead and Churchill, with Beaverbrook's encouragement from the outside. Nine months of 'educating public opinion', of repeated warnings of Communist infiltration and insurrection, had made anything less than total victory appear as capitulation. Even Baldwin was anxious that he had conceded too much. To confirm the mood of the cabinet hawks, the Postmaster General produced the previous night's intercepts from Eccleston Square and other trade union headquarters. They showed that telegrams had gone out to trans-port workers and men in the iron and steel industry ordering them to stop work at midnight. The strike was about to begin.

While the Cabinet plotted and speculated – he'd never been in a session like it, the cabinet secretary said later; it had been like something out of a cartoon strip, a Downing Street *Comic Cuts* – waiting to hear again from the TUC negotiating committee, the committee itself had learnt to its surprise that the miners had not waited to see if negotiations could be reopened, but had already left London for their own districts where the lockouts had begun. Although it had been referred to from the platform, the miners had not discussed this move with the TUC; only their secretary, Arthur Cook, now remained in London, and he refused to answer without his executive, whom he had now summoned back.

In their absence, Cook denied that the miners had ever agreed to accept the Samuel report and claimed the TUC was acting beyond the remit given to it by conference. ('It really looks tonight as though there was to be a General Strike to save Mr Cook's face. Important man!' MacDonald seethed in his diary later that night.) It was impossible to say when the miners and the TUC could consult, Cook stated. The TUC requested a meeting with the Prime Minister anyway, which was fixed for 9 p.m. that Sunday evening. Meanwhile, Cabinet, impatient with the delay, the reason for which had not been explained to them, drew up what they saw as an acceptable version of the statement that Baldwin's subcommittee had drafted with the TUC the previous night. Back into it went the express demand for flexibility on wages and hours in advance of agreement on reorganization. And now it also demanded the 'unconditional withdrawal' of the order for a general strike, which was 'a challenge to the constitutional rights and freedom of the nation'.

Despite the reservations of some of the Cabinet, the TUC negotiators were received again at the appointed hour; until 11.15 they resumed argument with Baldwin's subcommittee, while the full Cabinet waited. At 11.30 the miners' executive finally gathered at Downing Street. Privately, Arthur Cook indicated to Tom Jones areas for negotiation, and the TUC and the miners retired to agree a position, leaving the Cabinet to themselves. Very shortly afterwards, news arrived in Cabinet that some *Daily Mail* technicians, members of the National Society of Operative Printers and Assistants, NATSOPA, had refused to print an editorial denouncing as treachery a general strike. The newspaper would not come out in the morning. Led by Churchill and the Foreign Secretary Austen Chamberlain, the whole Cabinet was persuaded that this was proof that the strike really was under way. Baldwin was allowed no alternative but to present to the negotiating committee the strongly worded ultimatum on the withdrawal of the strike threat that Cabinet had agreed earlier in the evening. If he did not, there would be resignations.

The four-man TUC negotiating committee, who had been locked in discussions with the miners and the whole of the rest of the TUC General Council, were called in. Baldwin, 'exhausted' in one account, 'ill at ease' in another, handed them the ultimatum. None knew anything of the *Daily Mail* incident and were astonished to hear this was the government's reason for breaking off negotiations. Arthur Pugh protested that the miners had only just arrived; talks were just beginning. The Prime Minister responded wearily that the hotheads had made it impossible to reach agreement. Whose hotheads, he did not say. The trade unionists were shown out, but when they broke the news to their colleagues, there was general agreement not to give up but to continue trying to agree a form of words with the miners. For two more hours, as the lights in No. 10 and 11 flickered out, they struggled with a resolution. When Pugh and Citrine returned to deliver their reply to the ultimatum, based on Bevin's proposals for reorganization, they found everything shut up and dark.

The trade unions regarded the *Daily Mail* action as a pretext. In fact, matters were running beyond the control of both sides; NATSOPA, which had a powerful radical wing, was not officially behind the 'censorship', but nor was the *Daily Mail* incident the only occasion over the weekend when print workers had obstructed editorial and advertising with which they disagreed. In the final hours, as chances of a genuine settlement ebbed away, the only way to avert a general strike was to separate the TUC from the miners. That would have taken more than Baldwin's Cabinet was ready to give. Instead of making concessions to the miners that the TUC at least would have accepted, the government forced them back on to their commitment to stand by the miners. In the end, it was impossible to go on obscuring points of disagreement behind a gloss of vague language. 'If we live we shall meet again to settle it,' Baldwin had told Walter Citrine. 'If we live.'

PART TWO

6

THE STRIKE: 3–4 MAY

For the British Trade Union Movement I see a day of terrible disillusionment. The failure of the General Strike of 1926 will be one of the most significant landmarks in the history of the British working class.

Beatrice Webb's, Diaries 1924–1932, ed. M. Cole, 4 May 1926

In a technical sense it was never a General Strike. We at the Trades Union Congress always called it the 'national strike'. We regarded it as a large-scale sympathetic strike.

Walter Citrine, *Men and Work*

Tuesday 4th May. Went to Tooting with Spot, on foot because of the strike. The way in which people have accepted the inevitable is wonderful. The High Road is thronged with an unending stream of motor cars, and cycles. It looks cheery enough and to my mind, we will show the strikers and the trade unions that we are certainly not entirely dependent upon them for food supplies, papers and buses. Everybody is willing to give anybody help or a lift and the number of pedestrians is comparatively few. Had Connie to tea and afterwards walked part of the way home with her. Took Spot, nearly got run over at the Wheatsheaf but I still live!

Diary of Margaret Woods, aged fifteen

WORD THAT NEGOTIATIONS had broken down was first broadcast by the BBC at 1.10 a.m. on Monday 3 May. But when the country awoke, it was to a curious lull. For the past week negotiations had been constantly in the planning or execution. Phrases had been twisted, words turned, and although neither coal owners nor miners had seemed to believe a satisfactory compromise was possible, the general public still expected peace, not war. Yet, as Birkenhead said a few days later, there had never been any real chance of a settlement. The miners knew they had the backing of the trade union movement, the owners the backing of the government. Some mine owners and many others on the right believed a kind of bloodletting was essential, a lancing of the boil that would finally end the turmoil on the industrial front. A few on the left believed it might provoke revolution. In desperation, the miners and the owners who lacked the imagination to see another way out wanted to see the strike through; but although it was Churchill who defined the action as an attack on the constitution in the Commons – 'It is a conflict which, if it is fought out to a conclusion, can only end in the overthrow of Parliamentary Government or in its decisive victory' – fear about the civil unrest it might bring was not confined to the Tory right and Fleet Street. After his emotional words in support of the miners, Ramsay MacDonald reverted to his former position as opponent of the concept of a general strike, which in the next few days he managed to associate with Bolshevism in speeches both in the Commons and outside. In the parliamentary debate after the breakdown of negotiations, which took place on the Monday afternoon, Jimmy Thomas said the same, calling it 'the greatest calamity for this country'. It was not too late to avert it, he went on: 'I have never disguised that, in a challenge to the Constitution, God help us unless the Government won...'[1]

Such was the enormity of the idea that every trade unionist in the country might stop work, so incomprehensible the impact, that many still doubted that it would come, at least not to London. Hamilton Fyfe, discussing the strike with a shopkeeper, was told, 'But that's nowhere near London. It's the miners. Nothing to do with us.'[2]

'None of the leaders are strong enough to turn and tell their followers the truth,' Baldwin observed to Tom Jones. Baldwin had stood firm, but he knew that that alone would not be enough to hold back the 'old gang' of Churchill, Birkenhead and Austen Chamberlain, his tormentors, the men who regarded him as second-rate. His conduct of the dispute, now that it had begun, must tread the fine line between satisfying the hardliners' desire for a crushing victory, and his own instinctive desire to avoid provoking the strikers. 'Baldwin had complete faith in the commonsense and sanity of the working classes,' his closest political confidant J. C. C. Davidson claimed later. 'Many of the talks we used to have during the coal strike and the months which preceded the General Strike always resulted in our agreement that the British would reject dictatorship, whether from the right or from the left.'[3]

Baldwin's political difficulties were clearly revealed in his statement to the Commons that Monday afternoon, as he struggled to be simultaneously conciliatory towards the unions (or at least the working classes, whom he felt were often misrepresented by their leaders) and robust about the nature of the strike. After acknowledging that some would say his 'dreamy' speeches about peace were at an end, he continued: 'Everything that I care for is being smashed to bits at this moment. That does not take away from me either my faith or my courage. We may in this House be full of strife. Before long the angel of peace, with healing in his wings, will be among us again, and when he comes let us be there to meet him.'[4] He denied there was a general attack on wages. 'It is not wages that are in peril, it is the freedom of our Constitution ... I do not think all the leaders when they assented to a general strike realised that they were threatening ordered government and going nearer to civil war than we have been for generations.' The *Manchester Guardian*'s political correspondent listened sceptically. 'Mr Baldwin spoke his piece, but one had the feeling that the militants in his Cabinet had taught it to him.'

In his nightly report to the King, Baldwin said: '[The Commons] rose to its greatest heights ... the leaders of the Labour Party were sincerely anxious of finding an honourable way out of the position into which they have been led by their own folly'. The King may not have found this of much comfort; but he committed himself to remain in London throughout the strike. Troops were bivouacked in Kensington Gardens, ready at the hoisting of a red flag to gallop to the aid of palace or Parliament.

The proclamation of a state of emergency had triggered the government's strike arrangements. Civil commissioners were in post in the regions of England, and in Wales and Scotland. The Organization for the Maintenance of Supply announced it was handing over its register of volunteers to the individual commissioners. Within government, the Supply and Transport Committee, chaired by Sir William Joynson-Hicks, was to run the logistics of the strike-breaking operation; it included the service chiefs and Sir William Mitchell-Thomson, the Chief Civil Commissioner, as well as his deputy, Baldwin's friend Davidson.

The district civil commissioners had had months to prepare registers of available transport and volunteers, to organize routes by which essential supplies could be brought into their regions, and to arrange back-up supplies for power and fuel. It was the beginning of summer, and demand for domestic coal – immediately rationed – was slacking off. A national appeal for volunteers was launched on the Monday morning. Hyde Park in central London was closed, as preparations were made to transform it into a milk depot and food distribution centre. Army tents, wooden huts, generators and telephone lines were installed. A Transport Ministry official claimed they had 250,000 lorries on their register; all day commercial vehicles were turned away and instructed to wait until the next day before volunteering. But, particularly out of London, most civil commissioners were anxious not to be presented as leaders of strike-breaking organizations. Some explicitly distanced themselves from the OMS, and appealed to trade unionists to stay at work to help distribute foodstuffs.

Unions and management began to make last-minute preparations. NUR members were told: 'No trains of any kind must be worked by our members ... Allow no disorderly or subversive elements to interfere in any way. Maintain perfect order and have confidence in your own representatives. Perfect loyalty will ensure success.' Employees of the Great Western Railway received a communication from Felix Pole, the general manager: 'I appeal to all of you to hesitate before you break your contracts of service with the old Company ... Remember that your means of living and your personal interests are involved, and that Great Western men are trusted to be loyal to their conditions of service in the same manner as they expect the Company to carry out their obligations and agreements.'[5] In Plymouth, the GWR promised to stand by staff who chose not to strike, after it was reported that they were being warned by NUR members that they would not return to work until the blacklegs were dismissed.

On Monday evening a crowd of around five thousand gathered in Parliament Square. Some sang 'The Red Flag'. Others responded with 'God Save the King'. Police had to clear the road to allow ministers, MPs and members of the TUC General Council, in search of a last-minute settlement, to get through. Inside the House of Commons, there was a flurry of excitement when Jimmy Thomas challenged Churchill in the midst of his speech: if the strike notices were withdrawn, would the lockout notices come down too? Churchill did not rule it out, and there was a general exit from the government front bench which MPs and journalists took to mean that some kind of concession was in the air. But the Miners' Federation, already disavowing the power it had ceded to the TUC and crying treachery because negotiations had continued over the weekend in its absence, issued a statement reiterating the impossibility of accepting any wage cut.

The TUC, the miners and the Parliamentary Labour Party now met in different groupings and all together, arguing over tactics. After discussion, it was decided that Bevin's plan for reorganization, which was being considered when the government called the talks off, should not be raised in the House for fear of appearing panicked. (Bevin always believed it could have provided a basis for settlement.) Tensions between the miners and the TUC flared. Again, the miners defended the inviolability of their pay rates. Bevin retorted angrily: 'Well if that is your decision, the General Council must make its own decision. There are three and a half million men who must have their position considered.' Later, he insisted that the TUC was 'not committed to any slogan of any kind'.

Very late, when the last trains before the strike were already arriving at their destinations, MacDonald and the respected veteran Labour politician Arthur Henderson, who had been present at some of the earlier Downing Street negotiations, met Baldwin and Churchill. In angry exchanges, Churchill evoked Mussolini's takeover in Italy. The workers could not dictate to the government; Steel-Maitland, the Minister of Labour, told Henderson 'it was about time you were put in your place'. Henderson accused Churchill of resorting to the heavy-handed tactics he had used fifteen years earlier as a Liberal Home Secretary, when he personally commanded troops to capture anarchists in the East End: 'It seems to me, Winston, that you are trying to give us a dose of Sidney Street.' Churchill, stung by the reference to an episode that had enhanced his reputation as a self-publicist more than his reputation for cool judgement, retorted, 'You will be better prepared to talk to us in two or three weeks.'

If tempers were fraying at the top, the message going out to strikers could not have been more pacific. 'Keep everybody smiling,' was the slogan of the strike. The TUC leaders were timid, but they had some justification for fearing that violence on picket lines or elsewhere could be taken as justification for the use of troops and an escalation into serious unrest. It was only seven years since the Glasgow general strike had led to looting and rioting. There were suspicions that both Communists and Fascists might try deliberately to incite violence. This was the subject of the TUC's first order of the day and it was reprinted in full in the last pre-strike edition of the *Daily Herald*: 'Let none be disturbed by rumours or be driven by panic to betray the cause. Violence and disorder must be everywhere avoided, no matter what the incitement.' An editorial in the same newspaper elaborated: 'The General Council has warned us against spies, against scoundrels who incite to riot, to attacks on persons or property. Deal with such pests immediately –

whether they are in capitalist pay or are trying to make trouble from another motive.'

On Tuesday 4 May, in towns and cities across Britain, people awoke to silence; it was the most remarked-upon fact – no hammering or shouting on building sites, no trains, no buses, no ordinary rush hour. Not a tram or a bus left a depot in any major British city. Barely a train ran. The response to TUC instructions had been absolute. The solidarity startled everyone, including the TUC, which could not keep a note of surprise from its first bulletin. 'We have from all over the country, from Lands End to John O'Groats, reports that have surpassed all our expectations,' began the first report from its publicity department. 'Not only the railwaymen and transport men, but all other trades came out in a manner we did not expect immediately.'[6] The railways in particular were unexpectedly solid: the booking-office clerks and signalmen and even some stationmasters joined the strike, the first time members of the Railway Clerks' Association had ever struck. The GWR's reassurances had failed to win a single strike-breaker.

The plan hastily drawn up by Bevin and Purcell setting out which members of which unions would be in the first wave of the strike had outlined only broad categories. It was up to individual unions to call their members out and to sort out any complications that arose, in particular within the building trades and among the engineering and steel workers. But often the complications only became apparent at a local level. In Merthyr, the trades council took it upon itself to arbitrate, but many other strike committees, most of which had only just been set up, panicked and sent representatives by road to London to try to establish the proper procedure. In disastrous cases, like Braintree, a thousand steel workers belonging to three different unions were called out: three separate journeys were made to London to find out what should happen. In Wellingborough, the Plebs League – a working-class intellectual forum that promoted the idea of a general strike and gathered evidence about it in the weeks immediately after it was settled – was told later, the secretary had called a mass meeting.

'Each affiliated society secretary was on the platform ... each with differently-worded instructions, each of which called on the members to cease work, and then went on to lay down rules and regulations which no one could interpret, but which made it impossible for the members to do so.'[7]

In Birmingham, eighty-two different unions had each to decide which of their members were covered by definitions such as 'All workers engaged on building except such as are employed definitely on housing and hospital work'. Or, harder, instructions such as 'Trade Unions connected with the supply of electricity and gas shall co-operate with the object of ceasing to supply power.' Often, different unions reached different conclusions from the same instruction. Coventry council of action reported that it had discovered trade unions it had not known existed; the Brighton Boilermakers sent off to their headquarters in Newcastle in a desperate bid to find out if they were supposed to come out, but grew tired of waiting and came out anyway.

At the TUC headquarters in Eccleston Square, a short walk from Parliament, the chaos was magnified by the number of people trying to work with only an uncertain idea of what they were hoping to achieve. The call had gone out for despatch riders and car drivers to come and volunteer. Outside the building, the pavements were crowded with the enthusiastic, the bewildered and the merely bored, waiting to be given a task. Journalists came and went, pushing their way through delegates from the provinces seeking an interpretation of their orders. Inside, plain-clothes police mingled with visitors to protect them from the danger of a Fascist attack, while the inadequate clerical staff struggled to cope with a General Council in permanent session whose members, Citrine complained, expected their office 'to be run with the orderliness of an automatic machine'.

Conflicting instructions continued to be handed down. The flow of requests for clarification about the procedures construction workers were to follow came in such numbers that the building unions were hived off to new offices in Clapham. Typists came close to hysteria as they struggled with orders that cancelled each other out. In the general secretary's office, Citrine and Bevin vied with one another to control the management of the strike. Bevin refused to allow the local trades councils to take over powers from the unions' local branches; Citrine thought that it was the only efficient way to work. Later, they fell out even more noisily when Bevin declared outright that he needed to take over the overall organization. He won. In his diary, Citrine let rip: Bevin 'did not like to suggest it but could anyone doubt that with his unrivalled experience of strikes and [given] that nature had endowed him with a constructive brain, the Deity had specially ordained him to run the first general strike in Great Britain'.[8]

ALTOGETHER, two and a half million workers went on strike on the first day. The government confirmed it as the 'completest strike we have ever had, especially on the railways'. The only prominent report of trouble came from the appearance of the Communist MP Saklatvala at Bow Street on charges arising from his May Day speech in Hyde Park, where he stood £200 bail and agreed henceforth to speak only in the House of Commons until his case was heard later in the week.

Two and a half million on strike left about sixteen million others to find their way to work without public transport. The result was chaos. Roads and pavements were choked with pedestrians, cars, bicycles, horse-drawn carts and charabancs. Traffic was moving, if at all, three abreast. Private cars gave pedestrians lifts; small boys were reported to be travelling around London in luxury for the fun of it. It was a moment in history; ordinary people felt the weight of great events. The writer and journalist Arnold Bennett found Victoria Station shut up and deserted although the platform newsagents, W. H. Smith, was open. The populace he thought 'excited and cheery', but during the day he observed that there was 'a noticeable increasing gravity in the general demeanour'.[9]

Bennett regarded the strike as a 'political crime'; Beatrice Webb, from a rather different perspective, agreed. 'A General Strike aims at coercing the whole community and is only successful *if it does so* [Webb's italics] and in so far as it does so. Further, if it succeeded in coercing the community it would mean that a militant minority were starving the majority into submission to their will, and would be the end of democracy, industrial as well as political.'[10]

Gravity was the prevailing mood. It was picked up even by schoolchildren like Margaret Woods (whose diary is quoted at the start of these chapters). Margaret, the fifteen-year-old daughter of a prosperous draper in south London, was a faithful recorder of a small suburban world, and an unexpected echo of the daily editorial line taken by *The Times*. The stock parallel, in speeches and in newspapers, was with August 1914, a sense of long days of fruitless negotiation and disappointed expectation, followed by a stiffening of the upper lip and a determination to see it through; and then a long and bloody conflict. The language on both sides was military: discipline and loyalty were the cardinal virtues once more among the front-line forces; stoicism and sacrifice among those at home. The strikers called the first day of the strike 'zero hour'. One Free Church Minister, an ex-miner, spoke of it in terms reminiscent of Rupert Brooke on the eve of war: 'When the lock-out happened, I needed something to sweep me out of my miserable, bourgeois concern for security and popularity – something big and clean and explosive. When the miners came out I never hesitated for a second: I had found what I wanted.'[11] The generation of men and women who had lived and fought through the Great War were to be found on both sides. But this time the conflict was at home, not abroad, and however much Labour politicians and the unions might try to deny it or disguise it by careful language and frequent reiteration, it was taking place between the Labour movement and the government. There was no shortage of people, like a Conservative councillor in Plymouth who refused to let a Labour councillor see the government's emergency instructions, who thought it was class war.

Yet that remained a minority interpretation: on the whole,

Britain conducted itself as it always had, with studied moderation. Fortitude in times of hardship had been a supreme characteristic of the English at least since the Earl of Uxbridge lost his leg at Waterloo. It was, most newspapers thought, 'the natural expression of a nation which always shows to the best advantage in a crisis'. This was the spirit that Baldwin embodied and consciously strove to promote against the excitability and histrionics of colleagues like Churchill and Birkenhead. He was a politician who believed that, as well as the common man, he had God on his side. He once wrote to Davidson's wife Mimi: 'The longing to help the bewildered multitude of common folk is the only motive power to make me face the hundred and one things I loathe so much. And the longing only comes from love and pity.'[12]

If the response of the trade unionists had been beyond the expectations of the TUC, so was the response of the volunteers – to the relief of the more peace-loving members of the government who otherwise feared recourse to soldiers. Long queues formed at the Foreign Office, the main London recruitment centre. The upper classes turned up to register for work at their clubs in Pall Mall and St James's; they staffed canteens and enlisted as special constables – 'the thug-militia of St James's street', the young poet Osbert Sitwell called them indignantly, 'bands of young, steel-helmeted clubmen'. Around the country, naval ratings were on call to keep the power stations fired up. In Manchester twelve thousand volunteers enrolled, including a local aviator, with aeroplane. But what the volunteers could actually achieve was rather more questionable. Thousands who turned up at Paddington Station no doubt hoped to be allowed to drive an engine, but it took several days' training for even the most rudimentary understanding, as the rail companies discovered when their locomotives ground to a halt on hills and stalled deep inside tunnels.

On the first morning, there was an urgent need for porters to unload the perishables. Even before dawn broke, Paddington was blocked with trains that had no drivers to take them out again, and more trains continued to arrive. Throughout the strike, the GWR never managed to use more than 40 per cent of the volunteers, and many of those it did use were company pensioners or senior staff.

The day before the strike began, C. R. Clinker, a young railway clerk in Bristol, volunteered to work as a signalman.

> After lunch all suddenly became tense. The staff was handed copies of a telegram from the General Manager ... at four we were summoned to the Board Room [and] asked to indicate on a list whether we intended to remain at work and, if we did so, what we would undertake. It was an awesome decision ... I signed up for 'any work' with no clear idea of what this might involve. We were told to go home and sleep and report for duty at 6 am.

Early on the first day of the strike, he turned up at Bristol Temple Meads and was sent in the station car to the remote village of Codford, between Warminster and Salisbury, some fifty miles distant, where the stationmaster had gone on strike leaving his two crossing-gates shut across the lines.

> At the station I telephoned up and down the line to see if any train was about but there was no news. A farmer arrived with a dozen milk churns. I had no idea how to charge or invoice milk ... towards midday, the stationmaster's wife spoke to me over the hedge separating the garden from the platform. She said her husband had gone out and would I like some lunch on a tray? ... Just as I was sitting down ... a train arrived unheralded; it had come up the line ignoring signals. It was manned by a retired driver and his very juvenile son as fireman; the guard was a regular man. I unlocked the gates, passed the train through and rode with it for about half a mile to the second crossing. Here I encountered the crossing keeper's wife, a foul-mouthed unpleasant woman who shouted abuse at me whilst I handled the gates.[13]

Perhaps the most controversial order made by Bevin's Strike Organization Committee was to call out the printers; it was not a decision that had been taken lightly, but the view had been reached that the majority of newspapers were so right-wing in their coverage that the danger of the inability to communicate with the rank and file could be more easily overcome than their damaging propaganda. The *Manchester Guardian* wrote pleadingly to the TUC requesting exemption on the grounds of sanity, but despite conceding that it was normally 'very fair', the Organization Committee refused to relax the ban. In an inexplicable gesture, it even closed down its own newspaper, the *Daily Herald*.

THE GOVERNMENT had anticipated the loss of the national press. At noon on the first day, Churchill announced to Baldwin that he had commandeered the offices and presses of the *Morning Post* and was going to edit a government newssheet to be called the *British Gazette*. It was less of a unilateral action than at first appeared. The Newspaper Proprietors' Association had decided they did not want to risk trying to bring out their own newspapers, but they would do what they could to help the government bring out a small bulletin that could be posted up in town halls and other public places around the country. Initially, Churchill had favoured the premises of the *Daily Mail* for this task, but its location in Carmelite Street, part of the warren of lanes behind Fleet Street and close to the offices of the *Daily Herald*, defied basic military strategy. It was too easy to cut off. The *Morning Post* editor H. A. Gwynne, a former Reuters war correspondent, condemned the 'mugwumpishness' of the other newspapers and volunteered his offices, splendidly located at the west end of the Aldwych, and his printers. Unfortunately for the exercise, the printers were instructed by their unions not to cooperate, and by the time the non-union staff had rounded up a handful of other volunteers willing to work in defence of the government, it was running very late. As a result, some of the type that had already been set for the *Morning Post* was used in the government paper, and below a long attack on the reprehensible greed of the miners appeared details of the will of an eminent coal owner, Alderman William Edwin Pease, who left £295,213 (about £90 million at today's prices).

'I'm terrified of what Winston is going to be like,' Baldwin told his confidant Davidson when they were discussing contingency plans. 'Why don't you give Winston the *Gazette* ... it will keep him busy, stop him doing worse things.' The news that one of the government's leading Bolshevik-baiters was in charge of the government mouthpiece was viewed with alarm by those who wanted to keep the temperature down. 'He sees the whole affair as a film producer would see it,' observed Hamilton Fyfe, 'with this difference. Film producers do not act; Winston intends to appear as the hero of the story himself.'[14] Fyfe intended to run a rival newspaper from the offices of the *Herald*. The TUC approved; the printers' unions did not. Fyfe, an ex-Liberal, exploded with impatience against the unions. 'Trade unionism is a means to an end ... to make it an end in itself, to regard its machinery and regulations as if they were sacred, is to misapprehend and misuse it.' In the end, he persuaded the General Council to order in all those required to work on the newspaper. So as to deny the other side the monopoly of patriotism, it was to be called the *British Worker*.

Churchill had other plans for making sure the government's case was heard. He wanted to commandeer the British Broadcasting Company. John Reith went immediately to tackle Davidson, who was running all of the government publicity from an office in the Admiralty. The newspapers were strenuously opposed to the new medium sweeping away their readers by pre-emptive broadcasting of the news, and the BBC had never before been allowed to run its own news service. At the end of the year, its contract would expire and a choice would have to be made between the Reithian vision of an independent but government-funded corporation dedicated to education and information as well as entertainment, and an American-style, advertising-funded network of independent stations. At this delicate moment when its future form and content were in the balance, the BBC was caught between its own vision of its future and the government's demand for its services.

Reith and Davidson were neighbours at home in Westminster, and they had already talked during the weekend about the role the BBC would play during a strike. Aware that the government had the power to commandeer the network if it thought it necessary, Reith persuaded Davidson that consultation would work better than orders, and that the BBC should maintain a semblance of impartiality: it could not broadcast only the government's point of view, which might anyway trigger action by strikers that could paralyse the service. Ultimately, Reith suggested, the BBC might in some way promote an end to the strike. But Davidson had not committed himself, and on the Tuesday morning told Reith that he thought the BBC should after all be some kind of offshoot to the *British Gazette*. Reith dismissed the idea and retreated with a view to improving the news output which, he frankly admitted, had got off to a rocky start. He appeared oblivious to the sensitivities of his staff, who in less than twenty-four hours had set up the BBC's first newsroom.

At its headquarters in Savoy Hill just off the Strand ('hotching with police,' Reith reported to Baldwin when they bumped into one another in the Travellers Club that Tuesday lunchtime), the news staff had commandeered one room, five phone lines, four typewriters and an uncertain number of reporters, one or two of whom, adventurously, went out looking for news, an activity prohibited in normal times by the wire services such as Reuters that supplied the BBC. The quality was indeed patchy, but the BBC promised it was doing its best. 'The BBC fully realises the gravity of its responsibility to all sections of the public and will do its best to discharge it in the most impartial spirit that circumstances permit,' it told its listeners.[15]

If Reith believed he was maintaining the BBC's independence, it was not the impression created outside. The *Daily Herald*, in its final edition on Monday, had warned that the BBC would only broadcast propaganda, and advised listeners who possessed the technical equipment to 'oscillate' in order to disrupt transmissions. The BBC appealed to listeners not to follow that advice: the public would be left prey to wild rumours. But Beatrice Webb, listening at home, thought it was immediately obvious the BBC had, whatever it said, been commandeered. She could hear the 'agonised whispers' of the 'evidently harassed' announcers; however, she acknowledged that announcements from the TUC General Council – including the news that the response to the strike had been one hundred per cent – had been given the same weight as announcements from government. The BBC's bulletins, even if they were treated with scepticism, were eagerly awaited. As the strike wore on, neighbours who had no wireless of their own were invited in to listen, and enterprising individuals typed up the news and sold it on roneoed sheets, or stuck it in a front window or in a shop. For the first few days – until distribution problems were sorted out by the local papers, almost of all of which stayed in production – it remained the least compromised source of information.

One national newspaper did manage to stay in production. *The Times*, jealous of its long tradition of unbroken publication as a newspaper of record, was as dismissive as the *Morning Post*'s editor of the other newspapers' decision not to risk printing during the strike. *The Times* had recently been bought by the Astor family. On the Monday night, the chairman Major J. J. Astor called together all the Fathers of the Chapels – the leading union branch officials – and bade them a warm farewell. He understood the strike was not of their making, he said, and hoped they would all meet again as friends when it was over. He was loudly applauded. As they had stayed late producing the last pre-strike edition, Astor suggested that for getting home they use the emergency transport already laid on for the volunteer labour intended to keep the paper coming out.

In Printing House Square, the first day of the strike was spent teaching middle-aged journalists to carry heavy loads of paper upstairs to the temporary printing press that was to be the base for the first night. By the time it came to print, the atmosphere, it was later reported, resembled the 'accouchement of a Queen of France under the ancien régime'. In the audience that had gathered to watch as the machine operators struggled with unfamiliar equipment and unsuitable paper were a French diplomat and an Italian Fascist. The paper had to be printed one side at a time, but by 4 a.m. seven thousand copies had been despatched to subscribers and a provincial edition had been sent to Bournemouth. Why Bournemouth is not quite clear. In total, they ran off forty-eight thousand copies of the paper that they called 'the little sister'. *The Times* was on the streets; no revolution yet.[16]

7

DAY 2, WEDNESDAY 5 MAY

What are [the trade unions] fighting for? Are they fighting for the moon or for something attainable? And if it is attainable why do they not say what it is?

Manchester Guardian leader, Wednesday 5 May

May 5th Wednesday. School reopens [after holidays]. Mother thought that I ought not to go to school on my bicycle but I went. It was lovely. You could not stop but had to keep on with the long line of moving vehicles. Winnie walked. We were swept across the Wheatsheaf and, had I alighted by Trinity Tavern to walk across the road, without much doubt I should have been run over. There were no girls absent or late in our form and very few in the whole school. Miss Mason is delighted to send an excellent report to the council. Miss Mason said very earnestly to us, 'you will have to [be] true to your first two s's girls, during this strike. Carry on Steady & Straight and I can trust you to make no fuss.'

Diary of Margaret Woods

'LONDON AGAIN PRESENTED a wonderful spectacle this morning,' reported the first edition of the *Brixton Free Press*. Brixton was then a Pooterish suburb for City commuters.

From an early hour the main roads leading from the suburbs were thronged by charabancs, lorries, and motor vehicles of every kind and description. Thousands again made the long tramp to business on foot. Owners of private cars again came to the rescue and conveyed many weary and foot sore pedestrians to the City. By 9.30 am the traffic is practically normal, the tens of thousands having been conveyed to their places of business without any extraordinary difficulty.[1]

In most major cities, the second day of the strike was as solid as the first. An attempt to run trams from Camberwell in south-east London was abandoned because of the threatening crowds. Windows were smashed, and arrests made. In Hammersmith, Poplar and Canning Town other violent attempts were made to stop buses; a handful did operate, but only with a policeman sitting beside the driver and with netting over the windows.

In the hundreds of strike newssheets that had burst into print overnight to replace the newspapers silenced by the decision to call out the printers, wild rumours of mutiny and insurrection fought for space with self-congratulatory accounts of the phlegm and stoicism of the British people. There were reports of 'ugly scenes' in Leeds involving 'several thousand strikers' attacking an emergency tramcar with lumps of coal, then rushing another, before the police intervened. After a police charge to disperse them, two more tramcars were attacked. In Nottingham, a strike procession was reported to have broken up. A London train left Manchester at 9.30 a.m.; it was due to arrive at 5.55, stopping at all stations.

Alongside the more blood-curdling reports there would sometimes be a disclaimer, as the newspapers' desire to flatter their readers' more public-spirited sentiments struggled with the better story of revolution. Although crowd trouble from 'organised gangs of youths' was reported in Poplar in the East End where a valuable motor-car was destroyed, the *Brixton Free Press* added: 'We are instructed, however, by the Chief Commissioner, to announce that the general position throughout the country is satisfactory and no rioting has been reported by the police.' In a neighbouring column: 'One day of the strike was sufficient for Londoners to display their great characteristic adaptability to new situations, and today they have acted like born philosophers ... Flower sellers in Covent Garden were at their pitches by 9 o'clock surrounded by spring

flowers in abundance ... Livestock left on hand at several railway
stations is being fed, watered and made comfortable.'[2]

The great majority of the country, not directly involved and
now deprived of reliable news, had only their prejudices to fall
back on. There was widespread sympathy for the miners and alarm
that negotiations had been allowed to fail when such a potentially
devastating threat to civil order might result. Thousands volunteered through the government's recruiting centres, and a BBC
broadcast by the Home Secretary appealing for thirty thousand
more to sign up as special constables fuelled the mood of alarm.
Hundreds of unemployed responded to local appeals for labour. In
areas where they were strong, the Communist-inspired National
Unemployed Workers' Movement claimed it was successfully per-
suading its members not to blackleg. On the railways, men who had
been apprentices but had been laid off when they reached adult
pay rates were taken back as volunteers and promised permanent
jobs after the strike. Stationmasters and company directors and
undergraduates signed up to be engine drivers. Later in the strike,
there would be fatal consequences from this determination to
establish a sense of normality.

The universities were a principal recruiting ground for volunteers. In London, the great East European specialist Professor
Walter Seton (one of the originators of the OMS) was accused of
hinting that students' degrees might be affected by the enthusiasm
with which they supported the government. Cambridge was considered diehard Tory; Oxford, partly under the influence of the
Socialist Master of Balliol, A. L. Lindsay, had some Labour sym-
pathies. Hugh Gaitskell, then a second-year New College undergraduate destined for the Indian Civil Service, felt the government
'practically declared war on the strikers'. He offered his help
through the University Labour Club. 'The impact of the Strike was
sharp and sudden, a little like a war,' he wrote later, 'in that
everybody's lives were suddenly affected by a new and unprecedented situation, which forced us to abandon plans for pleasure,
to change our values and adjust our priorities. Above all we had to

make a choice.' He drove the Oxford academics Geoffrey and Margaret Cole, theoreticians of Labour, to London and brought back bundles of the *British Worker*, racing to get home before his college's midnight deadline. He told his mother: 'Henceforth, my future is with the working classes.'

Two other Oxford undergraduates, Tom Driberg and A. J. P. Taylor, tried to volunteer at the King Street headquarters of the Communist Party, but there was no one there except a caretaker, who told them to go away. 'The only instructions I ever took from the Communist Party,' Taylor always claimed.[3]

In Eccleston Square, Bevin was taking control through his Strike Organization Committee, watched rather bitterly by Citrine. ('The committee appointed practically every member of the General Council to a particular function; some of them of little use, I am afraid.'[4]) Bevin intended to channel all key decisions to a duumvirate of himself and Alf Purcell in which, although Purcell remained as chairman, he himself would be the senior member. He and Citrine and Jimmy Thomas bickered over tactics: Bevin saw the strike as a kind of military exercise, in which different groups of men could be treated as battalions and called out on strike as if being ordered into the front line. While there were still reserves, the strike would not yet have reached maximum effect, and there would still be potential to negotiate from a position of strength, which would keep up the men's morale. Citrine doubted that there was enough order and discipline to keep the groups separate, and pointed to the confusion among power workers over lighting and power which was already leading to angry accusations of blacklegging.

Most seriously, the railmen and the other transport workers disagreed over the movement of food. The railmen were against carrying any food because it would mean bringing in 75 per cent of their men. The transport workers, in lorries, could carry food and still keep most of their members out on strike.

The transport of food was proving highly controversial for other reasons. The TUC's initial offer, made before the strike began, to cooperate with the government in the movement of essential goods had been angrily rebuffed by an administration that saw the gesture as a reinforcement of the idea that the TUC was a rival and comparable authority to itself. But at a local level, issuing food permits to delivery drivers often became the core activity for the strike committees that were in the process of being set up. Deciding who could have permits was an irresistible opportunity to mark the realignment of power brought about by the strike. In some cases, it was seen as poetic justice, as a steelworker wrote in his union journal:

> I thought of the many occasions when I had been turned empty away from the door of some workshop in a weary struggle to get the means to purchase the essentials of life for self and dependants ... I thought of the many occasions I had been called upon to meet these people in the never-ending struggle to obtain decent conditions for those around me, and its consequent result in my joining the ranks of the unemployed; of the cheap sneers when members of my class have attempted to rouse consciousness as to the real facts of the struggle ... only a rigid examination of the stern facts of the case moved our actions. The cap-in-hand position reversed.[5]

Occasionally, the permits were used as a cover for pilfering. As protection, Aberdeen fish traders put a basket of rotten fish at the back of their lorries; elsewhere, elaborate arrangements were made to allocate permits, and scrupulously carried out. Sometimes, sheer bossiness took over. In Kilsyth, near Glasgow, all transport was diverted on to the football ground and impounded, while the drivers were sent – some distance – to get permits. The ground was permanently manned with a picket and a large supporting cast of miners.[6]

Often the trades council worked harmoniously with the local civil commissioner and other authorities, particularly over matters of policing where thorough consultation played an important part in reducing confrontation. In Lincoln, for example, the Chief

Constable invited the trades council to provide all of the special constables. Occasionally, the conflict between cooperation – which reflected on the power of the trades council – and confrontation, the desire to maximize the impact of the strike, was decided in favour of confrontation. In Northumberland and Durham, possibly influenced by the Communist Robin Page Arnot who had been released from prison and had returned to his home area to contribute to the strike organization, all the main unions had decided to work together on a joint strike committee that covered the same area as that of Sir Kingsley Wood, the region's civil commissioner, a moderate Conservative, Baldwin's junior Health Minister and a man committed to sound administration. Trade unionists, working 'under permit' to move food in the docks, refused to work alongside blackleg labour. Sir Kingsley, rather daringly conciliatory, proposed some sort of dual authority, and there were two meetings to try to establish a modus operandi. The trade unionists refused to concede the principle of blacking volunteers, and talks broke down.[7] In the Commons, one of the local MPs declared that the government forces had lost control, a misrepresentation that entered strike mythology, confirming the TUC's worst fear – the capture of the strike by the revolutionaries.

The strength of revolutionary intent in each area tended to decide whether the trades councils formed themselves into councils of action or strike committees. Organization was ad hoc; as in so much else, there were no clear central directions. Both types of committee performed the same function of sorting out contradictions between individual unions' instructions, deciding local policy on transport issues, organizing picketing, entertainment and, above all, despatch riders who travelled the highways like medieval traders, collecting and passing on news. By the end of the strike, parched for reliable information, many had started up their own strike bulletins, most of which were launched just in time to report that the strike had ended. But the Communists had been advocating councils of action for the previous six months, to 'mobilize all the forces of the working classes in [their] locality', and on the whole where there was a council of action, Communists were locally influential. Councils of action were intended to bring together the industrial and political wings of the movement, ready to take over all local powers. They were frowned on by the TUC as threats to their own central control, while trades councils and strike committees tended to be dominated by trade unions.

ON THE AFTERNOON of the second day in the House of Commons, the Home Secretary Joynson-Hicks set out the powers the government had taken under the emergency regulations. They included the use of military force to ensure the maintenance of supplies and civil order; they also, more controversially, included the right to arrest without a warrant, a draconian move that added fuel to the sense of crisis that Jix himself plainly felt. Labour, aggrieved that it was being blamed for provoking the strike, took the opportunity to put the trade unionists' case. In breach of convention, and in breach of the agreement on confidentiality reached at the time the talks took place, Jimmy Thomas set out in dramatic tones his account of the negotiations that had continued until the early hours of Monday morning. He dwelt on the trade union side's shock at hearing that all negotiations were at an end when their discussions with the miners' executive had only just begun. He reiterated that they had known nothing of the *Daily Mail* printers' refusal to print the 'treachery' leader. At this point, Ramsay MacDonald intervened to declare that when they had returned to the Prime Minister's room to present their response to the government's ultimatum on the withdrawal of the strike threat, they had found it shuttered and dark. At this, there were cries of 'shame!' To great excitement on the Labour side, Baldwin confirmed the substance of Thomas's account. 'You know, Baldwin is a damned honest fellow,' Thomas said later that night. 'He'll never be a politician.'

Baldwin's critics in his own party agreed. Confirmation that the negotiations had ended so abruptly rebounded badly on the government. Even supportive newspapers like *The Times* thought it unwise to have precipitated so grave an event for so spurious a reason. But

Labour had no effective outlet through which to exploit what they were determined to present as a Conservative admission of guilt. With all national newspapers shut down except *The Times*, there was no vehicle for independent analysis. The papers that resumed publication either as tiny strike sheets or, like the *Daily Mail*, by printing abroad, were vigorously supportive of the government. The Liberal newspapers – like the *Daily News* – reflected in their publishing decisions the ambiguous attitude of their party to the strike. They attacked the principle but were unwilling to challenge its effect, and simply decided it would be too difficult to publish a paper during the strike. As a result, a source of reasoned criticism of the government from a non-Labour viewpoint was silenced and the *News* was restricted to publishing all its editorials, most of them sympathetic to the strikers, in one batch the week after the strike had been defeated.

That left the BBC. The manner in which it interpreted its role would decide whether Labour – its politicians or the strikers – was to be allowed an effective national voice. Of the 151 Labour MPs who had survived the pasting in the 1924 general election, well over a third were sponsored by trade unions, and of those the greatest number were miners' MPs. A few had reservations, but all supported the strike. John Reith had to decide whether the BBC should recognize that the party nonetheless remained as entitled to comment on the General Strike as the government. Two senior Labour backbenchers, the former Liberal Charles Trevelyan and William Graham, who as a member of a parliamentary committee had been closely involved with the Company's development, were despatched to discover Reith's approach. With uncompromising Reithian certainty, a request for a broadcast was refused. Reith ascribed his decision to a desire to avoid provoking the government; he had been clear from the start both that the government had to defeat the union challenge and, to this end, that it was right and necessary for the BBC to offer its complete support. But however forcefully he might present himself – particularly to those he was to disappoint by denying access to the airwaves – as constrained by the government's threat to take over the Company, the truth was that Reith believed, first, that the government was right and the strikers wrong, and second, that it was for him alone to determine the BBC's editorial line. It was, for example, on his initiative that Baldwin was invited to broadcast, an offer being held in reserve for the crisis Downing Street believed was inevitable.

Although it often contradicted official government sources, news from trade union bulletins was regularly broadcast; but the absence of a Labour or trade union voice, contrasted with the frequent visits to the BBC studios of ministers and supportive Liberal politicians, was much criticized. Instead of the stimulus of controversy that in his long-term planning Reith had declared himself determined to introduce, instead even of generating the heady air of something resembling impartial reporting, it was to be by 'the droning of train times ... as soothing as the blessed word, "Mesopotamia"',[8] that the BBC's first contribution to a national crisis would be remembered. From the Liberal and intellectual capital of Bloomsbury, Virginia Woolf complained of the broadcasting of trivia, of the values that made the Prince of Wales's return from Biarritz a news item of significance. But she also recognized the uniqueness of the moment. 'A voice, rather commonplace & official, yet the only common voice left, wishes us good morning at 10. This is the voice of Britain to wh[ich] we can make no reply.'[9] A David Low cartoon of the time shows crowds gathered at a shop doorway to hear the BBC intone: 'Mr Baldwin has eaten a good lunch and is hopeful. It is denied that the Albert Memorial has been wrecked. There will be several trains tomorrow and the other six million of you can walk.'

The first edition of the *British Gazette* had run off the *Morning Post*'s presses in the small hours of Wednesday morning. By 6 a.m., 232,000 copies had been printed and sent about the country on a distribution network generously donated by one of J. C. C. Davidson's constituents who, through his firm, appropriately named International Combustion, owned a fleet of motor vehicles. Each evening the cars gathered across the road from the Aldwych in the quadrangle of Somerset House where the Inland Revenue, an arm of Churchill's Treasury, was also based. The Inland Revenu offices themselves were being used as dormitories for the *Gazette*'s workforce.

On its front page, the first edition bore an article stamped with Churchill's authorial personality. The *Gazette*, it declared, 'is published to prevent this great nation being reduced to the level of African natives dependent only on the rumours which are carried from place to place … if this were allowed to continue, rumours would poison the air, raise panics and disorders, inflame fears and passions together, and carry us all to depths which no sane man of any party or class would care even to contemplate'. Had any hope remained that the newspaper might be used to promote a spirit of conciliation, it would have been disappointed by a robust attack on the unconstitutional nature of the strike, to submit to which would leave 'our rights and destinies in the hands of a body of men … representing only a section of the public … the democratic state cannot possibly submit to sectional dictation'.[10]

George V, watching from Buckingham Palace where his guard had, for the first occasion in peacetime, shed its scarlet tunics to parade in battlefield khaki, received almost hourly updates. Despite his sympathy for the miners' condition, he was appalled by the challenge to the state posed by a general strike. Just such a strike had, after all, led to the downfall and murder of his cousin the Czar. He took up the *Gazette*'s cry. In a letter from the palace to Baldwin, he echoed the proposal that it was time trade union power was curbed. Baldwin refused to be provoked. It would, he thought, be 'highly controversial and so inopportune'. Next, the King began to worry about picket-line violence and intimidation. His private secretary wrote to Baldwin: 'The King is somewhat concerned to find from the official reports that the people who are ready and desirous of assisting the Government in the maintenance of law and order are suffering considerably from intimidation from the strikers and other evil disposed parties, with the result that

transport, which is the mainspring of the Government arrangements, is threatened.'[11]

Hamilton Fyfe, preparing to bring out his trade union paper
the *British Worker* for the first time that evening, had first been
shown the *Gazette* at five in the morning by an enthusiastic
supporter, who had been driven round to hammer on the door of
Fyfe's flat by a sympathetic *Daily Mail* man. The trade union line,
which Fyfe was to devote himself to extolling, was for steadiness,
peace and constitutional rectitude. Still battling with trade union
reservations, Fyfe had a team of censors foisted on him by the
General Council, whose purpose was to prevent anything creeping
into the paper that might cause 'uncontrollable irritation and
violence'. With this objective, the TUC was determined that it
should control all propaganda, lest it be captured by Communists
using strike sheets for their own purposes. Strike committees were
banned from printing anything other than 'material supplied by the
[TUC's intelligence] Committee'.

Among other restrictions imposed by the union bureaucrats that
nearly drove the highly professional Fyfe to distraction – and
within the year prompted his resignation from the *Daily Herald* –
volunteer drivers were not allowed to transport the newspaper
without a Paperworkers' Union card, journalists were not allowed
to use the politically loaded term 'council of action', and the
workers at the paper were paid full union rates whereas most
people working with union permission took only strike pay. On
the first day, and every day thereafter, the *British Worker* carried
a paragraph declaring that the strike was an industrial dispute
and not a threat to the constitution, and exhorting readers to be
'exemplary in [their] conduct and not to give any opportunity for
police interference'. Pickets in particular were instructed to confine
themselves 'strictly to their legitimate duties'.

Early in the evening, as the *British Worker* was prepared for the
presses, crowds began to appear outside the *Herald* offices. Some of
the staff addressed them from a first-floor window. Soon police

were there too; but not, as Fyfe first assumed, to keep the peace. They had come with a warrant to search the building and seize papers, nominally because of the advice given in the final pre-strike edition of the *Herald*, to those readers who owned wirelesses, to oscillate them in order to block BBC transmissions. Curiously, however, the police also wanted to take away copies of that night's *Worker*, which the city commissioner wanted to see. With these in their pockets they retreated and peace descended; until the TUC, who had been told in a fine burst of rumour inflation that a hundred mounted police had surrounded the building, raced to the scene. Citrine found its despatch room packed with about two hundred people in their shirtsleeves singing 'The Red Flag'. Outside, the crowds took up the chorus. Citrine nervously pondered the dangers of a riot when peace-loving men were inflamed by the clumsy activities of the authorities. Within half an hour, the paper was given permission to go ahead. MacDonald claimed the credit; he contacted Baldwin, who contacted the Attorney General and discovered he had not been consulted. Any action against the *Herald* was cancelled.

In Birmingham, where on the first day of the strike there had been nothing but a cyclostyled single-sheet edition of the *Birmingham Mail*, by Wednesday there was both a Communist strike paper and one produced by the strike committee in a desk-top publishing operation that had been set up through the money and influence of Oswald Mosley. Mosley, married to the daughter of Baldwin's former Foreign Secretary Lord Curzon, had as the Labour candidate nearly defeated Neville Chamberlain, the last of the Chamberlain dynasty in the city, in his Birmingham Ladywood constituency at the 1924 election, and it remained his base. With another Labour candidate, the writer John Strachey (whose father edited the *Spectator*), he set up a strike bulletin which, like similar bulletins that emerged more slowly elsewhere, was to be indispensable in combating rumours about a drift back to work.

Throughout the afternoon of Wednesday 5 May, London had been lost in a 'thick brown fog' that had settled about lunchtime, adding to the mood of foreboding. When Tom Jones met Baldwin and his wife before lunch, they were sitting in the dark in the drawing-room of 10 Downing Street, not wanting to waste electricity. Together Jones and the Prime Minister composed a brief appeal for the following day's *Gazette*, on behalf of a government that had 'undertaken to preserve the liberties and privileges of the people of these islands'. Arnold Bennett, lunching at the Reform Club, found 'General opinion that the fight would be short but violent. Bloodshed anticipated next week.'[12]

In Bloomsbury, Virginia Woolf recorded the fog as she entertained her brother-in-law Clive Bell, who supported the government, and Maynard Keynes, anxious to promote a Liberal perspective. 'It is all tedious & depressing, rather like waiting in a train outside a station. Rumours are passed round – that the gas wd. be cut off at 1 – false of course.'[13]

Liberal politicians were slowly preparing to move. In Monday's debate in Parliament, Lord Asquith, the former Liberal Prime Minister, had made a speech strongly condemning a general strike but sympathetic to the strikers. Despite the strident tone of much of the newspaper coverage, his was not an unusual point of view; many ordinary people were impressed by the willingness of the strikers to forgo not just wages but also, potentially, their jobs in support of a cause that was not directly their own. Anxiety about the derisory level of miners' wages was widespread. There was a mood for peace that was not entirely motivated by fear of what would happen if the strike ran on.

THE CHRISTIAN CHURCHES, and in particular the Archbishop of Canterbury, came to play a leading role in the search for a negotiated settlement. It was not the first time that the Anglican Church had tried to mediate in an industrial dispute. Encouraged by a succession of effective interventions in local disputes at the end of the nineteenth century, the Archbishop of Canterbury, Randall Davidson, now in his seventies, had offered to intervene in both the 1919 rail strike and the 1921 miners' strike. There had been no interest – as well as a nasty put-down from his own bishops, after the second, that had left him contemplating resignation. Even so, Anglicans had continued to be concerned about the Church and its relations with the working classes, who had deserted it so conspicuously during the Industrial Revolution. Another important influence was R. H. Tawney's report, *The Living Wage*, which identified the need for wages to do more than ensure the barest subsistence, while suggesting their payment should be the first charge on any employer in every industry. That had been followed, in 1924, by a Conference on Christian Politics, Economics and Citizenship (Copec) to deliberate on the challenge posed to Christianity by the modern world. Unhappily, no persuasive answer to the rise of materialism had been found before May 1926.

On that second day of the strike, the Archbishop made his first intervention: he echoed Lord Asquith's condemnation of the strike as 'intolerable', demanding total support for the government. But he went on to say, sympathetically, that it had been a response to the fear of a general cut in pay, and he urged the government to 'explore every possibility of reaching a settlement'.[14] On the same day, he met both Baldwin and MacDonald to put forward an eccentric idea from the Bishop of Liverpool involving continuing the subsidy by public subscription. It was politely rejected, but Baldwin as well as MacDonald encouraged him in his attempts to mediate.

Archbishop Davidson also met, among many others, R. H. Tawney, who was an intimate of Tom Jones's and familiar with the detail of the final round of negotiations. Most unexpectedly, he spoke, too, to Lord Londonderry, one of the largest and most intransigent of the coal owners. To his surprise, he found him full of 'suggestiveness [and] resource', although it seemed that part of Londonderry's purpose had been to impress on him the government's utter determination to make no move until the strike had been called off. This seems to have convinced the Archbishop that pressure had to be exerted to persuade both sides to drop their preconditions simultaneously. Encouraged by leaders from the Free Churches, who had also been meeting to discuss potential courses of action, he began to make preparations for an appeal.

At about the same time as the Archbishop was meeting the Prime Minister, the most authoritatively reported act of sabotage was taking place against the only national newspaper still printing in London. At the offices of *The Times*, petrol was poured through a shaft usually used for loading newsprint from the street; the petrol was followed by lighted matches. A terrific blaze ensued, producing a wall of fire thirty feet high. However, it was a concreted area, and tightly rolled newsprint is slow to burn. The fire was swiftly contained, and – according to *Strike Nights at Printing House Square*, a slim volume privately published shortly after the strike that was to do much to shape memories of May 1926 – its principal effect was to rally most of London society to *The Times*'s offices. For the remainder of the strike, it became *de rigueur* in some social circles to spend a few hours working at *The Times* as volunteers. These included 'a strong contingent of the Chairman's [Major Astor's] friends from the House of Commons ... on the chance of a turn-up with the pickets', as well as 'statesmen, sailors, and school boys', directors of *The Times* and City banks and public companies, and a governor-elect on leave before going out to Australia. A section of the Women's Legion, 'which included at least two duchesses', scoured the provinces for skilled men to work the presses and set the type.[15]

The attempt to torch *The Times* was almost certainly an act of sabotage by the pickets who thronged the area in and around Fleet Street in the early days of the strike. But men like these were highly visible. The great unmentionable for those charged with maintaining order was some kind of insurrection or, worst of all, mutiny, among the troops. Rumours abounded; their publication was the serendipitous basis for imprisoning many local Communist leaders in the early days of the strike. MI5 was on permanent standby. As the likelihood of a strike had grown over the last days

of April, the War Office prepared. One branch, MI(B),[16] was set up
for emergency home defence, with a subsection responsible specifically for military security and intelligence. Rooms were allocated,
telephones installed, stationery, bedding and candles ordered. A
house in west London was earmarked for overnight accommo-
dation. Another subsection, I(B)ii, was responsible for military
security among the civilian population: soldiers, dressed in civvies,
were sent to spy in East End pubs.

Inevitably, when the strike actually started, a few oversights
were identified. Although a small band of retired generals and titled
women were available to drive volunteer cars (including Dame
Adelaide Livingstone who in the 1930s was to organize the Peace
Ballot, a mass petition, the success of which delayed rearmament),
there were no despatch riders. Nor, embarrassingly, was there any
official source of news. 'C. J. Saunders, RASC [Royal Army Service
Corps], a clerk, displayed considerable enterprise in bringing his
crystal wireless set to the War office on May 1st. [He] circulated
copies of the Wireless Bulletin to several WO Depts including
MI(B) during the first few days of the General Strike. These copies
were of great use at a time when newspapers were almost
unobtainable.'[17]

Agents briefed to fall into conversation with the strikers were
despatched around the country; reports flooded in. The railmen in
Leamington would go back at the drop of a hat, it was asserted,
provided they were guaranteed protection. The transport workers
had successfully recruited a large number of men who worked for
the War Office and Admiralty in Portsmouth. Salisbury Court
training centre for ex-servicemen took regular delivery of an
alarming twelve copies of the Communist journal *Workers' Weekly*,
but, the report added, that was probably because of the large
number of Communists held in the city jail. Ipswich was a 'hotbed'
of red railwaymen where 'a great deal of socialism' was taught in
the elementary and secondary schools. Even the agricultural labour-
ers were 'rather unsettled'. From Liverpool came a report that one

J. Walsh, 'about 34, dark complexion, slim, clean shaven, dirty, slight twist to both eyes, very shabbily dressed, decidedly verminous' was 'one of the intellectuals of the party'.

More agents mingled with guests at the National Hotel in London where Arthur Cook, secretary of the Miners' Federation, was staying, but they discovered little beyond his room number and a report that he was visited regularly by the hardline Communist Andrew Rothenstein. Bevin was said to have telephoned him 'frequently'; but the agent had been unable to hear their conversations. Curiously, the chambermaid reported that Cook was also being watched by private detectives whom she recognized from their work in a recent divorce case.

A posse of agents descended on the barracks town of Aldershot, always feared to be a potential site of mutiny. The agents adopted various personae: one was a South African visiting a friend, with another agent as his chauffeur; a third man was in search of work, two others were partners in a small motor business. Their evidence, considering the effort expended, appeared disproportionately low-key. A grocer's wife told the 'South African' and his driver that there was 'a great deal of anti-king feeling', a report they somehow got substantiated by a housemaid. Others gleaned that a particular regiment was absolutely reliable, that a messenger from Eccleston Square was expected at 10 p.m. but did not arrive, that there had been intensive Communist propaganda at the barracks, with 'leaflets thrown over the walls, pavement chalking etc.'. But attempts to get soldiers to be subversive got nowhere. 'In most cases, when political arguments were started the soldiers finished their beer and left at once.' It was a very wet night, the agents reported sadly, and although there was a distinct tendency to sympathize with the miners, no Communist propaganda was observed.

8

DAY 3, THURSDAY 6 MAY

May 6th Thursday. Third day of the strike. England has a very efficient way of getting food supplies and protecting her people against unruly strikers. It makes me proud to think how loyally the men and women from all quarters have responded to the call for volenteers [sic]. Mother said that later, of some of the strikers, if they are true Englishmen they will be ashamed to have shirked their work (especially the 'bus & train & tram drivers) when they see the cheery city people struggling to work on any conveyance that will carry them, and also to see how quickly and steadily England's people are being supplied with food, conveyance and news. Mother added too, that all along she thinks the strike will soon end, because sound British common sense will come to the fore & all will be well.

Diary of Margaret Woods

DISPLAYED ON THE FRONT of the second issue of the *British Gazette*, Baldwin's statement, drafted in the gloom of the Downing Street drawing-room the previous morning, was an emotive call to patriotism and to history. It said nothing about the underlying causes of the dispute, nor opened any avenue to negotiation. It was drawn up in haste. But although it was propaganda, it was the most effective kind of propaganda: at its core was Baldwin's fundamental belief in the Conservative duty to preserve national institutions:

Constitutional Government is being attacked. Let all good citizens whose livelihood and labour have thus been put in peril bear with fortitude and patience the hardships with which they have been so suddenly confronted ... The laws of

145

England are the people's birthright. The laws are in your keeping. You have made Parliament their guardian. The General Strike is a challenge to Parliament and is the road to anarchy and ruin.

What academics later called the 'impact of Labour', which so troubled the Churches, also preoccupied Baldwin. Plainly there were political implications attached to a powerful workers' party, but Baldwin, like the bishops and many on the middle-class Left, agonized at least as much about the moral degradation of a life with only material ends as they did about the inadequacy of the working class's standard of living. Baldwin believed people's lives, and accordingly government, must have a moral purpose – although that did not validate intervention in what should be the self-regulating activities of employer and employee. Government must promote and maintain order and the stability in which prosperity and, with the right encouragement, goodwill, could flourish. The laws of England were indeed the people's birthright, and the framework for a civilized society; and so too was that sense of Englishness that Baldwin embodied, a mythologized version of the vanished past, the community of the village and the family firm, that made your neighbour's fortune a proper responsibility of your own. Baldwin's instinct was to find a way around a fight; but if in the end the fundamental structures of society risked being damaged, then he would stand firm. Hence his apparently contradictory stance over the following days, when he continually offered the prospect of negotiation without ever removing the principal obstruction to it – his insistence, before all else, on the ending of the General Strike. There was also, of course, the pressure from the majority of his Cabinet, who were determined to force the issue to the point of surrender for more overtly political reasons.

The TUC, in the pages of the *British Worker* and through its members' conversations with journalists, portrayed Baldwin as a puppet at the mercy of the cabinet diehards, left with nothing to do by the thrusting Churchill and the paranoid Joynson-Hicks, reduced to 'mooning about' in Hyde Park surveying milk churns in what had become the main London food distribution centre. There were even rumours, which surfaced in a French newspaper, that the Prime Minister had had some kind of breakdown – which must have had enough truth in them for the Cabinet to draw up, although not in the end to publish, a denial. People close to him observed that the long hours of meetings and negotiations in the days immediately before the strike had left him anxious and ill at ease, but according to Tom Jones, once the strike began his spirits recovered and his purpose became unwavering.

Since Baldwin was unable to pursue negotiations himself, the more public spirited – or the more nervous – among the great and the good put themselves forward as surrogates for the government, to act as unofficial mediators. From the shores of Lake Garda, Sir Herbert Samuel had been watching the careful work of his Commission wilfully misrepresented and ultimately destroyed. Once again he laid aside his books of philosophy and prepared to intervene. Other Commission members, too, were angry at the fate of their work and felt they should have been asked to interpret the disputed points in the report. Sir William Beveridge had had to be restrained by the Labour Minister, Steel-Maitland, from going to the press to complain that the mine owners had ignored their recommendations for national wage settlements, while another member, Sir Herbert Lawrence, had written to Baldwin pointing out that the pay cut the employers were imposing was quite unreasonable.

Samuel, despite being advised by a friend in government to stick with Pliny, hastened back to England. On Thursday the 6th he reached Folkestone and – having had the forethought to tele-gram the Postmaster General to ask for transport – he was met by a motor-racing ace, one Major Seagrave, for what was evidently a thrilling drive to London. 'We sped along one of the newly built motor-highways, all the roads empty of traffic because of the strike. At times we touched eighty-five miles an hour; and although Seagrave drove cautiously through the villages and suburbs, we

reached the Reform Club in Pall Mall from Folkestone in one hour
and ten minutes.'[1]

Samuel was warmly welcomed by the railmen's leader Jimmy
Thomas, and rather less enthusiastically by the other members
of the Commission who thought no intervention likely to help.
Members of the government to whom he spoke echoed their
views. But Samuel was confident that something should be done,
and that if no one else would do it, then he must; and with only
the most discreet encouragement from the government, the only
option he had left was to work with the TUC alone.

The weapon Tom Jones had been looking for, that would
separate the TUC from the miners, appeared to be at hand. The
TUC was already suspiciously watching Thomas. At Thursday's
General Council session, the miners had tackled him directly with
the accusation that he and MacDonald were plotting to sell them
out behind their backs, particularly since Thomas had said in the
Commons that he had accepted the form of words agreed with
Baldwin on the Saturday night, a proposal that had never been
agreed with the miners. And suspicion of Thomas was not the only
cause of unease in Eccleston Square. From the provinces, pressure
was mounting to escalate the strike and clear up the confusion
between who was and who was not allowed to come out.

The government's case, as Baldwin had restated in the *Gazette*
that morning, rested on the unconstitutionality of the strike; now
came the first assertion that it was also in breach of common law.
Sir John Simon, a barrister with a glittering reputation and later
Lord Chancellor, decided, allegedly on a whim as he came into the
chamber of the House of Commons, that the strike was illegal. He
delivered a magisterial judgement against the strikers. They were
in breach of their contracts, he said: the 1906 Trade Disputes Act
that protected individual trade unionists and trade union funds
from damages could not be held valid. It was as wrong for them to
leave work without notice as it would have been for the mine
owners to have turned the miners away without notice on 1 May.
'I am not saying this with the slightest desire to blame or to praise,

but it would be lamentable if the working classes of this country go on with this business without understanding that they are taking part in a novel and an utterly illegal proceeding.' It would be no defence for the striker to say that he was obeying orders, on pain of forfeiting his union benefits. Unlawful orders should not be obeyed, and no trade unionist could lose his benefits on those grounds. Twisting the knife, he addressed the case of the railwaymen. 'Every railwayman ... who is now out in disregard of the contract of his employment is himself personally liable to be sued in the County Court for damages.'

Within twenty-four hours, a summary of the speech was posted in railway stations; the Conservative Party had five thousand copies run off and distributed.

It was a terrifying blow to the TUC; if this ruling was upheld, it threatened the existence of every union. At the start of the strike, there had been anxious talk about the entire General Council being arrested; but that would have left the trade unions themselves, although leaderless, fundamentally undamaged. To be exposed to claims for damages, on the other hand, would be an almost irrecoverable reverse. Simon's declaration had a further effect. Trade unionists were respectable, law-abiding people. They knew, whatever the government said, that they were not trying to undermine the constitution. It was much more difficult to be confident that they were not breaking the law.

Labour's first Solicitor General, Sir Henry Slesser, author both of *The Pastured Shire*, a volume of poetry, and more significantly of a textbook on labour law, argued for an immediate rebuttal of a case that he, and most lawyers subsequently, regarded as flawed. But MacDonald hesitated to appear to challenge so eminent a jurist. Slesser was restrained until the following Monday, and Simon's interpretation had a free run for the next four days. Three days into the strike, and the General Council's resolve, never very stable, was damaged beyond recovery; Sir Herbert Samuel had fertile territory in which to work.

*

Away from the smoky rooms and snatched meals of TUC headquarters, the country was settling into a new and relatively
untroubled pattern. In Birmingham and many other cities, there
were no gas or electricity cuts to disturb domestic life; as the long
spring evenings turned to dusk, street lights came on as usual. Post
and telegrams, and telephones for those who had them, worked
with their customary efficiency. In some towns and cities where
most workers were not in the front line there was almost no
evidence of the dispute. Even in a manufacturing centre like
Birmingham, the great majority of workers were non-unionized;
jewellery- and gun-making, the main occupations in the inner city,
had escaped the attentions of the strike committee. Shops and
offices began their days and ended them according to the normal
routine. Lorries making food deliveries were remarkable only for
having 'Food Only' chalked on their sides. Groceries were in stock,
and supplies of meat were available at the butchers', who had access
to plentiful stocks in cold stores. Under the aegis of the civil
commissioners, transport committees had been set up, lorries req-
uisitioned and a network swiftly established to replace the rail
system whereby food was normally transported (the railways would
never recover all of the trade). Of course it was unusual that the
lorries tended to travel in convoy, with a police escort, but few
shoppers finding the normal goods on the shelves would have
known how they got there. Birmingham, in the heart of a market-
gardening area, had a surplus of green vegetables: cabbages and
broccoli were taken to a number of ports and traded for onions.
Fish was brought in by enterprising fish merchants who converted
charabancs into lorries: five tons arrived from Milford Haven,
stowed where the passengers had formerly sat.[2]

For many, the most prominent reminder that there was a strike
on was the morale-boosting parades of strikers. In Brighton, an
invitation to the leaders of the trades council's transport committee
to call at the town hall to discuss the possibility of resuming work
on an inconveniently halted construction job led to several hundred
strikers marching through town accompanied by a brass band. On

Day 3 in Exeter, where on the Sunday before the strike began the Bishop had preached on the virtues of community over the interests of the individual, two thousand five hundred men marched to a special service in the Cathedral, at his invitation. In York, the strikers marched through the city every afternoon.

Coal rationing had been introduced as soon as the lockout began. Supplies were now further rationed, sometimes by a system devised by the local trades council, sometimes by the local authority. The most complex arrangements related to the Co-operative stores, which simultaneously wanted to support the strike and supply their customers. Birmingham's Co-ops provided transport for pickets and banking facilities for trade unions, enabling strike pay to be paid. But their own lorries were being picketed and the position of their drivers was uncertain. After much discussion they decided, in a contradictory solution to a contradictory problem, to use government transport and send home their union drivers, even if they wanted to work.

Few people outside the trade unions had any sense of the chaos within. Virginia Woolf, reluctantly attracted by the compelling drama of a national crisis, found the lack of newspapers disorienting and longed for it all to be over, for someone to say 'kiss & be friends – as apparently we all desire'. But she also felt people settling into a pattern, 'occasionally thinking of other things'. 'Of course one notices lorries full of elderly men & girls standing like passengers in the old 3rd class carriages. Children swarm. They pick up bits of old wood paving … over it all is some odd pale unnatural atmosphere – great activity but no normal life.'[3]

Unsparing effort was devoted to getting the buses working again in London. Unsurprisingly this effort became a focus of picketing activity, and the most frequent source of violence. Arnold Bennett reported seeing eleven buses passing the top of Sloane Street within five minutes, two with their windows smashed and a policeman and a special constable on each. Pickets gathered at tram and bus depots, and often that was enough to put off any volunteer drivers. But where they persisted, there were frequent attacks as they left.

There were disturbances at Camberwell, and seventy buses failed to return to their depot at Chiswick because they had been damaged en route. A common strikers' tactic was to remove the sparkplugs or some other vital piece of the engine while the driver was absent. In the Walworth Road, south of the river, a bus was said to have driven deliberately at pickets, and nearby at the Elephant and Castle a bus was set on fire. The volunteer driver and conductor were forced to get off and were roughed up as they tried to run away. Despite police arriving at the gallop, another bus was stopped after it nearly crashed into a pub, and there was an accident involving a van and a motorcycle. More than forty men appeared in the police courts charged with stone-throwing and, in at least one case, with striking a bus inspector with a bottle.

The authorities also finally plucked up the courage to imprison an MP: Shapurji Saklatvala surrending to his bail at Bow Street on Thursday, refused to be bound over, and was sent to Wormwood Scrubs for two months convicted of sedition. At the end of the strike the Communist Party, which claimed a membership of six thousand (it rose sharply immediately after the strike and fell even more sharply in the following year), estimated that a thousand of its members had been arrested, and that a third of all court appearances involved Communists. Police had extensive powers 'under the regulations', and it was easy enough to find reasons for picking up the known local CP members; having an interest in provoking trouble, they were also more likely to draw attention to themselves. Retribution was swift and harsh, although how harsh depended on geography. In Darlington, where there had been trouble among the pickets, a man got three months for throwing a stone at a car. In Birmingham the climate was slightly milder – only a month for smashing a tram window, but six months' hard labour for assaulting a civilian assisting the police.

Reports of such street drama were the staple of the strike newspapers, absorbing reading, even if their accuracy was treated with scepticism. The *Daily Telegraph*'s strike issues even had a column headed 'Reckless Rumours', enabling it to circulate gossip that it knew to be untrue, such as reports of the murder of a policeman and the wounding of a cabinet minister. It took only the addition or omission of a word or two for a completely different perspective of what had actually happened, to emerge. In York on 6 May, a train was held up at a level crossing on the edge of the city where around three hundred people were waiting. Extra police arrived and went to open the crossing-gates, but because the latch on one of them was already lifted, it swung back on to the engine, broke, and knocked a police constable into the path of the approaching train. He was rescued in the nick of time by a local coal merchant, and the 'very hostile' crowd fled. This appeared in the government's Supply and Transport Committee's news digest as: 'At York police were obliged to disperse strikers who were holding up a train at a level crossing. The gates were smashed and a constable thrown in front of the train but rescued.' When the *British Gazette* reported the incident, verbatim, it added: 'Order has been restored.' By compression rather than inaccuracy, the picture of a difficult incident was turned into an ugly one.

The battle for control of public transport got worse as the strike wore on, producing the bulk of the most dangerous episodes that took place.[4] Meanwhile the MI(B) operation, somewhat at a loose end in the Admiralty, decided they should prepare a rogue's gallery of the men and women most likely to be in the vanguard of the coming revolution, presumably so that they could swiftly be arrested if things took a turn for the worse. This occupied several people for the next ten days, and the strike was over before it was complete.[5]

Evelyn Sharp, suffragette and novelist, was also diarist in the *New Leader*, the Independent Labour Party's newspaper, for the duration. In fact, the *New Leader* did not publish during the strike but subsequently produced a record of the events. Sharp suspected that it was the same blackleg bus that was burnt, allegedly, in Poplar, Camberwell and Hammersmith. She went down to the Docks, where the reports of violence and confrontation had been most vivid, to find out for herself the truth of what was happening.

Here she reported nothing but 'lean-faced men in rough working clothes, without collars or spats, standing for weary hours, animated only by loyalty to their mates and a cause'.

Less alarming, but perhaps an even greater affront to the millions of working-class people who expected everyone to play by the rules, was the suggestion that strikers were prepared to cheat. It was becoming commonplace for private cars to offer rides. The RAC had printed stickers so that drivers could show their destinations; people put charity collecting-boxes in their cars. So the *Brixton Free Press* knew its relatively well-heeled readers would be outraged by the news that 'it is the dastardly practice of strikers in various parts of London to jump into vehicles in order to prevent legitimate pedestrians securing a lift. If these are their instructions for playing the game,' it added indignantly, 'they did not emanate from England.'[6] However, a similar sense of correct conduct animated the strikers. In one town a strikers' meeting was angrily told that bags of sugar had been looted from the local Co-op. The point was made that looting damaged the strikers' cause. However, the speaker added ominously, it was known who the men responsible were – the bags had leaked.

THE NEWSSHEETS played a vital role, and not only for their propaganda value. For although the national press with the exception of *The Times* and the *Daily Mail* – which was being printed in Paris and flown in – was silent for most of the first week, the provincial papers were soon back in production if only as roneoed sheets and on the whole proving almost as supportive of the government as the *British Gazette* itself. The *Western Morning News*, in its first strike edition, declared: 'Owing to the high-handed action of the trades union leaders, the *Western Morning News* and its associated papers have been driven to take part in the struggle against those subversive forces which seek to bring ruin and misery to the country by paralysing national services.' The *Exeter Express and Echo* took an even stronger line: 'The question is no longer one of wages and hours but the infinitely graver one – who shall govern the country … if they win their battle to starve us into submission they will be rulers of the state.'[7] Provincial newspapers goaded those local councils they discerned as backsliding, unwilling to take on the strikers. 'It seems to us with a little energy and initiative that Birmingham could have 500 buses or charabancs operating. If the police cannot cope, call up the special constables,' demanded the *Midlander Daily Bulletin*.

Distributing the *Gazette* and the *British Worker* became another surrogate contest that divided strikers and their critics. Getting copies on to the streets in large numbers required organization and endurance, especially for the *British Worker*, which had no fleet of cars to match the *Gazette*'s. Instead it relied on volunteer drivers such as the young Hugh Gaitskell – who twenty years later would serve as Chancellor in the postwar Labour administration before becoming Labour leader – equipped with the appropriate temporary union membership card to meet the bureaucrats' objections and ferrying as many bundles of the *Worker* as would fit in the back of his car. A motley assortment of cars queued in Carmelite Street, outside the *Herald*'s offices, taking what they could get. Birmingham's driver would bring around twenty thousand copies a night into the city – as long as his car was working. 'Car conveying today's issue from London konked out 8 miles this side Northampton, send relief,' one desperate telegram went.

As the strike wore on, local strike papers started to copy the whole of the *Worker* into their own pages; where the printers allowed, it was produced locally, with local news inserted alongside. On this third day, the TUC was embarrassed to discover that the electricians at the power station that supplied the *British Worker* had come out on strike and been replaced by naval ratings. It could continue to publish – but only thanks to blackleg labour. Citrine now decided propaganda was more important than scrupulous observance of trade union propriety.

Churchill, relishing his unexpected opportunity to be simultaneously a press baron and a newspaper editor as well as Chancellor of the Exchequer, was busy developing his empire at the

Gazette with the help the emergency powers regulations gave him to requisition buildings and property. Within thirty-six hours of the start of the strike, he had commandeered – in addition to the *Morning Post* offices – the Argus Press in nearby Tudor Street, the Northfleet paper-making works, Somerset House, the W. H. Smith despatch warehouse in Carey Street and the Phoenix Wharf for paper storage. At Somerset House the cars were lined up in convoys. They then processed to Carey Street, where they picked up neatly labelled parcels to take off to various parts of the country.

The Times, hampered by its tiny courtyard that could only be reached down narrow alleys, had to rely on a rather more makeshift distribution system. Each car had to reverse in, at the right moment in the darkness of the early morning, to pick up its load. But after Wednesday's sabotage incident the newspaper enjoyed the services of a glamorous protection squad, largely composed of its sporting department which had taken on several fit young sportsmen who became the shock troops, drilled to get the cars loaded and past the pickets as swiftly as possible. The Jazz Band, as they became known, turned up for work in Fair Isle sweaters, avid for a 'scrimmage with the pickets' and eager to put wartime expertise in planning and protection to good use. But after a single episode of fisticuffs in the early hours of Thursday morning, and with the backing of the local police who had been invited to use *The Times* canteen whenever they wanted to, they had no further trouble. Their most reliable driver was a director of the paper, who lived in Beaconsfield and used to take a supply of papers to Oxford in the small hours, leaving them in a secret hiding place in a church tower before going off home to sleep in his own bed.

The status of the BBC remained unresolved. During the day J. C. C. Davidson took Reith to discuss the issue with Baldwin in the cabinet room. Baldwin walked up and down while Reith, tall and good-looking and still only thirty-six, lounged against the mantelpiece. Baldwin, cautiously, would only say that it would be 'far better to leave the BBC with a considerable measure of autonomy and independence'.[8] Not quite the guarantee for which

Reith had hoped. At Baldwin's suggestion, he went on to attend the daily meeting of Joynson-Hicks's Supply and Transport Committee. Through Baldwin, Jix's support was supposed to have been secured, but the Home Secretary was not, he admitted, 'strong in the chair' when faced by Birkenhead and Churchill. Sure enough, when Churchill 'emphatically objected' to the idea that Reith should be in charge of the BBC, asserting that it was 'monstrous not to use such an instrument to the best possible advantage', Jix climbed down and said feebly that it could be raised in Cabinet if anyone felt strongly about it. Reith went off to prepare a statement on the position of the BBC that he later sent to Baldwin. In it, he argued that although the BBC had to be 'for the government' in the present crisis, it was essential that it should be able to define its own position to the country. He saw that unless the public retained confidence in the Company's independence, 'its pioneer work of three and a half years will have been undermined ... an influence of almost unlimited potency ... shaken'.[9]

That night, he broadcast a statement he had received from Labour declaring that, contrary to the government's assertion, the strike was purely industrial in motive. This may have salved Reith's conscience, but although they listened along with everyone else, among trade unionists everywhere the BBC remained the BFC, the British Falsehood Company. Reith's decision to continue to negotiate over the BBC's status left it an effective prisoner of the government, censoring itself in the interest of an external authority. Where it might have exerted some editorial independence, it was only necessary to hear the word 'commandeer' breathed for the Company to fall meekly into line.

In the evening, the *British Worker* published a statement that to the acute observer could be seen as an overture in response to Baldwin's inflexible declaration in that morning's *Gazette*: 'The General Council is ready, at any moment, to resume negotiations for an honourable settlement. It enforces no conditions for resuming preliminary discussion with the Government on any aspects of the case.' The statement went on to reiterate the arguments against withdrawing the strike notices; but the window had been opened a crack. That same evening Tom Jones dined with a group of like-minded friends: Lord Astor, brother of *The Times*-owning J. J. Astor, the liberal-minded Philip Kerr, 11th Marquess of Lothian, and the Warden of Toynbee Hall, J. J. Mallon. They drew up a framework for a settlement that closely followed the lines on which agreement had nearly been reached five days earlier. The Samuel report was to be accepted by government, owners and miners as the basis for the settlement; subsidy would continue for a fortnight to allow negotiation on disputed points, with a specially convened Coal Commission waiting in the wings to arbitrate. As before, the government would help with the costs of reorganization. But the stumbling-block remained: it would be impossible for anything to happen until the General Strike notices had been withdrawn.

9

DAY 4, FRIDAY 7 MAY

The end of the fourth day of the strike sees the stoppage of productive work more widely spread, with no sign whatever of weakening among the strikers, who regard themselves as pioneers in a glorious movement, aimed at freeing humanity from the tyranny under which millions of wage-earners are expected to accept a disgracefully low and degrading standard of life.

Hamilton Fyfe, *Behind the Scenes of the Great Strike*

May 7th Friday. School. All the mistresses are here: there have been very few lates and still fewer absent girls. The council has replied to Miss Mason's letter and says he is very proud of us. So we have to 'keep on keeping on' so to speak. Dad is splendid in the strike. He takes up people every morning and keeps a weapon on the seat beside him, because many of the Bolshy Roughs like to demonstrate their feelings on the hardworking citizens and their doings is not [*sic*] by any means pleasant. People are all well protected though by police and special constables and riots have been quickly suppressed by baton charges. Anyhow, the strikers have not ruined the press and as long as we get a piece of paper 12″ × 8″ for the 'Times' we are perfectly happy.

Diary of Margaret Woods

THE FIRST FRIDAY without wages: the moment, Hamilton Fyfe thought, when iron enters a strike. The question was, which way would it go? Would the strike start to crumble? Or would extremist elements capitalize on the apparent stalemate? There was plenty of evidence to support both points of view. The government had to decide whether a clampdown and a show of military force would strengthen the extremists, provoke the wavering or convince them that the game was over. Even allowing for exaggeration, the overnight news was bad. On Thursday evening, the Home Secretary Joynson-Hicks had broadcast an anxious appeal for fifty thousand more special constables. As if to illustrate why, there had been a night of rioting in Glasgow, which began after rumours circulated that students were staying overnight in the tram sheds ready to take trams out the following morning. A mob threw stones and bottles at the depot, and nearby shops were looted and liquor stolen, although the most popular target was the boot shop. There was disorder in Hull, where a Royal Naval vessel standing off the docks landed a party of ratings to break up a mob attacking trams. In the City Square, mounted police were reported to have charged into a crowd of three thousand. Seven people were injured, including two innocent bystanders. More rioting was reported in Liverpool and Ipswich.

Churchill's deputy, the financial secretary to the Treasury Ronald McNeill, told his Canterbury constituents that the country was nearer civil war than it had been for centuries. As the number of cases mounted, magistrates dealt harshly with those convicted of violence – few who came up in the police courts got off. In some places, notably Cardiff but also Brighton, prisoners travelling from cell to court were marched through the town in chains. There were to be no exceptions, as the west London magistrate sternly announced: under emergency powers legislation those convicted of damaging buses at Hammersmith were liable to up to six months' imprisonment. 'Women will be treated the same as men. They often inflame men's passions.'

Some trade unions, especially those with a majority of members on strike, were now struggling to realize the huge amounts of cash needed to pay benefits to the hundreds of thousands of strikers. Other unions levied members in work to pay those on strike. Thousands were forced on to the beggarly amounts available under Poor Law relief.

And for those not on strike, the excitement and novelty were wearing thin. Factories hit by a shortage of supplies were laying men off. By Monday 10 May, York's unemployed, as distinct from strikers, would have nearly quadrupled, from 1,363 to 4,301.[1] The 'Great Trek' in and out of work was losing its appeal, particularly in London where it had been wet all week. Stirring verse by 'Tom Fool' (the poet Eleanor Farjeon, perhaps best known for the hymn 'Morning has Broken'), like this from the pages of the *British Worker*, was not enough to repair soaked boots and shoes.

> It's the great, great Trek
> On the road that is unseen
> To the goal of the future –
> And the obstacles between
> Will seek to daunt the hearts
> And hold the march in check
> Of the Workers who are following
> The great, great Trek.

At the TUC's Strike Organization Committee meeting that morning, Bevin 'in a state of considerable perturbation' insisted that no notes be taken; the government had announced extra powers to raid premises in search of seditious material, and had already swooped on the Communist headquarters in King Street after persistent reports in their strike leaflets alleging mutinies. There was even greater disorder than usual: the *Gazette* had published the statement that the TUC negotiating committee and Baldwin had drawn up but which the miners had never agreed to, despite the understanding that all conversations at the negotiations were without prejudice and any documents arising would be destroyed – although Thomas had already revealed their existence by referring to them in the Commons. The statement, of course, recognized the Samuel Commission as the basis for a settlement, and ended with the controversial assertion that it was accepted that a cut in wages might be involved. The negotiating committee was again forced on to the defensive. Citrine felt particularly vulnerable. 'I sometimes wonder whether Baldwin is as honest, plain and straightforward as he appears, or whether he is a hypocrite and a humbug. When in personal contact with him he conveys the feeling of sincerity, but his subsequent actions can only be justified by the assumption that he is dominated by his Cabinet.'[2]

The general committee also had to admit that the administration of the food permit system, initially the responsibility of local strike committees, was too chaotic to continue in its current form. 'Eccleston Square this morning was crowded with huge vans and carts and motor vehicles of every description, all of them bearing the usual label "Food Only",' Citrine complained in his diary. The Westminster *Worker*, the local edition of the *British Worker*, claimed that they had found rocking-horses, bedding for blacklegs and coal all labelled 'Food Only'. Beyond the outright determination to flout what was increasingly being described as an illegal exercise of authority, those who were willing to submit to the TUC's system had an elastic idea of what constituted food. Was salt counted? It was vital for the fish markets and butchers and bakers. The TUC simply threw up its hands and stepped back from the management of perhaps the most sensitive aspect of the strike. All decisions in future would be made by a central permits committee of the transport and railway unions. That body swiftly issued a total ban on all food movement – as the railwaymen had always wanted; then that too was modified, under pressure from the Co-ops, who had received bewildering and contradictory instructions.

In York, the Co-op branch of the National Union of Distributive and Allied Workers first came out on strike, then went back to work, but later they were instructed that it could only be 'for the purpose of delivering milk and bread directly to their members'. Like the Co-op in Birmingham, they decided to rely on government transport. Despite it all, apart from beer, which was getting hard to come by in many areas, there were no reports of serious food shortages.

The *Gazette* at once announced that the TUC was trying to starve the country into submission. Churchill had to be restrained from writing a 'wild article' calling up the Territorials. But that morning the President of the Board of Trade, Lord Eustace Percy, received a letter from one of the main operators of meat cold storage in London, UCS (Universal Cold Stores). Staff were being 'continually threatened with violence from the crowds of strikers in the vicinity ... Many serious assaults have taken place and we have been forced to close these premises today.' This appeared to be confirmation that some strikers at least were now genuinely ready to hold the country to ransom, to control the movement of foodstuffs until they could control every avenue of commercial activity. The letter demanded protection before an attempt was made to reopen the three riverside premises that had been forced to shut down. There were also hints from elsewhere that the government had received information that tension was mounting, or that it intended to ratchet up the stakes itself. That day's official communiqué reprinted in the *Gazette* declared that the climax was not yet reached.

There was trouble elsewhere on the docks. Eighty men had arrived to unload cargoes of lard, bacon and butter but were found not to have the correct (TUC-issued) documents. Nor was there the expected transport from Hyde Park. Before anything could be done, the TUC intelligence committee was told, 'a large and hostile crowd had gathered ... the eighty men demanded police protection'. By the time the police arrived, the men had gone. The TUC blamed the police: 'the dock gates are in one police area and the remainder of the dock area is in a different division. A spirit of complete co-operation does not seem too readily forthcoming from the police side.'[3]

The TUC was rattled. Citrine noted that Bevin, the Napoleon of trade union leaders, was fading beside the conciliatory Thomas. The main business in Eccleston Square that Friday morning was to prepare the ground for negotiation. Bevin was the first to move: he suggested that there were influential businessmen interested in helping to secure a settlement. It was agreed that 'even though we are certain of the strength of our strategic situation' – Citrine again

– this potential opportunity was worth pursuing. Thomas, in the manner of one triumphantly laying down a royal flush, revealed a series of contacts with the grand, the rich and the powerful, starting with a letter from Lord Londonderry received the previous evening. The letter criticized the government, and declared that 'something' had to be done. Earlier, another magnate, Lord Mansfield, the vice-president of the Federation of British Industries, had confided in Thomas: 'If Winston gets his way, we will have no country left.' Finally, Thomas announced that he had been in contact with Sir Herbert Samuel, who was willing to meet the TUC's Industrial Committee in secret that very afternoon.

Baldwin too was steeling himself to talk of negotiation, to the hardliners in his Cabinet. From early in the morning discreet meetings took place in Downing Street. Ramsay MacDonald took Sir Allan Smith, chairman of the Engineering Employers' Federation, to see Baldwin with his own scheme for a settlement. As soon as he had gone, Tom Jones advanced the ideas that he, Astor and Philip Kerr had worked out the previous night, and which Astor had had typed up early in the morning. He read to Baldwin the passage in the previous evening's *British Worker*, which offered to resume negotiations without conditions for 'preliminary discussions', and pressed him to respond to it with some conciliatory remarks in the Commons.

Baldwin was in as delicate a position as the peacemakers on the TUC. To concede, after a week of widespread industrial action, any point that would have prevented it in the first place could hardly be acceptable to anyone, least of all to the Cabinet. And after Red Friday, neither he nor his party could afford any gesture of apparent weakness. Nor, personally, was he prepared to concede the constitutional point. But equally, at any moment a march might get out of hand, a commissioner might lose control, some unstoppable process could begin. Neither the experience of the moderates during the Russian Revolution, nor the evidence from MI5 of a deliberate strike strategy leading to civil war, was ever far from

Baldwin's mind. If he submitted to the will of a Kerensky, Lenin would not be far behind.

Jones knew that Churchill was the chief obstacle to a settlement. In an extraordinary move, as Baldwin prepared to meet his Cabinet, Jones set off for the Treasury to try to square him. It was, he wrote later, 'one of the fiercest and hottest interviews in my life'. Churchill immediately saw what was coming, and let fly 'a cataract of boiling eloquence'. It was too late, he said, the ground had changed too much, to negotiate now. 'You must have the nerve.' Jones said it would take something more than nerve. Churchill accused him of undermining Baldwin's resolve: 'You have a terrible responsibility, in advising a man so sympathetic as the Prime Minister.' When Jones said that the TUC leaders Pugh and Thomas were as loyal to the state as was Churchill himself, Churchill exploded again, leaving Jones 'tossed about like a small boat in an angry sea'.[4]

THE SENSE THAT the strike was approaching a watershed, fostered by the lurid accounts in that day's newspapers, was a general topic of conversation. Beatrice Webb reported that Sidney returned from London 'far more apprehensive of a long strike and bloodshed in the streets before it ended'. Reports from Glasgow and Newcastle – where the failed negotiations between the commissioner and the Strike Organization Committee over blackleg labour had just been revealed – showed, they feared, that in some industrial areas 'there is a very ugly spirit which, if the stoppage continued and there were hunger, might mean outbursts of violence between the workers and the police'.

The same forebodings reached the poet Osbert Sitwell, a young man known at the time, as he would admit in self-mockery, as little more than a music-hall joke. The eccentric son of an archaic family, brother of Edith and Sacheverell, he had spent the fortnight before the strike working with his sister on an all-absorbing production of *Façade*, the unprecedented alliance of Edith's verse and the young William Walton's music, which after a rocky start had become a great hit. When Osbert, on whom the Old Etonian mantle of public responsibility lay heavy, looked around him and saw the strike had begun, he took it personally. He was aghast at the complacency of his friends, volunteers on the buses proudly sporting their sticking-plaster medals, all combatants in the war against Bolshevism – it must have been one of these who, it was said, when working as a volunteer driver, pulled his bus up outside the family house in Eaton Square and invited the conductor and the only passenger to come in for breakfast. Osbert saw instead the potential for an irreversible split in the nation that, in the curious way of the exceptionally privileged, deeply offended his sense of Englishness. Over a large martini and a long lunch at the Embassy Club he confided his anxieties to Lady Wimborne, whose husband was a former Viceroy of Ireland and first cousin of Churchill's. Wimborne, it emerged, was another of the public men with much to lose from a serious disruption of the status quo, but a desire to compromise rather than confront. He had already offered himself to the miners as a go-between, but had been politely rebuffed. Osbert proposed that Lady Wimborne, a celebrated political hostess, should dis-creetly bring representatives of all the sides together in her dining-room at Wimborne House, in Arlington Street just behind the Ritz. She should lunch for England.

That Friday afternoon, in the house of the South African magnate Sir Abe Bailey in Bryanston Square, barely a bread roll's throw from the Embassy Club, Sir Herbert Samuel was entertaining the TUC negotiating committee. In the first-floor drawing-room, Citrine was admiring the paintings – Gainsborough, Reynolds, Lawrence – and discussing philosophy with his host, before they settled to business. Samuel reiterated that his Commission had wanted nationally decided wage rates with some district variation; the coal owners were wrong to insist on district rates. He was also interested in the coal owners cooperating in and across districts in a cartel, so as to end the cut-throat competition that drove down wages. He thought the idea of a wages board, like the one in the railway industry that negotiated wages nationally, drafted by Bevin

during the previous weekend's negotiations, was too adventurous a
proposal. The TUC was equally negative about Samuel's proposal
that there should be international agreement on miners' hours: this
would have meant British miners matching the longer hours worked
by miners in Germany.

The two sides separated, planning to meet again the following
day. 'If my own position was weak,' Samuel commented later,
'theirs was weaker still. The Government had not crumpled under
the shock ... the public in general were rallying to their support ...
working class families suffered the most, and the strike was unpopular in the homes of the people.' Samuel gives no authority for this
final remark.

The negotiating committee slipped back into Eccleston Square
one by one 'so as not to arouse suspicion, as so many press sleuths
are hanging about'. Since many members of the General Council
were known to retire to the pub to discuss the progress of the strike
with the journalists they found there, it was a futile precaution.
Before the day was out, the evening papers were advertising the
possibility that the strike would be over by Monday.

By that evening, the Churches too had agreed a precise form of
words for an appeal to restart negotiations. It was not hard to identify
the three hurdles that had first to be cleared: the subsidy must be
renewed, the strike must be cancelled, and the mine owners must
withdraw their notices. The difficulty was to evade the government's
constitutional objection to negotiating with the strikers; the phrase
'simultaneously and concurrently acted upon' was devised to overcome it. Londonderry, who again just happened to drop in on the
meeting of clerics, approved the statement and advised the Archbishop to see Baldwin and MacDonald and then to issue it immediately. MacDonald subsequently told the Archbishop it was 'inspired',
but said that ending the strike had to come at the top of the list.
Baldwin was locked in Cabinet when the Archbishop arrived, arguing
over the possibilities of negotiation. But through intermediaries it
emerged that he was not convinced by 'simultaneously and concurrently'; he was still determined that the strike should be ended first.

Here the Archbishop put his foot down, apparently for the prosaic reason that it was too late to reset the type.

The final part of the plan was to broadcast the appeal that night. Baldwin, indicating that he was himself intending to make an appeal the following day, said he would rather the statement was not broadcast, though he would not ban it. Plainly, he would rather not appear to be acting at the behest of the Archbishop. The Archbishop and the BBC conferred. It is unclear who made the approach. The Archbishop held that the BBC had invited him, sight unseen, to make the broadcast; but it was intercepted by the BBC Chairman Lord Gainford, a Quaker coal owner and former Liberal minister, a man whom the Archbishop subsequently accused of 'being most unhelpful throughout'. Gainford, by curious coincidence, was of the same family as Alderman Pease whose will was inadvertently published in the first edition of the *Gazette*.

According to Reith, however, the approach came from the Archbishop, and when Reith saw that the statement contained the suggestion that negotiations should begin at the same time as, and not after, the strike was called off, he consulted Ronald Waterhouse, Baldwin's private secretary, who relayed Baldwin's views. Reith decided to turn the Archbishop down, but rather than blame the government he decided, controversially, to maintain the appearance of independence, and telephoned the Archbishop to tell him that he personally had decided that he should not broadcast, 'putting it as nicely as I could'.[5] In his memoirs, he gloated: 'A nice position for me to be in between Premier and Primate, bound mightily to vex one or other; at thirty-six years of age.'[6] The Archbishop sent off a stinging letter: 'The position is that yesterday morning the authorities of the Churches in England, not sitting formally but carrying the imprimatur of the two Archbishops, several Bishops, the leaders of the Free Churches ... agreed upon a statement ... Are we to understand that if the Churches desire to put something forth their grave utterance must be subject to the approval of its wording by the Broadcasting Committee?'[7]

A further account came from J. C. C. Davidson, who was in

charge of publicity. (Confusingly, the Archbishop – Randall David-son – and the Deputy Chief Commissioner shared a surname.) According to J. C. C. Davidson, it was he who told Reith that '[the broadcast] could not go out, and [Reith] could not give those who might wish to, such an opportunity for taking over the BBC'; he added: 'whatever SB[aldwin] had said, I knew that he certainly hoped the Appeal would not be broadcast'.[8] Davidson recalls Reith being 'very disturbed'.

Davidson also vetoed the inclusion of the appeal in the follow-ing day's *Gazette*. 'It ignored the constitutional issue,' he thought, and could mislead those 'unthinking' people who were so desperate for peace that they would not realize it. Later it emerged that Davidson placed the Archbishop among the unthinking. 'To call the Archbishop's message statesmanlike is a complete travesty of what the public thought at the time.' He thought the Archbishop 'weak and waffly' and much better kept out of politics.

The following day Reith replied to the Archbishop's letter to explain in greater detail his reasoning:

> We were in a position of considerable delicacy. We have not been commandeered, but there have been strong representa-tions to the effect that this should be done ... we have maintained a considerable degree of independence hitherto and the matter is still *sub judice*. It would therefore be inadvis-able for us to do anything that was particularly embarrassing to the Government, by reason of the fact that it might lead to the other decision that we are hoping to obviate.[9]

It was an ill-judged decision, 'the low-water mark of the power and influence of the BBC', Asa Briggs judged it. 'Protests from listeners poured in immediately.'[10] It was bound to leak out, for only that morning the BBC had reported that the Churches were conferring. Virginia Woolf, an avid wireless listener, reported it, adding that Leonard, her husband, had remarked sceptically: 'if the state wins & smashes Trade Unions he will devote his life to Labour: if the archbishop succeeds, he will be baptised'.[11]

Friday afternoon's *British Worker* had come out in a smaller format than the previous two issues. The newspaper explained why: 'The reason is that the Cabinet has stopped our supply of paper. At the docks and in a mill there are supplies belonging to us. The Cabinet refuses to let us have them.'[12] Churchill had decided that his *British Gazette* did not have enough paper for the circulation that he thought appropriate to the government's principal propaganda weapon; he would use his powers to requisition more. The demands of the *Gazette* were also a cover for trying to close down, or at least limit the availability of, the *British Worker*, without drawing attention to the embarrassing contradiction between a government that had broken off negotiations with the trade unions, ultimately, because they had interfered with the sacred principle of a free press, and a government that was endeavouring to gag its opponent's only mouthpiece. The Chancellor had already commandeered a paper mill, but it was in 'a rather disaffected area' and needed both an army and a naval guard, and the entire company of volunteer workers had to sleep and eat and work on site. It was, however, already producing enough paper for a million and a half copies a day of the *Gazette*, but for a tyro press baron like Churchill, a circulation of a million and a half was just a beginning. It was reported that distribution was less than perfect. MI(B) had to rescind a decision to get it to all London troops as there were no copies at all in other areas, which therefore had to rely on the news to be found in the *British Worker*.[13]

It was not just the *British Worker*'s supplies that were taken over, as Churchill pointed out when, as soon happened, he was accused of trying to suppress the opposition's news. He also commandeered all other sources of paper, including *The Times*'s. Geoffrey Dawson, recently reappointed its editor and an intimate of Baldwin's, found Churchill insufferable. When Dawson wrote *Strike Nights at Printing House Square* soon after the strike ended, it seems he was still enraged. 'It was,' he wrote of the *Gazette*, 'produced from the office of the *Morning Post* with a staff reinforced by a strong contingent of generals and admirals ... and rapidly lost all the character of a stop-gap or supplement and threatened to hamper, if not to prevent altogether, the revival of ordinary newspapers.'[14] The *Gazette* took staff that the independent newspapers (that is, *The Times*) might have used as well as newsprint that *The Times* desperately needed.

Dawson began his campaign in defence of his newspaper with a letter to the Prime Minister, arguing that with his own, and other papers, now printing successfully there was actually no justification for the *Gazette* at all:

> Official propaganda is always suspect, and therefore ineffective, and a newspaper for which the Government is avowedly responsible but which it cannot possibly control in every detail [not a kind reflection on Churchill] may at any time cause it very serious embarrassment. If the result of pushing the circulation of the *British Gazette* with all the resources at the disposal of the Government should be to drive every independent newspaper out of existence, I do not think that the policy would easily be defended or commonly approved.[15]

Baldwin, instinctively sympathetic, left Dawson with the impression that *The Times*'s arguments were in his opinion justified. But any optimism Dawson may have felt was swiftly soured by the formal response to his letter which came not from No. 10 Downing Street but from No. 11. The Chancellor's response reveals a showman revelling in his new vehicle:

> The *British Gazette* printed 836,000 copies last night,' Churchill wrote. 'I hope to print over a million on Monday and over a million and a quarter on Tuesday. It is devouring paper at a terrible rate. But remember this is the one means which at present exists of holding together, in direct contact with the Executive Government and Parliament, the whole loyal mass of citizens throughout the nation on which success depends.

Braggadocio then turned to a maudlin appeal to Dawson's public spirit – but one that must have reflected Churchill's genuine concerns about what was at stake: 'I hope you will remember what a frightful task it is to feed all these millions of people in the face not only of desertion, but of widespread obstruction. Any serious breakdown in supplies or vital services might lead to an appalling local catastrophe. We cannot really afford to take needless risks or neglect any possible precaution.'

For Churchill, the strike was a war, a war almost more serious than the war against the Hun – a war between the established order and the trade union movement. He had convinced the government that no compromise was admissible. Now he had to persuade the country to view it in the same way. 'One of the difficulties of the situation is that large numbers of working people feel quite detached from the conflict; and they are waiting as if they were spectators at a football match, to see whether the Government or the trades union is the stronger.'

10

DAY 5, SATURDAY 8 MAY

May 8th Saturday. Music lesson. Mr Holland at the end said I should pass but I don't believe him yet. Mother said he ought not to have told me I should pass, as it would stop me practicing but she need fear not in that direction. Came home and helped mother. Saw Mr Grable on his beat (he is a special constable). Dad brought home the British Gazzette [*sic*] (2 pages for 1d) I am saving the papers as relics. Some buses are running. The volunteer [*sic*] drivers and some conductors are being guarded by a special constable and the bonnet by barbed wire. Mr Stanley Baldwin sent a cheery message to everybody, saying that every man who did his duty would not be forgotten and telling us all to keep calm and support the govt.

Diary of Margaret Woods

VERY EARLY IN the morning of Saturday 8 May, the fifth day of the strike, there were signs of unusual activity in the army encampment that had sprung up in Hyde Park. More than a hundred lorries were drawn up, in a convoy said to be two miles long, interspersed with an escort of twenty or more armoured cars bearing soldiers. These were Guardsmen, wearing the same uniform they had worn on the battlefields of Europe less than ten years earlier, steel helmets and grey greatcoats and, at the controls, Tank Corps soldiers in their distinctive black caps. As dawn broke, they drove east out of the park, past the grand houses of England's aristocracy, heading towards the City, and on down to Victoria Docks in the East End. The government was laying on a show of strength. The dockside warehouses were to be reopened.

'London needed the flour and London had to have it,' the *British Gazette* trumpeted when it had a chance to report the event on the Monday. The Home Secretary, Joynson-Hicks, was said to have told the army that they could use whatever force was necessary as long as the docks were opened. By 7 a.m., the dock gates were secured and the volunteer labour force had begun work. By 11.30 the whole convoy, armed troops sitting on sacks of flour, was on its way back to Hyde Park. The thin Saturday morning shopping crowd – many shops were shut – cheered it as it went, as if it were the Lord Mayor's parade, some thought, and Davidson won his bet with Joynson-Hicks, struck after a bad-tempered cabinet arguing with Churchill, that the show of force was entirely unnecessary. The BBC reported, without apparent irony, that no attempt was made to interfere with the convoy. The *Gazette* almost sounded apologetic. 'Curiously enough,' its reporter observed, 'there were few expressions of hostility from the crowd, and no open demonstrations against the soldiers.'

Churchill had wanted hidden machine-guns along the route, as well as the inclusion of tanks in the convoy, but calmer counsel prevailed. This was Sidney Street revisited, the moment when his urge for direct, irresistible action, for excitement and drama, overwhelmed any sense of the political. It was the action of a man who, Lloyd George thought, 'like a chauffeur who is apparently perfectly sane and drives with great skill for months ... suddenly takes you over a precipice'.[1]

To most of England, Bow and Poplar, where the docks lay, were a foreign country. They were among London's poorest boroughs, a place of joblessness and a degree of lawlessness, where even in normal times the forces of law and order trod carefully; a place where life was lived on the edge. From the beginning of the strike, the pro-government strike sheets had painted Poplar as if it were fomenting revolution. The first day had been dubbed 'Black Tuesday': there were reports of cars being held up, deliberately damaged and sometimes set alight, their occupants left to make the rest of their journey on foot. Special Branch reported intimidation, and a strict rota on picket lines that had to be kept in order to claim strike pay. The local strike committee, a 'sinister body ... attempting to usurp lawful authority ... impertinently issued diktats and arbitrarily denied transport permits,' the *Daily Telegraph* reported afterwards; here, large numbers of men living on unemployment pay 'have become a grave menace to the community'.

The representative and defender of these people was the Christian pacifist MP George Lansbury, 'a wild Socialist, passionate and shouting', the *Gazette* (or its editor) thought. Lansbury later became leader of the rump Labour Party that emerged after the disastrous 1931 election. His daughter Dorothy was married to another Labour Member of Parliament, Ernest Thurtle, who had been seriously wounded during the war and had then become a leading figure in the Ex-Servicemen's Movement. MI5 had received information that he was a secret member of the Communist Party. (But so, they were told, often on the flimsiest of grounds, were many other individuals. MI5 agents generally had only a weak grasp of the shades of left-wing opinion.) As mayor of Poplar, Lansbury had led thirty Labour councillors to prison in a dispute over the government's refusal to provide central funding for welfare in the borough. He was a powerful critic of his own Labour leadership, and a constant irritant to Ramsay MacDonald, against whom he tried to launch a coup after the first Labour government. In 1911 he had founded the *Daily Herald* as a strike newspaper, but had been forced out when the TUC rescued it from bankruptcy in 1922. He continued the radical tradition with *Lansbury's Labour Weekly*, notable for its uncomfortably vigorous criticism of TUC and Labour policy.

The orthodox Labour view of Churchill's convoy was reflected in the *British Worker*.

For no reason whatever except to delude the public mind, the Cabinet gave these lorries an 'escort' of ... armoured cars, cavalry and mounted police. There was no risk of attack whatever. The lorries were as safe as ordinary traffic is at ordinary times. The object of making this ridiculous unnecessary demonstration was clear. It was to make people afraid, by making them believe that the strike had violent revolutionary aims.[2]

Many others agreed. But against this must be set the anxious reports of violence in the docks that flooded in almost every night. There was an active local Communist Party, pickets at every factory and dockyard gate, knots of men on corners and 'a state of mental tension leading to a state of mental chaos'.[3] If there was to be serious trouble in London, this is where it would emerge. After the previous day's problems in the docks, the transport workers' ban on all food movement, and other warnings coming into the Board of Trade, Churchill's gesture had perhaps more justification than many felt at the time.

There was trouble elsewhere that Saturday morning. At about the same time that the convoy was preparing to leave Hyde Park, police raided the offices of the *Birmingham Worker*, a Communist newssheet, for publishing false reports of mutinies. Four men and a woman were convicted, under the emergency regulations, of 'committing an act likely to cause disaffection'. Birmingham's police were unusually energetic in pursuit of sedition; the Labour-controlled city council stood accused in pro-government newspapers of covert sympathy with the strikers, and a lack of will to get the trams and buses back on the road. An MI(B) report suggested the NUR men were ready to go back the moment they were offered adequate protection. A couple of days later, on the Tuesday, the entire editorial and production team of the strike newspaper set up by Oswald Mosley the previous week was arrested. Early in the strike, the bulletin unfortunately misreported proceedings in Parliament; by a genuine error, it had alleged a government defeat on a key aspect of the emergency powers legislation. This was close enough to treason to merit the arrest of the editorial board, including John Strachey, the editor. As there were so many of them, the police superintendent rang the secretary to the trades council to tell her they were all to be arrested, and would she telephone round to ask them to report to court the following morning.[4] Mosley, however, the bulletin's financial backer, was not named, and was in fact speaking elsewhere. He rushed back to Birmingham to give himself up, but to his chagrin the police were not interested. In court a few days later, the magistrate asked Chief Superintendent Burnett, 'All the men are of excellent character and standing?' 'I would not go that far, quite,' he replied.[5] They were all fined £10 each. Mosley paid. Strachey claimed to regret not being sent to prison.

THE SPORADIC BATTLE to get public transport running again continued to occupy time and energy. In Plymouth, the council tramway committee, which employed the men, had issued notices for them to return to work. On Saturday morning twenty-six had responded and, with volunteers and inspectors, launched a service. A crowd, estimated by 11.30 at four thousand, swiftly gathered in the centre of town at Drake Circus. When other traffic held up the first tram to come along, it was surrounded by angry strikers. Only when police actually got on to the tram was it allowed to go on. The next tram had its destination board torn off, and the one after that had stones thrown and windows broken. The police launched a baton charge. Pandemonium ensued. When it calmed down, however, one of the strike leaders marched the men off to Guildhall Square and warned them of the harm that violence did to their cause. For a few hours, they resisted the temptation, even when a woman on the top deck of one bus stood up and thumbed her nose at the strikers. But more trouble began again later, and a handful of arrests were made. They were later prosecuted by the formidable, faintly biblical figure of Isaac Foot, father of Michael, who in the early 1980s would briefly be leader of the Labour Party.[6]

As the near-riot continued in the centre of Plymouth, a more celebrated incident was taking place on the local football ground in the city's Home Park. Strikers were playing the police at football. The idea had come from the local strike committee as a demonstration of the peaceful and law-abiding intent of the striking men. The Chief Constable's wife kicked off; the strikers won 2–1 in front of a crowd of ten thousand. At half-time, the tramway band struck up, apparently oblivious to the ongoing uproar in the town centre. 'The English are not a nation, they are a circus,' a French journalist wrote when he heard of the story. But the nation's press lapped it up. If the *Western Morning News* thought it a fraternization too far, most other commentators saw it as the essence of Englishness: the passion for sport, the sense of fair play – above all, the shared sense of identity that, even in the midst of a general strike, showed there was more that united than divided even strikers and police. However, when Davidson told Churchill about the game, and exhorted him to include it in the *Gazette*, Churchill refused. 'Winston thought I was a perfect ass,' he wrote later. So deep was the division between confrontationists and conciliators in Baldwin's government that the decision to run the story had finally to be endorsed by the entire Cabinet.

The *Gazette* was continuing to absorb Churchill's energy. Afterwards, he described it unapologetically as 'the combination of a first-class battleship and a first-class general election'; soldiers were called in to protect the *Morning Post* offices, naval engineers to mend the presses, and Churchill himself provided much of the rousing propaganda as well as trying his hand at every other aspect of the production process, butting in 'at the busiest hours and insist[ing] on changing commas and full stops until the staff is furious'.[7] But his energy was exhausting the *Morning Post* staff involved in the paper's production. H. A. Gwynne, the *Post*'s editor in normal times, wrote to Davidson begging him to keep Churchill away: 'We have produced the *British Gazette* under very trying circumstances, but we are by no means satisfied that we cannot produce a much finer paper. In order to do this however, it is essential that all orders, communications, instructions and suggestions from the Government should come through one channel, and that channel would naturally be you and your department.'[8] In a memorandum he wrote afterwards for the record, Davidson observed that the 'Chancellor occupied the attention of practically the whole staff ... it was unfortunate that he tried so persistently to force a scratch staff beyond its capacity ... he thinks he is Napoleon'. Beaverbrook, from whom Churchill was also commandeering newsprint, remembered: 'Churchill on top of the wave has in him the stuff of which tyrants are made.'[9]

That morning's *Gazette* had struck another provocative note which, taken with the food convoy episode, marked an abrupt ratcheting up of government resolve. 'All ranks – the armed forces of the Crown – are hereby notified,' it stated, 'that any action they may find it necessary to take in an honest endeavour to aid the civil power will receive both now and afterwards the full support of HM Government.'

There was a storm of protest, not least from the King. George V was already distressed to be the subject of bitter criticism among trade unionists, who saw him firmly on the side of the government, responsible for both the proclamation of emergency, which was made in his name, and the *British Gazette* which, as a publication of HMSO, the official stationery office, carried the royal coat of arms. He wrote at once, through his private secretary Lord Stamfordham, to the Chief of the Imperial General Staff Sir George Milne, who conveniently was also an aide de camp, in the understated terms that signify royal irritation: 'His Majesty cannot help thinking that this is an unfortunate announcement and already it has received a good deal of adverse criticism.'[10] The message was not repeated.

The government's appeal to service and duty worked like a dog whistle on the consciences of young officers and cadets at home on leave. C. H. Drage, a naval officer recovering from appendicitis who had volunteered at the start of the strike, was called in to work that Saturday in the 'U.C.' department of the Admiralty. 'U.C. stands for Unrest, Civil,' he wrote in his diary; 'The Section was working at top pressure and expanding at the same time. At noon a parcel of 12 service pistols were brought in by an old Admiralty messenger – so now we can defend ourselves.' Drage was to be an assistant to the director of the operational division of a temporary department that seems to have been explicitly established to oversee the use of the military in strike-breaking and policing. He went on:

> The news is not good: food stocks are becoming depleted throughout London, but on the other hand the first food convoy has been successfully run up from the docks ... The story goes that when the convoy came out through the dock gates, an old lady in the very hostile crowd picked on one tank and followed it along abusing it. The tank took no notice until presently she called it a 'bastard'. Then a small iron window in the tank opened and a Tommy's head poked out. The head remarked, "'ullo muvver, fancy meeting you 'ere!' and then withdrew: the iron window closed and the tank continued on its way.[11]

This tale, like the Plymouth football match, became part of the mythology of the strike, undermining the attempts to portray it as class war. It later appeared in strike sheets and in Drage's 'U.C. jest pack', a collection of jokes that had circulated in the nine days the strike lasted.

Joynson-Hicks continued to appeal for volunteers. On the first day of the strike he had appealed for 30,000 special constables. On Friday, although he reported reassuringly on the numbers who had already responded, he had asked for 50,000 more. On Saturday it was officially announced that there was to be an entirely new full-time volunteer police force in the capital. It would be additional to the 25,000 in the Metropolitan Special Constabulary Reserve and Metropolitan Emergency Constabulary; it was to be called the Civil Constabulary Reserve. It was immediately noticed that the proposed daily pay rates, at five shillings for a constable and twice that for a commander, were above the daily rate miners could earn, even before the pay cuts. It was intended to recruit men already serving as part-time soldiers in the Territorial regiments, and public schoolboy soldiers from the Officers' Training Corps. It was necessary, the Home Secretary explained, 'owing to the tactics employed by ill-disposed persons who are taking advantage of the present crisis' – another hint that the great majority who were on the side of the government were being threatened by a tiny, probably Bolshevik, almost certainly foreign, minority.

This was a way of recruiting men with some military training without, as Churchill had been demanding, calling up the reserves, and it produced a gleeful response. Every drill hall in London became a recruiting office. The Royal Naval College in Greenwich was ideally placed as a barracks from which to police dockland. But it was correspondingly vulnerable, a lightly defended Winter Palace that a large mass of men could reach comparatively easily. 'The officers in College were all organised & yesterday sworn in as Special Constables to be used as a reserve,' one cadet wrote home. 'On Monday we were organised for repelling boarders. I found a very efficient weapon in the centre of my riding boot tree [a long thin piece of wood with a handle at the top] but this was superseded on Tuesday by a lighter but possibly handier "Truncheon"! If the alarm was given at night we were all to wear cap covers & monkey jackets for distinction.'[12]

Meanwhile, the news of the BBC's suppression of the Archbishop's appeal, singularly missing from Saturday's *Gazette* as well as from the airwaves the previous night, was becoming a matter of general discussion. *The Times*, although unremittingly supportive of the government's constitutional case, was determined that it should retain its reputation as a newspaper of record. It continued to publish details of births, deaths and marriages, and it would certainly publish a pronouncement from Lambeth Palace. It duly appeared in Saturday's paper. P. T. R. Kirk of the Industrial Christian Fellowship and Henry Carter, secretary of the Wesleyan temperance and social welfare department, both of whom had been involved in drafting the appeal, drove round distributing it to as many manses as they could reach. A surge of support across the country ensued, although perhaps not uniformly. An attempt by Birmingham's Church leaders to raise a march to push for a negotiated settlement foundered on apathy. In London, Reith, a man given to agonizing if strictly private self-doubt, spoke again to

the Archbishop's chaplain. A compromise was found. The Archbishop was due to give a sermon the following day, which would
be about the churches' proposals for conciliation; under the
onslaught, Reith no longer found it constitutionally unacceptable
and agreed to broadcast it. '[The Archbishop] reverted to the
Church's manifesto,' he noted in his diary, 'but it was quite
innocuous.'

Behind the public preparations for a quasi-military clampdown,
efforts to find common ground for negotiation quickened. In the
morning Herbert Samuel, who had made little progress trying to
squeeze negotiating room from the owners, spent two hours with
Baldwin. Samuel tried to persuade the Prime Minister to make
the acceptance of the main principles of his report the basis for
agreement. The permanent secretary at the Ministry of Labour,
Horace Wilson, and his minister Steel-Maitland, as well as Birkenhead and Neville Chamberlain, rushed to stiffen Baldwin against
such an acceptance of government intervention. Birkenhead argued
against any expression of the government's position being transmitted through Samuel; there could be no question of negotiating
during a general strike. Chamberlain insisted the promise of a
subsidy had to be conditional on a settlement, Steel-Maitland that
there should be no 'vestige' of official authority behind any discussions. Wilson, who kept in careful contact with the miners' leaders,
believed they were now ready to accept a pay cut as long as they
got copper-bottomed assurances on reorganization of the industry.

In the afternoon, Tom Jones saw his old LSE friend Harold
Laski. Laski, a veteran of the Labour movement, was as close to the
trade unionists as any outsider although prone to exaggeration. 'I
spend all day at Eccleston Square,' he told Jones reassuringly.
'I take Pugh home every night. I think I know their minds there.
Of the twenty-six known to me not more than three are out and
out revolutionaries.' He too believed the miners were prepared to
accept a formula involving a pay cut. At about the same time,
Samuel was holding another meeting with the trade unions in
Bryanston Square. He told them the government was still not

prepared to negotiate, even in private. He proposed that grounds for a settlement should be agreed between themselves, and that he would then set them out in a public letter in the knowledge that the TUC would welcome them, thus leaving the government the responsibility of rejecting them. Of the owners, he had little hope. The miners would have to have government behind the settlement in order to override them.

THE TUC's HOLD on the General Strike was faltering. Some groups of workers, like the electricians, were demanding to join it, but others wanted to go back to work. They were watching their jobs go to volunteers, and daily read the government's repeated assertions that, if they did return, they would be protected from victimization by their unions. Reports that came in to the TUC intelligence committee were several days old, and there was little way of verifying or contradicting the claims that the strike was crumbling and violence growing. Worse, relations between the TUC leaders and the miners were increasingly poisoned by suspicion. Handed the loaded revolver of a general strike, the miners would not relinquish it until it had secured victory. The TUC thought the strike was merely a negotiating instrument; they were reluctant to consider what to do if the government did not comply, but they were becoming increasingly aware that the question could no longer be ignored. With their precious funds draining down the plughole of solidarity in a battle that, increasingly clearly, was not only of no immediate benefit to their members but looked increasingly likely to cost them their jobs, the TUC believed there was no option but negotiation. But they were haunted still by Black Friday, by their previous conviction for betrayal.

The miners' leaders Arthur Cook and Herbert Smith were both publicly insisting that they be party to any negotiations. On Saturday morning, Citrine's diary records 'a heated discussion' between the miners and John Bromley of ASLEF, the train drivers' union. ASLEF, with a smaller, better paid and skilled membership, had never had the same enthusiasm for group action. 'By God,'

Bromley said, 'we are all in this now and I want to say to the miners, in a brotherly, comradely spirit, but straight ... but straight – that this is not a miners' fight now. I am willing to fight right along with them and to suffer as a consequence, but I am not going to be strangled by my friends.'[13] Smith challenged him back: 'If he wants to get out of this fight, well, I am not stopping him.' Reluctantly, Smith conceded that although no definite negotiations could take place without himself and Cook, it would be acceptable to hold 'conversations'. In his later account, Smith – who dated the news of the talks to the following day, the Sunday – denied even that concession. 'The miners had had plenty of Sir Herbert Samuel, we knew him quite well, and did not want anything to do with him.' (They did, however, go and meet him two days later, on the Monday.) That evening, after the afternoon session in Bryanston Square, the miners' negotiating committee together with the General Council were shown Samuel's draft proposals in which he clung to the hope that his report offered the basis for settlement. 'I could not see any concern among them,' Citrine wrote defensively.

Meanwhile the Wimbornes' eat-your-way-to-peace initiative, which held out the best hope for finding a solution acceptable to the mine owners, continued with another lunch at Wimborne House. Sitwell, of course, was there, and Lord Wimborne had persuaded two influential figures from the coal industry to join him, Lord Londonderry and Lord Gainford, also Chairman of the BBC, described by Sitwell as the 'restrained, tight-mouthed ... typical ennobled master of industry'. J. H. Thomas was present, according to Sitwell, 'worried and tired almost beyond bearing', and the 'affable Caesar ... slightly damaged by life', Lord Reading, newly returned from India where he had been Viceroy. Ethel Snowden, whose husband Philip was the dry-as-dust Chancellor in the first Labour government, made up the party, whose exchanges, Sitwell's dramatic account continues, swiftly became too inflammatory for the servants. 'So important in its matter, so vehement in its manner, so frank was the talk, that the footmen, I recall, had to be told almost at once to leave the dining-room.'[14] Confusingly, this was so even though Lord Reading was so trained in discretion that, Sitwell also remembered, he would discuss only golf.

There was, again according to Sitwell, such excitement when Thomas 'finally committed himself to the admission' that the miners would accept the entirety of the Samuel Commission, including wage cuts, that Lords Reading and Wimborne departed immediately to Parliament, drafting a peace formula as they went. There they met Birkenhead and Churchill; to their chagrin, neither was in the mood for compromise. Sitwell, together with the war poet, former literary editor of the *Daily Herald* and all-round radical Siegfried Sassoon, decided the best they could do was to persuade their various journalistic contacts to listen to them and modify their attitudes. They camped out on the doorsteps of Arnold Bennett, who was earning hundreds of dollars writing on the strike for the American press, and of Beverly Baxter, the editor of the *Daily Express*. But neither was in the mood for peace-making. 'One brief but angry chapter of the Class War had opened and both sides were enraged,' Sitwell recorded.[15]

News of these meetings spread through London society, embroidered and inflated. Within twenty-four hours Virginia Woolf had heard that Lady Wimbore [*sic*] had brought Thomas and Baldwin together through Asquith – but then learnt that Asquith was sixty miles away, and not unnaturally she discounted the entire story.

On this fifth evening of the strike, in another indication that a watershed was approaching, Baldwin, who had been almost invisible up till now, decided to make a broadcast – the first time a prime minister had ever used the wireless to communicate directly with the country in an emergency. All day, drafts of his words had circulated between the Ministry of Labour and No. 10. When the moment for the broadcast came, though, Baldwin was still trying out phrases in his head. Reith had decided that the Prime Minister should broadcast not from the BBC's Savoy Hill base, nor from Downing Street. Instead, in a fine show of power and ambition, he should make an outside broadcast sitting at Reith's desk, in Reith's own study in his house in nearby Barton Street. At ten past nine, he personally collected Baldwin from Downing Street and, escorted by a carload of police, they motored the short distance back to Barton Street. Baldwin handed his script – 'this tripe' – to Reith and invited him to comment. They discussed the ending: Baldwin wanted something about peace. After a little thought, Reith proposed: 'I am a man of peace; I am longing and working and praying for peace; but I will not compromise the dignity of the constitution.' The word 'surrender' was inserted for 'compromise'. Leaning over Baldwin's shoulder, Reith now announced the Prime Minister. Baldwin lit his pipe and began. 'The General Strike has now been in progress for nearly a week, and I think it is right that, as Prime Minister, I should tell the nation once more what is at stake in the lamentable struggle that is going on.'

The broadcast went on to distinguish carefully between the legitimate miners' dispute and the unconstitutional General Strike – 'a direct attack on the community ... [by] a body, not elected by the voters of the country ... [aiming,] without consulting the people, without consulting even the Trade Unionists ... to impose conditions never yet definite ... [striving to] dislocate the life of the nation ... [starving] us into submission.' Baldwin rejected appeals for some 'conditional' end to the strike. No door is closed, he said, but there could be no negotiations until the strike was called off 'absolutely and without reserve'. The strike could 'only increase in misery and disaster the longer it lasts'. As he neared the end of the broadcast, according to his diary, Reith, in an action that illustrates both a sensitivity to language and an imperviousness to risk, decided that 'dignity' was an inappropriate word to utter in relation to a crisis. He reached over and took the last sheet of paper from under Baldwin's hand, crossed out 'dignity' and inserted 'safety and security', then slid the paper back to the Prime Minister seconds before he reached that point in his statement. Baldwin paused, but 'almost imperceptibly' before reading on.[16] Sadly, Davidson, who was in the room throughout, remembered a much more prosaic version of events.

Special Branch had received a warning that the signal transmitting the broadcast was to be interfered with by the Communists. HMS *Hood* was instructed to jam any rival transmissions. Davidson claimed later that the only complaint came from an old lady listening in bed on her earphones and crystal set who said her eardrums were burst by the volume of the *Hood*'s rival signal.[17]

DAY 6, SUNDAY 9 MAY

May 9th Sunday. Quite a peaceful day. All of us went to church in the morning. Met Vera and went for a walk with her after church down the High Road. Bought a small page titled 'Sunday Pictorial' for 1d and from it I gathered that the miners' question was almost forgotten and the union's [*sic*] and the strikers are attacking the Government. I read in the official papers that Mr Baldwin said there are two alternatives to the present Government 1) Fascist Govt 2) Socialist Govt and he was right declaring that no true British man would stand those. I hope everybody will loyally support Mr Baldwin and our present Parliament. Went with Mother to Uncle [illegible]. Gran was there. Came home with roots. Saw Newton coming home. Took Spot out after and he trundled with me. Quite slick.

Diary of Margaret Woods

ON SUNDAY the Prime Minister went for a long walk on Hampstead Heath with his son Windham and the indefatigable Tom Jones. They barely mentioned the strike. In the afternoon, although Regent's Park was shut because troops were setting up camp, as they were in Victoria Park in Bow, Baldwin visited the zoo. He was the very image of a man with time on his hands, confident he had only to wait and the strike would collapse. His calm amiability contrasted with rumours of imminent arrests and reports of Saturday night violence; and the evidence of military and quasi-military activity, as lorries full of soldiers in steel helmets thundered about the streets of the capital and carloads of undergraduate volunteers motored off to the docks.

Baldwin's demeanour also belied the fury among both clergy and congregations that the Archbishop had been gagged by the government. Many clergy read Randall Davidson's appeal from their pulpits. Lord Astor, a Tory, also welcomed it. He told the Methodists that 'the all-important thing was to maintain the moral claim and witness of the Church ... for the spirit of the Churches would be needed to fight against the Mussolinis in the Government camp and the Lenins in the labour movement'.[1] In Oxford, under-graduates took it from house to house as a petition. A. D. Lindsay, the Master of Balliol, a Christian as well as a Socialist, ensured its distribution through the Society of Friends and the League of Nations; from there it spread to Sussex, where a thousand people gathered in Horsham to hear it read. It was also read in Carlisle and Peterborough and in Bradford Cathedral. 'Its effect in the industrial areas here has been wonderful,' the Bishop of Birming-ham later wrote. The Birmingham clergy, disappointed by the lack of support for a march, united to pass a resolution supporting the appeal.

Dr Norwood, the minister at the City Temple, declared: 'There is no attack on the constitution. It is impossible to witness the remarkable order on both sides and believe that we are in the grip of reckless revolutionaries. The conviction behind the strike may be mistaken, but it is honest and sincere.'[2] In Poplar, *Lansbury's Labour Weekly* told its readers to go to church. 'You will come to our meetings at night, but I would like you to attend the Church Services nearest your home ... It is Christ's gospel of passive resistance which you are practising today.' The Dean of Manchester spoke of the strikers' chivalry: 'Willingly the great mass of them threw their present and future prospects of livelihood to the winds for the sake of a handful of men in another industry ... that, and no sinister blow at the Constitution, was the backbone of the strike.'[3] In Preston, the strike bulletin carried a message from Canon Donaldson of Westminster urging the strikers to stand firm: 'If they stand firm, they will win. But if they begin to doubt and quaver and to blackleg – all will be lost and lost for a generation.'[4] In Wigan, the Sunday strike bulletin exhorted strikers to keep the Sabbath day holy, and repeated the first commandment – 'Thou shalt love the lord thy God with all thy heart, soul, mind and strength and thy neighbour as thyself.'

In many towns and cities, despite the general divorce between the majority of the population and the churches, strikers marched into the pews and joined in prayers for the police as well as for the men taking action, for the King as well as the TUC. Many, following an instruction from TUC headquarters seeking to deny reports that ex-soldiers were out of sympathy with the strike, wore their war medals. Eleanor Farjeon was prompted to write another rhyming indictment of the government's promise to stand by the men who only twelve years earlier had gone to fight for King and Country. At Eastbourne, Victoria Crosses, Distinguished Conduct medals and other war decorations were worn in a procession, and banners were carried bearing the legend, 'Miners were comrades in 1914, they are comrades today.'⁵ In some towns, like Plymouth where a powerful strike committee worked hard to promote a peaceful attitude, strike committees and churches had arranged for daily services. In Shrewsbury, strike committee meetings were preceded and followed by church services. In Reading, 'the spirit of love, sacrifice and service embodied by the carpenter of Nazareth' was held by the strike newsletter to live on in the strikers. The vicar of St Mary Magdalene in Barnstaple suggested that since national warfare was a crime, so too should be industrial warfare, and it should be possible 'to fasten the guilt of that crime on those morally responsible'. Across Devon, many vicars and ministers spoke out for the strikers, although there were some strident exceptions. The vicar at Paignton thought that 'if the worst came to the worst, [it might] go like Russia'. The vicar of Norwood in south London, the Reverend Heaton-Renshaw, went so far as to rewrite the national anthem:

> God save all Englishmen,
> Make us all friends again,
> God bless our men.

Children and homes and wives,
Grant to them peaceful lives,
For this each Christian strives.
God save our men.[6]

On Sunday night, the Archbishop's sermon was carried on the BBC – 'a really moving appeal', Hamilton Fyfe considered, unwittingly interpreting it exactly as J. C. C. Davidson, in effect the government censor, had feared. 'For the first time in its history, I think, the Church of England has put itself on the side of the People against the Privileged Class. The old Archbishop has been splendid.'

But the Christian Churches did not uniformly view the strike as an opportunity to exhibit the New Testament virtues of love and conciliation. A Brixham vicar became an engine driver and took over the shunting at Newton Abbot, conducting his church services before starting work. More seriously, Cardinal Bourne, England's leading Catholic priest, declared the strike 'a sin against God'. The government ensured that the Cardinal's views got widespread publicity. Catholic Labour MPs were among those who objected: 'We have striven for peace and peace has been denied us by the Government ... with all respect, yet with emphasis, we protest against a high dignitary of the Holy Church making a statement which neither the morality nor the theology of our faith justifies.'[7] For the Communists, the Catholic Church, its nearest rival in scale and control, became the leading enemy. But the scorn heaped upon the Cardinal, and the wide if not universal welcome given to the Archbishop's words, were small consolation for the trade union movement's leaders as they wrestled with the government, the press and – it was feared, after Sir John Simon's ruling that the strike was illegal – the courts.

Astor's support for the Archbishop's appeal for a reopening of negotiations based on the concurrent withdrawal of the strike and the lockout notices took him back to Downing Street. He had learnt from Jimmy Thomas that the government was refusing even the indirect contact that Sir Herbert Samuel was offering. Nor was he impressed by Baldwin's broadcast: it had not opened the door far enough for the unions to squeeze through. MacDonald, who like Astor had been told by Thomas that there were to be no contacts between the protagonists, wrote to protest. The weekly press, taking its first opportunity to comment on the strike, was critical of the government. The *New Statesman*, the Fabians' newspaper, ducked the constitutional question and blamed the government for allowing the negotiations to break down. The *Spectator*, from which the government might have expected support, instead attacked it for asking the miners to accept an unspecified cut in wages for an uncertain future reform; and though it conceded that the strike was unconstitutional in the sense that it could only be won by the unions if government became impossible, it was nonetheless 'persuaded there is still a clear opportunity for reopening negotiations. Mr Baldwin, we may be sure, will not be blind to it. The one duty of every patriotic man, while doing his share in keeping the life of the nation going, is to engender peace.'[8] These were sentiments uncomfortably close to those of the *Daily Herald* on the first day of the strike.

But Baldwin's broadcast was having an effect in some quarters. Initially, Sitwell and the Wimborne House peace warriors had thought, like Astor, that it was discouraging in its refusal to compromise. However, Tom Jones, who was aware of the discussions, let it be known that from Baldwin's apparently intransigent words on Saturday night it might be deduced that the PM wanted to encourage unofficial talks like the Wimborne House sessions; he also hoped the TUC might review its position. Furthermore, Jones may have been intending to encourage the coal owners to declare their support for the Samuel Commission report as the basis for a settlement, as the TUC was already prepared to do, thus isolating the miners.

FOR THE STRIKERS, meanwhile, Sunday was just another day for demonstrating solidarity. From the start, the TUC had advised local strike committees to find the strikers useful work, or at least entertaining relaxation, lest the devil, in the form of agitators or fifth-columnists, find their hands idle. 'Keep everybody smiling' was the motto; and 'the best way to do this is to smile yourself'. On the front of its first issue, the *British Worker* had relayed the message from the General Council: 'In all districts where large numbers of workers are idle, sports should be organised and entertainments arranged. This will both keep a number of people busy and provide amusement for many more.' In many places, the instruction was taken to heart. Rallies, meetings and marches were obvious ways of keeping up morale. Educational lectures and study circles, play centres and games, cinema shows, concerts, dances and other social gatherings were all recommended.

In Croydon the conductor Rutland Boughton, the man who invented the first Glastonbury Festival, was helping to organize music and concerts, a cricket team was being selected, acrobatic displays were taking place on the lawn of the trade union centre at Ruskin House, and there were daily readings of the *British Worker* to 'a cheering and enthusiastic crowd'. The *Bradford Worker* cited the No More War Movement as chief organizers of entertainment, and added that, since everyone was walking everywhere, chiropodists were doing very well. In Herne Hill, south London, strikers lined up in fours and marched around Brockwell Park, attracting a large crowd and making a collection of £55. 'Do something,' exhorted the *British Worker*. 'Hanging about and swapping rumours is bad in every way. Do the thing that's nearest. This will occupy you and steady your nerves if they get shaky.' A JP chipped in: 'Don't touch anyone. Smile on and we'll win through.' In Cardiff too strikers were encouraged to keep smiling, and not to hang about the city centre where, although 'good feeling' prevailed between the strikers and the Cheshire Regiment, which had been billeted there, 'trouble might arise'. Instead they should go out into their gardens or parks or into the countryside – advice keenly taken by some with a view to sheep rustling. This, though rewarding when successful, was not as easy as it sounded, as Jenny Evans, the daughter of one Maerdy family of Communists remembered fifty years later:

> My mother's brother he was going to go out this night now with a gang of men … so now they told my mother's brother, 'Now you stop down in the hitch [*sic*] by here, and we will chase the sheep towards you and surely you will be able to catch one.' Well they chased the sheep towards him and they were talking among themselves, 'Well Dick is bound to have caught one of the sheep by now,' but when they came now to my uncle the sheep had bowled him over and knocked him unconscious. There was no lamb or anything that night.[9]

Strike newsletters buoyed morale with praise for enterprise and appeals to decency. This was a strike for fair play as well as fair pay, and fair play must rule when, for example, shopping for food. No hoarding by customers, but the shopkeepers should also, the *Preston Strike News* urged, 'play fair and prevent customers from benefiting themselves … remember you depend largely on the support of the working class for your profits, not they depend upon you for their usual weekly supply of food'.[10] The Preston bulletin called on the women, like the men, to pull together and 'show their usual unselfish pluck which, in these trying times, is always foremost, [or] the efforts of your men may be seriously imperilled and the fight for justice will prove a very hard task'. Down in Berkshire, the *Reading Citizen* reported:

> All is Well … From every quarter come heartening reports of a cheery courage and determination to go forward unflinchingly … We would like to pay a special tribute to the brave, enthusiastic and effective co-operation that has been given by the wives and other women relatives of the strikers. The women, perhaps, more than any others, feel the pinch of struggles such as that in which we are engaged and their loyal and unselfish support of the cause will be a big factor in the successful issue to which we all look.

But the great majority of people were still at work; even at its short-lived peak, the strike actually involved only around three million out of a workforce of nineteen and a half million people. The non-striking workers, however, were not redundant. They were the invaluable extras in the portrayal at home and abroad of this extraordinary national event. The law-abiding strikers who, for example, played football against the police were plainly English, but how much more English were the new middle classes, the men and women who daily made the Great Trek from the suburbs into the shops and offices where they worked. What made them such quintessential embodiments of the virtues that had made England great was their endurance, their stoicism, their capacity to soldier on, the uncomplaining victims of a hardship they could not change. The authors of their suffering were variously the fat-cat union bosses, reported in pro-government newspapers to be living like emperors, swishing past the workers in the untypically cold, wet spring in chauffeur-driven motors while puffing on their cigars, or, more sinisterly, the swarthy and often verminous characters who peopled the reports of the more susceptible MI5 agents.

The newspapers were quick to identify and glorify these heroes whose stalwart character stood between Britain and revolution. 'Whatever may be in store for us,' pondered the *Mirror*'s strike newspaper, 'it is at least our consolatory thought at this stage that the first round has exhibited the finest qualities of our race and made it clear once for all that its vital resources are not to be lightly attacked while the spirit of mutual service lives and thrives among us.' The *Ladies' Mirror* offered a collection of positive ideas: a cold buffet should be laid out ready for the hungry workers whenever they struggle home. It might include, the paper recommended, 'corned beef, hard-boiled eggs, sardines, fruit, cheese, cold ham and sausages', which can make 'quite a tempting meal'. Women who can drive can offer lifts, and those who have a spare room can offer a bed to someone from further away. And there were social opportunities: 'Broadcast parties have become quite a social feature during the strike. People with wireless sets invite as many friends as their rooms will hold to come in and hear the announcements. "Come and listen tonight," has taken the place of "Come and play a rubber."' Another day there was advice on what to wear to meet that everyday dilemma of needing a coat when walking, but then finding oneself too hot should one be offered a lift. 'The ideal, I think, is a silk jumper-suit and a light tweed coat with perhaps one of the snug little furs that the Americans call "throwers" . . . I always think that if you look to your shoes and stockings and gloves first, providence seems to reward your virtue.'

The respectful acceptance of social inequality that remained a powerful strand of Englishness threaded its silken, diamond-studded way through the newspaper coverage. On the outside pages, the threat of revolution over a few shillings a week for the miners; inside, the doings of the five hundred families who by birth and inherited wealth made up English Society. Some Society activities had been cancelled: the Chester Vase race meeting at York, for example. Debutantes and their mothers were informed that King George and Queen Mary had retired from the social whirl because of the Emergency, and no Courts were to be held in May. The King, always punctilious about matters of turnout, was concerned that 'it would be difficult for the dressmakers to cope with the orders'. Australia was beginning an Ashes tour and was warming up by thrashing county sides, though England went on to win a rain-affected series; and most theatres were still open. The season at Covent Garden had begun with a triumphant performance of Mozart's *Marriage of Figaro*, conducted by Bruno Walter with Lotte Lehmann, Elizabeth Schumann and Richard Mayr: 'Let everybody who wants to know what genuine, pure unadulterated artistry is go to hear Bruno Walter's performance of Figaro,' declared the *New Statesman*'s reviewer. Osbert Sitwell, genuinely concerned by the threat of class war, took comfort in the idea that at the very least lunch with Lord Wimborne would have shown Jimmy Thomas that some of the aristocracy understood the anxieties and concerns of the working classes. When Communists in Rotherham, during a royal visit before the strike began, tried to preach republicanism, they had to flee an angry mob. There was no market for newspapers that preached social equality.

Foreign correspondents were genuinely impressed by the unselfishness of the strikers, and, it was reported in British newspapers, delighted to have their prejudices about the English so satisfactorily confirmed. On Sunday night it was reported that there had been fewer casualties in the whole of the strike's first week than in that day's Joan of Arc celebration riots in Paris. Told by Arnold Bennett of what Osbert Sitwell paraphrased as 'revolutionary workers versus the chivalrous, true, brave, good, gentle and generous middle-classes',[11] the American newspapers, reported the *Brixton Free Press*, praised the English as 'a people who think clearly and in every emergency keep their feet on the ground'. One American commentator, however, more familiar with the black arts of marketing, added: 'These traits in the national character are constantly referred to by leader writers and convince them that in the end right and justice will prevail.' The French were inclined to gloat at the spectacle of the English enduring the consequences of their vanity in overvaluing the pound at the time they returned to the Gold Standard – France had let the franc fall, a move that in some analyses was responsible for the failure of Britain's economic strategy.

But the newspapers were careful not to get too far removed from the reality of life as experienced by their readers. 'These tranquil and improving appearances,' the *Brixton Free Press* remarked, 'and the evident power of the government to carry on the life of the people must not, however, lead anyone to forget the increasing arrest of all business and production, or the growing hardships and impoverishment to which the mass of the people are being subjected.'

Once more the spirit of England was invoked. Englishness, as it had been since Elizabeth I declared she had the heart and stomach of a king – and a King of England too – was a lifebuoy in uncertain times, a potent set of values to be held aloft like a standard before strikers and non-strikers alike, and to which all must cleave. Strikers and non-strikers were playing different games, but by the same set of rules. Thus, for example, the TUC kept to hand a copy of Debrett, the bible of English society. And so, early on this Sunday afternoon, at Eccleston Square, its general secretary was immediately available to see a man without an appointment but with a double-barrelled name and a plausible manner. A small, sunburnt individual 'with hawk-like features' presented himself. His name, he said, was Rivett-Carnac – 'you can look my family up in Debrett' – and he had come with the news he had just picked up in his Club, that Churchill was out to smash the union movement. The self-proclaimed Rivett-Carnac – the real one was the financial adviser to the King of Siam – suggested that for a mere £1,000 and a hundred strong men he would attack Downing Street and murder the Cabinet, prior to taking Princess Mary's children hostage. He was shown the door, and a little later appeared in court for defrauding elderly ladies of large sums of money.[12]

THE TUC NEGOTIATING committee was considering how to handle Samuel and the miners. Thomas was now convinced that without a willingness on the part of the miners to negotiate on pay, there was no point in going on. Faced with a strike that had been expected to last a few days at most but that was now heading into its second week, the whole General Council, Walter Citrine believed, was coming to the same conclusion. One trade union leader said, 'Judas Iscariot played a dramatic part in history. There could have been no Jesus Christ without him.'

The realists on the General Council had always put their faith in securing a commitment to restructure, backed by a subsidy, as a more realistic objective than preventing any reduction in pay. Now Citrine began to doubt that even a subsidy would be forthcoming, and the strike could last no more than another two to three weeks at the most. Legal penalties on some strikers, the risk of permanently losing jobs to blackleg labour, fears for pensions – all, in Citrine's view, made a drift back to work and the internal crumbling of the strike a serious danger. 'The logical thing is to make the best conditions while our members are solid. We must retreat, if we have to retreat under compulsion, as an army and not as a rabble.' The inadequacy of communications made it hard to judge the accuracy of the government's claims of a return to work; and the government's high-profile food convoys, while having little to do with supplies, damaged men's morale and heightened the risk of violence.

Another factor was the money. Strike pay was haemorrhaging union funds; daily, the *British Worker* reminded readers at work to levy themselves five shillings a week to support the strikers. Without funds, the strikers could not stay out. Agonizingly, they had just received a telegram from the All-Union Central Council of Trade Unions in Moscow offering £26,000. Reluctantly, they decided not to take it. MI5 was told that the NUR had discovered it could not realize £8 million of war loan and gilt-edged railway stocks; 'great deficiencies had been discovered in the TUC's War chests,' the agent reported.[13]

Also at an advanced stage of discussion, unknown to the TUC, were cabinet plans originating with Churchill to introduce two potentially devastating pieces of legislation. The first would stop all trade union funds immediately. The second would outlaw sympathy strikes. These proposals would not just cut off any funds from Moscow, they would also make it impossible for the trade unions' own legally held and legally raised funds to be used for strike pay, a powerful weapon to drive trade unionists back to work. These plans appear not to have been known about beyond a small handful of the Cabinet. But Thomas was in regular, if informal, contact with several senior ministers, and it is possible that it was this proposal, rather than a separate problem with NUR money, that the agent had been told about. MI5 thought its information explained why that Sunday night – in a speech to strikers which, the Plebs League said later when it reviewed the strike, 'made the Blue Hall in Hammersmith, bluer' – Jimmy Thomas chose to return to his attack on the principle of a general strike. The unions had not wanted one, he said, but the government would not force the coal owners to withdraw the lockout notices, so that the unions were thrown back on their only weapon, collective bargaining. This was not a challenge to the constitution. It was the duty of both sides to keep the door open. 'The task is a difficult one: responsibility is indeed a heavy one. But there will be a graver responsibility on whichever side fails to recognise the moment when an honourable settlement can be arrived at. The moment must be accepted, and everyone must work to that end.'[14] It was the most significant public indication that the TUC was weakening; and in the minds of millions of trade unionists, for ever more, Thomas stood condemned by his own words.

That same evening, another senior Liberal politician, Lord Grey of Falloden, came to the aid of the government. Like Asquith at the start of the strike, Grey believed that in a contest between 'freedom' and fairness, freedom had to emerge the winner. Among the Liberals, only Lloyd George repeatedly attacked the government for allowing negotiations to break down. Some Conservatives who also blamed the government for the strike looked on the Liberals with renewed enthusiasm. Other long-standing Liberals like John Maynard Keynes believed that the party's response to the strike would mark its final downfall and leave the path clear for Labour. Keynes was backing a petition that was gathering support for the Archbishop's appeal; the entire Liberal intelligentsia were being asked to sign it. Such was the level of emotion that even Arnold Bennett, despite his robust disapproval of the strike, was persuaded to put his name to it. 'I can always comfort myself with thoughts about the great traditional British policy of compromise,'[15] he wrote gloomily. With all the Liberal newspapers silenced, a new one, the *British Independent*, was launched with the same aim of promoting a negotiated settlement. But Grey was on the Liberal Party's traditional wing. And, having written an attack that appeared in the *Gazette* (critics remarked on a similarity of style shared by all the government's supporters when contributing to the *Gazette* and suspected Churchill of 'improving' them all), he was to make what turned out to be a much more conciliatory broadcast on the BBC.

'The strike with its threat to the life of the community is a challenge to the sense of freedom and divides us. Renewal of negotiations would appeal to the sense of fairness in all of us and unite us.'[16] Afterwards Reith, chauffeur to the powerful, went to collect him from Churchill's house, where he was having dinner. Churchill left the table and rounded on Reith for the BBC's lack of partiality; Reith suggested he should call at Savoy Hill when he was feeling indignant, and was supported by Grey in his defence of the BBC's independence. 'I told him that if we put out nothing but government propaganda we should not be doing half the good we were.'

12

DAY 7, MONDAY 10 MAY

May 10th Monday. School again. Miss Mason says we shall be docked of milk supplies so the alternatives are cocoa and water. The papers report that shipping and the transportation of food etc is improving and that many men have defied the union orders to strike and have returned to work. I'm so glad. It's about time some of them came to their senses. I feel positive that the strike cannot continue much longer and mother is so optimistic and cheerful about it, that Miss Firewash [?] and Mrs Bush declare her a regular comfort. Dad all along has had forebodings about its duration and often tells us that we shall have no jam etc soon. He has had a baton made for him and so has Mr Fourniss – they mean business evidently. Dad took Mr Fourniss out to teach him to drive.

Diary of Margaret Woods

OF ALL THE ASPECTS of the propaganda campaign against the strike, the most important was the claim that public transport was functioning again; and of transport networks, the railways were the most significant.

In practical terms, the more trains that ran the more normal working people's lives became. Symbolically, the railways to a unique degree represented the power of organized labour. Restarting a rail service by the use of volunteer and blackleg labour was the objective of the government's daily promises, made with increasing vigour, that it would protect all strike-breakers from victimization. The railway companies, having experienced one national strike and several smaller ones since 1919, were as willing as the government to do all they could to curtail the power of the rail unions.

On Monday the 10th the BBC claimed 'a tendency' for railmen to return to work, even though statistics released after the strike showed that only about 3 per cent of drivers and firemen went back before the end. In one curious case, South Lambeth, men worked throughout the strike and then walked out on 14 May over the reinstatement terms.[1] Guards and less skilled workers were only slightly less committed. The real value – if not the purpose – of the BBC's daily broadcasts of the number of trains the companies claimed to be running lay not in helping the occasional listener plan his or her journey, but in the impression they created in the minds of strikers and non-strikers alike that the strike was crumbling. It was spoofed in one strike bulletin: 'The Strike is over. Only 400,000 NUR men are now on strike, plus 1 million miners and 2 million others. But three trains are running in Manchester and there is a five minute service every two hours on the tube.'[2]

On this, the seventh day of the strike, it was reported that nearly four thousand trains would run, the most since the action had begun. It was *not* reported that on a normal Monday, nearly three and a half million would travel by train; even if each train was carrying a hundred passengers (and most travelled more or less empty), they would carry barely a tenth of the normal number. On Southern Railways 200 trains were claimed to be running. The normal number was 1,880. On North Eastern Railways, 500 trains ran: Newcastle alone normally had 954 through in one day.[3] But it was true that volunteers were emerging from training and that more trains were in service. As a result there was a sharp increase in accidents. This Monday there were four fatalities, three in a single smash on the Edinburgh line where a passenger train ran into some goods wagons. A similar disaster killed another passenger at Bishop's Stortford. A derailment, caused by suspected sabotage, occurred near Newcastle. Sporadic sabotage was discovered several times a day, in some cases potentially lethal incidents involving dynamite. In one instance, incompetent driving by a senior clerk (who blamed a greased rail) put the leading carriage of his train through a wall and into the Oswestry station parcel office.

These sometimes tragic incidents illustrated at what risk the trains had been brought back into service. Great Western Railways' statistics after the strike, which cost the company £5 million in lost receipts alone, showed that despite claims of daily improvements, they trained only 886 volunteers; and in all important grades, more than 80 per cent of their staff remained on strike from beginning to end. The drivers and firemen were 95 per cent solid. Volunteers had flooded in from the start; but though fifteen thousand from outside the company were enrolled, fewer than five thousand could be used, despite intensive training and an instruction book praised subsequently for its clarity. 'Imagine yourself,' began the introduction to the concept of distant signals, 'the engine driver of a non-stop train travelling at a mile a minute … if suddenly you come to a signal showing "Stop", what would happen…?'

Of more use to the company were the tiny handful of strike-breakers, and young men who had been made redundant when they reached the adult rate and who were taken back on when the strike began. But Sir Felix Pole, the general manager of GWR, refused expenses for men stranded away from home unless they were ready to do any work that was asked of them, regardless of their own job. In a foretaste of the attitude it would take at the end of the strike, the company was similarly remorseless with those who wanted to come back to work. When a night inspector in the Exeter area appealed 'with tears in his eyes' to be re-engaged, 'having lost his nerve a bit on Tuesday', he was turned away again.[4]

The chaotic organization of the volunteers further reduced their effectiveness. Competent men were stranded without trains, or with trains, but in the wrong place. Signalmen were thrown into unfamiliar boxes at short notice, and unskilled volunteers were accused of causing thousands of pounds' worth of damage. 'Fire-boxes full of fused clinker, firetubes wedged with lumps of coke and hot axleboxes were a few of the maladies that had to be repaired afterwards. On the minimal one day's training received by signalmen it was as well that traffic was very light.'[5] Another writer estimated that it took two years to repair all the damage; the GWR itself admitted it did not return to full service until a year later. Strikers compounded the ignorant volunteers' difficulties. Some greased the rails on inclines, others hurled bricks through signalbox windows.

But often the volunteers needed no help in causing havoc. One was said to have driven his train straight through Bristol Temple Meads, unable to stop, and on to Bath, where he finally resorted to emptying his firebox. It was a relatively common occurrence for trains to hurtle through level-crossing gates and pass signals at danger, especially since in many places the signals did not work. Where lines were open, non-striking supervisory staff manned several boxes at once, bicycling the mile or more between each, ahead of the train. Strikers joked that the trains that did run took so long to get anywhere, lunch was being served on the commuter services. The GWR, which had the lowest proportion of senior staff on strike, could never manage more than 25 per cent of its normal daily mileage for passenger and perishable goods services, and barely 5 per cent of its normal mileage for other freight. It took a day to organize a single fish train from Milford Haven to Padding-ton, a venture not repeated, particularly after angry complaints of a fish shortage in South Wales. Apart from milk, which continued to arrive in London in such quantities that the Hyde Park milk pool was rechristened the 'milk lake', most perishables had either to be disposed of locally or were lost altogether, although Channel Islands vegetables came in through Weymouth and intermittent banana trains got through to London from Avonmouth. Hundreds of boxes of the new season's asparagus waited wiltingly at Worces-ter to be brought to London; fresh meat from Ireland was eventually sent by road instead.

The King was said to be worried about the pit ponies, which either stayed down the mines looked after with union permission, or were brought up for a holiday. But the railways also had hun-dreds of horses, regularly used for road transport. At Paddington, staff from the bloodstock auctioneers Tattersalls came in to look after them. Elsewhere, the men who normally cared for them were exempted from the strike by their unions. In a few cases, normal carrier service was uninterrupted.

Strike-breaking efforts on the trams and buses, where less skill and fewer support staff were needed, had more success. Some of the amateur conductors, wearing the uniform of the golf course – plus-fours, gloves and ornamental stockings with tasselled garters – and liberally dispensing their 'Thanks awf'ly', caused delighted amusement. Virginia Woolf, travelling from Bloomsbury down to the House of Commons with material for a speech to be made by the Labour MP Hugh Dalton, took buses both ways, '& no stones thrown. Silver & crimson guard at Whitehall; the cenotaph & men bareheading themselves'.[6] In Birmingham, the tramways committee warned its drivers that if they were not back by Wednesday they would lose their jobs; by the following day the strike was almost at an end. But the same day, an intelligence agent reported that the men had gone back and been sent home by the city corporation, which was giving in to the 'rowdy element'. 'Unless a strong line is taken soon, there will be serious bloodshed...'[7] Subsequently, the tram men themselves denied they had been ready to go back, and claimed to have been the victims of black propaganda. They had been told that York men were working.[8]

There were still huge problems, but undoubtedly the Great Trek was being eased in towns and cities across the country. And other propaganda blows were dealt against the striker. Electricians at the West Ham power station cut off all power to the London docks at 4 p.m. on Day 7, imperilling the water level in the docks and most of London's frozen meat. By twenty past four, it was on again, running from the batteries of six submarines connected up in series.

Although there were unskilled jobs the volunteers could do effectively, on the whole they were not workers, but actors in a drama being directed by the government and its supporters in the press. They were the representatives of the indomitable will of

20. Non-strikers' good humour as they struggled to work was a constant source of self-congratulation in the press. 'One day of the strike was sufficient for Londoners to display their great characteristic adaptability to new situations, and today they have acted like born philosophers.'

21. The main central London recruiting office, in the forecourt of the Foreign Office, was almost overwhelmed with volunteers.

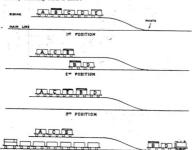

RAILWAY SHUNTING

FREIGHT TRAIN VEHICLES

PRACTICAL OPERATIONS

The example given in the first illustration shows in a simple manner how railway shunting work is done :—

SIDING **A B C D E**

MAIN LINE   POINTS

1ST POSITION

A C E

B D

2ND POSITION

A C E   **B D**

3RD POSITION

A C E   **B D**

HOW THE TRAIN TAKES ON THE WAGONS

Here are five trucks (lettered A to E) on a siding. Suppose you require to place the two marked " B " and " D " into a position to be taken on by a train which, later, will arrive on the main line. This is how you proceed :—
Join the engine to truck " E," see that " B " " C " " D " and " E " are coupled together, and that " B " is detached from " A." Draw forward the four trucks that are connected together. When " B " has passed over the points, detach " B " and push it on to the main line. Again reverse the points, and push " C " on to the siding. In like manner shunt " D " on to the main line, and " E " on to the siding. Detach the engine from " E " and attach it to the two trucks (" B " and " D ") on the main line. Then place these trucks on the siding. They will therefore stand at the " points " or " outlet " end of the other wagons.
When the train arrives on the main line, it must come to a stand a little distance short of the points. Its engine must be detached and sent into the siding to " pick up " " B " and " D." It must then push these wagons against the train on the main line. Then join the connecting (" coupling ") chains, and the train will be ready to proceed.

22. Great Western Railways was proud of its carefully designed instruction manuals for volunteers – although they did not prevent millions of pounds' worth of damage being caused to locomotives through ignorance.

23. Thousands volunteered to live out their engine-driving fantasies, but few had enough training to take out an engine before the strike ended.

24. The rail companies hoped to be able to break the strike by threatening legal action. But even the Railway Clerks' Association, which had never been on strike before, came out in support of the miners.

25. 'Mrs Sloane Stanley, Miss Coventry and the Honourable Mrs Beaumont exercising the horses at Paddington railway stables.' The King was said to be alarmed that animals, like these horses used for local delivery from Paddington station, might be neglected during the strike. Miners had special dispensation to look after the pit ponies.

GREAT WESTERN RAILWAY.

NOTICE TO THE STAFF.

The National Union of Railwaymen have intimated that railwaymen have been asked to strike without notice to-morrow night. Each Great Western man has to decide his course of action, but I appeal to all of you to hesitate before you break your contracts of service with the old Company, before you inflict grave injury upon the Railway Industry, and before you arouse ill feeling in the Railway service which will take years to remove.

Railway Companies and Railwaymen have demonstrated that they can settle their disputes by direct negotiations. The Mining Industry should be advised to do the same.

Remember that your means of living and your personal interests are involved, and that Great Western men are trusted to be loyal to their conditions of service in the same manner as they expect the Company to carry out their obligations and agreements.

FELIX J. C. POLE.
General Manager.

PADDINGTON STATION,
May 2nd, 1926.

7765-5-26

26. Many agreed with the government that a General Strike was an attack on the authority of parliament. But there was very little violence during the nine days.

27. The armed forces were drafted in and, generally with the co-operation of the local trade unions, unloaded ships in order to maintain essential supplies.

28. Undergraduates and officer cadets were encouraged to volunteer. Osbert Sitwell called them the 'thug militia of St James's Street, the bands of young, steel-helmeted clubmen'.

29. Osbert Sitwell watching with his brother Sacheverell as the manager and barman at the Savoy demonstrate shaking a cocktail.

30. A rare image of physical attack, at King's Cross station in London. Most episodes involved stone throwing and tampering with engines.

31. Tanks patrolled London streets, heightening tension and exacerbating trade union leaders'
fears of losing control of the strike.

32. Churchill insisted on an armed escort for a food convoy from the docks to Hyde Park.
Cabinet colleagues bet against a shot being fired. Trade unionists saw it as an attempt to alarm.
'For no reason whatever except to delude the public mind, the Cabinet gave these lorries
an "escort" of armoured cars, cavalry and mounted police.'

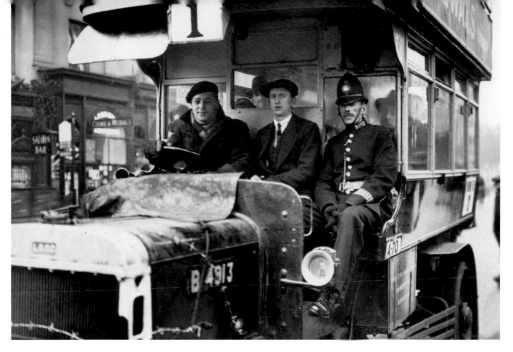

33. Where there was violence it was usually against the strikebreaking efforts of the public transport network.

34. In many cities, pickets attempted to prevent buses and trams leaving the garage. There were frequent reports of buses being overturned and set alight, but no reliable count was ever made.

35. With almost all newspapers closed down, Churchill became editor of the government's *Gazette*. He commandeered large amounts of newsprint, handicapping newspapers like *The Times* as well as his intended target, the union-backed *British Worker*.

36. People gathering to hear news. BBC bulletins were put up in shops and newspaper offices.

what was projected, without investigation, as a majority, against the revolutionary demands of a minority. Slowly a myth of the strike was being created, to be reinforced less than fifteen years later in the early years of the Second World War by the experience of the blitz. It was a demonstration of the power of the idea of national solidarity that required most people on both sides to behave according to a shared but unspoken code. The electricians, for example, walked out of West Ham only after they had discussed with the Navy a convenient moment for a handover.

Hamilton Fyfe wryly watched as, each evening, paper was delivered to the *Gazette*'s commandeered Argus Press, next door to his own offices. At the *British Worker* the reels were delivered in the customary fashion: a lorry arrived, the men slung the paper into the machine room, the lorry left. The arrival of the *Gazette*'s paper, on the other hand, was a military operation. There was a three-man guard, and the street was filled with special constables. 'There were also some mounted men caracoling up and down. What a perfectly ridiculous exhibition! There was no risk whatever, *and everyone knew there was none.* The display of force was melodrama,' Fyfe later wrote.[9] *The Times*'s experiences, after the early incident of sabotage, were similar to Fyfe's. 'The truth about the pickets is that comparatively few of them had their heart in a very cold and monotonous job,' Dawson wrote. The numbers out in the street fell off, the hooligans disappeared and the booing and truculent remarks died down. The Jazz Band, the newspaper's protection squad, was more or less redundant. 'After a time it became almost as difficult to prevent undesirable fraternization with the volunteers as to prevent recriminations.' Pickets demanded early copies of the paper, collected their back pay and asked for racing tips. They even continued to salute the chairman as he went in and out of the office.

DOWNING STREET on Monday morning was preoccupied with the idea of legislation to deprive the trade unions of cash and the strike of legitimacy. The idea had come originally from the bellicose

tendency, Churchill, Chamberlain and Birkenhead, eager now for a
sudden death. Baldwin had been pushed into it at a cabinet meeting
on Saturday, where it had been agreed that an order in council be
used to prevent the trade unions receiving money from abroad. But
Tom Jones and the King between them would now defeat the idea
of legislation that would specifically outlaw the strike.

It was one of the few sunny mornings of the strike. Jones walked
up and down the terrace behind Downing Street with Baldwin. He
believed the Prime Minister was on the verge of throwing away his
carefully sustained image as a peacemaker. 'Eccleston Square was
already beaten, and knew it was beaten,' Jones told him, but this
attack would 'come as a thunder-clap on the country which was
utterly unprepared for it, and would greatly confuse its mind'.[10] It
also risked fraying the peaceful temper of the strikers. Churchill
and the Chief Whip joined the group and Jones repeated his
arguments. A cabinet meeting was arranged for the afternoon.
Baldwin's private secretary Ronald Waterhouse suggested to Jones
that the only other route by which the Prime Minister might be
influenced was through the King. The King's power 'to advise and
to warn' could be brought in to cut off the diehards; George could
be relied upon to offer reinforcement to Baldwin's moderate
instincts. Jones, meanwhile, consulted the permanent secretary at
the Treasury and head of the Home Civil Service, Warren Fisher,
from whom he learnt that Churchill had at first wanted to arrest
the unions' funds without legislation or order in council, and only
the Governor of the Bank of England had ruled it out.

That afternoon two of the men struggling to break the strike on
the railways, Felix Pole, general manager of the Great Western
Railway, and Guy Granet of London, Midland and Scottish, also
warned of the danger of provoking the strikers by such aggressively
hostile legislation. 'They did not want to destroy the Unions, but
only wanted power to select the men who should return after
the Strike so as to eliminate undesirables.' Lord Stamfordham, the
King's secretary, alerted by Waterhouse, arrived to see Baldwin.
Stamfordham wrote later: 'Private information reached the King

that the Cabinet as a whole was by no means satisfied as to the proposed legislation: that there was a danger of the Prime Minister's being rushed by some of his hot-headed colleagues into legislation which might have disastrous effects, especially at the psychological moment when there is but little bitterness of feeling between the Government and the strikers.'[11] He warned that if money were cut off and there was no food, there might be rioting or looting of shops, or even bank robberies. Nor, he thought, would such legislation be popular in the House of Commons. The project was put on hold, and its death warrant effectively delivered in the Commons the next day.

Meanwhile, the Wimborne–Sitwell peace mission was reaching its apogee. Early on Monday morning Jimmy Thomas had once again been driven from his home in Dulwich to Arlington Street – he observed the electric trains running again on the commuter lines – to meet Lords Wimborne and Reading. Further long discussion produced a formula intended to break the deadlock: if there could be some assurance, not from the government but from a respected public figure, that negotiations to implement the Samuel Commission report could resume as soon as possible, the TUC would call off the General Strike and commit the miners to accepting a 'possible adjustment of wages'. Thomas was asking for a paper victory, an agreement to negotiate before the strike was called off. This was relayed to Tom Jones, who in turn passed it to the Prime Minister.

Baldwin was not impressed. He had already given all the assurances he was prepared to in the course of his broadcast, and the Reading–Wimborne–Thomas plan was 'tossed aside with some impatience'. Sitwell, later, was disappointed to find that in the two chapters of his memoirs devoted to the strike, Thomas did not mention his new lunching companions and their role in finding a way out. For what they had arrived at was broadly the formula that was to emerge from the Samuel–TUC negotiations and, if not quite in the paternalistic terms Sitwell imagined, the contacts made with the more imaginative of the employers did provide at least the

impression of their being ready to listen and to negotiate. But
Thomas was soon to be pilloried for his role in ending the strike;
perhaps his weakness for the aristocracy seemed an embarrassment
for a trade union leader engraving his name on posterity.

Thomas must have gone directly from the Wimborne meeting
to Bryanston Square, for another session with Samuel. Samuel had
prepared a memorandum – considerably more subtle and detailed
than the broad-brush approach achieved in the Wimborne talks –
on which, he believed, negotiations could be reopened. There
should be no wage cuts until progress had been made on reorganization, as proposed by the Commission. A board representing all
sides of the industry should oversee it. There should be, too, a
national wages board with an independent chairman, which would
take the final decision on pay levels; and, as Baldwin had proposed,
while negotiations continued, so should the subsidy.

The TUC's Negotiating Committee thought it might work. In
the afternoon, they came back with the miners' executive, old
acquaintances of Samuel's from the days of his inquiry. But they
were no more amenable to pressure from him than they had been
to their fraternal colleagues in the TUC. Samuel lost his temper
and asked how there was to be any progress when neither side
would concede an inch. The miners' president, Herbert Smith,
argued back. Samuel, in his memoirs, spoke of Smith with a certain
reluctant admiration. 'A burly Yorkshireman, full of courage ...
when his mind was made up he was not to be moved. Three hours
of argument in our conference left Herbert Smith's attitude on
every point precisely what it had been at the beginning.'[12] No
progress was made. In the evening, the General Council and the
miners met again to discuss the Samuel plan.

The TUC had now been in almost constant session for ten
days. The public image, energetically portrayed in the *British
Worker*, was of a bustling, efficient, purposeful organization. 'Every
few minutes despatch riders are arriving or departing, bringing and
taking news, instructions, and information to the different areas.
Cars with deputations, officials, members of committees and vol-

unteers are also going to and fro in continual procession. Everything is quiet and orderly, everyone doing his or her job without confusion or complaint.'[13] Citrine, shown in contemporary photographs as tall, stylish and fastidious beside the swelling bellies and well-worn clothes of the trade union leaders, a young man in an imperfectly defined role facing men with a generation's experience of bitter industrial fights, wrote of confusion and hysteria. Others heard of worse. The General Council were living, Beatrice Webb reported with distaste (but also at second hand), 'a thoroughly unwholesome life – smoking, drinking, eating wrong meals at wrong times, rushing about in motor-cars, getting little or no sleep and talking aimlessly one with another ... there were perpetual misunderstandings between the General Council and the miners; they were silent, or "rowed" [with] each other according to their moods'.[14]

Several of the miners' executive had never been back to London since the strike started. Smith and Cook, their general secretary, were left to carry the burden of decision-making on their own. Perhaps it is not surprising that they refused to say anything but no. Citrine described Jimmy Thomas resting his head on his hands. 'He tells me he cannot sleep at night, and has the exhausted look of a man completely worn out.' Thomas and Bevin never agreed, either: if one thought the strike had to fold, the other was relaxed to the point of driving his colleague to distraction. The following day, their positions might be reversed. 'And Maggie Bondfield calmly goes on with her knitting.'[15]

By the time of Monday night's meeting between the General Council and the Miners' Federation, the miners were scenting a sellout and the General Council was exhausted, uncertain of what was really going on, unable to see their way ahead. Their intelligence network was inadequate and patchy, and relied on the reports of local trades councils delivered already a day or more old, mainly by despatch rider, and written in a style as relentlessly and opaquely upbeat as the *Gazette*'s. 'All solid', 'Excellent response', 'No truth in the rumours', 'Picketing proceeding smoothly'. But, embedded in cheering news from Bethnal Green and Edmonton, on Monday there were more ominous reports from the East End, of military activity, tanks on the Embankment, Scots Guards in the Tower of London and dock bridges being guarded by troops.[16] Trade union leaders, used to negotiations with employers they knew, leading a workforce they understood, found themselves on an unwieldy committee nominally responsible for directing millions of men on an unknown project, with neither a clear objective nor an adequate chain of command. The government's rival organization, on the other hand, ran on generations of inherited wisdom, was operated by people who regarded themselves as the governing class, bred as they were on the experience of running an empire, of successful distant communication and delegated authority. The civil commissioners' regions were virtually autonomous, their objectives specific, their resources unlimited. Telephones and telegrams, petrol and despatch riders, and a bureaucratic culture that understood how to relay information – all lay within their easy reach. Towards the end of the strike, the Chief Constable of Barrow was surprised to find a second destroyer in the port. 'I didn't order it,' he told the War Office. Communication did, then, sometimes go wrong, but with results that, though spectacular, were not necessarily damaging.

The miners, Citrine thought as they sat down to the joint session that Monday night, looked hardset, their faces exhibiting no sign of compromise. Herbert Smith, who had been thought ready to persuade his men there was no alternative to pay negotiations, was 'as dour and dogged as ever'. Arthur Cook appealed to the General Council as if he was addressing a thousand men: 'Gentlemen, I know the sacrifice you have made. You do not want to bring the miners down. Gentlemen, don't do it.' It was left to Pugh, the chairman of the Council and the understated hero of the negotiations, to try to persuade them to see the TUC perspective. If the miners could not understand the case for negotiation, then, 'it is no use talking. We must go on with this struggle until the process of attrition has brought the whole trade union movement to its knees.' He repeated there was no possibility of negotiation with the government while the General Strike continued. The miners were 'in a fool's paradise' if they thought the subsidy would be restored. They must face their responsibilities.

The meeting broke up. The General Council reconvened to consider their position. Citrine, Bevin and Thomas believed a settlement must be negotiated while the unions' position was still strong. Citrine believed a 'dangerous split' was likely; but the others thought that an end to the strike would be less unpopular among the men than he feared. When the miners returned, they announced they would accept almost all of Samuel's memorandum. But they must exclude any scheme that did not rule out a reduction in wages. Pressed by the General Council, they still refused to put forward suggestions for a settlement themselves. They went back to their homes and hotels (where the chambermaids were in the pay of MI5 and the telephones and telegrams monitored by the Postmaster General) in dispirited mood.

ON THIS SEVENTH DAY of the strike, Labour politicians were still arguing with the BBC for the right to be heard. Reith had rebuffed deputations from the Parliamentary Labour Party, and letters from MPs. Again and again, he cited Churchill's opposition and the threat of takeover. Ramsay MacDonald, overshadowed by the dominance of both the TUC and the government, rang twice to urge Reith to allow him to put his point of view. Reith agreed to look at a draft broadcast, which MacDonald got to him by the early evening. Reith despatched it at once to J. C. C. Davidson, 'strongly recommending', he said in his diary, that MacDonald be allowed to broadcast. In the privacy of his diary, Reith railed against the bind he was in, without acknowledging that he had conspired with the government to achieve it.

I do not think that they treat me altogether fairly. They will not say we are to a certain extent controlled and they make me take the onus of turning people down. They are quite against MacDonald broadcasting, but I am certain it would have done no harm to the Government. Of course it puts me

in a very awkward and unfair position. I imagine it comes
chiefly from the PM's difficulties with the Winston lot.[17]

MacDonald was duly informed of the rejection, and wrote Reith an
angry letter, calling for an opportunity for the fair-minded and
reasonable public to hear Labour's point of view. Reith may have
been right that it would have done no damage to the government,
and to have heard an Opposition voice would certainly have done
something to restore the faith of millions of working-class people
who had lost confidence in the BBC's potential to be a national
institution and a reliable and trustworthy source of news. Reith's
ambitions for himself and for the BBC, which led him to play such
a dangerous game with the BBC's future, could hardly be disen-
twined. But at about this time he decided that his announcers were
sounding panicky, and to his other responsibilities – notably that of
driving eminent politicians to and from the BBC studios – he now
added that of reading most of the news bulletins.

The moment had come when the trade union movement as a
whole had to address the issue it had ducked for so long. If the
General Strike was not a revolutionary weapon, if it was not
intended to force the government to adopt a certain course of
action, to replace it as the highest authority in the land, but if,
as the TUC had always insisted, it was merely the heavy artillery
in the industrial battleground, then it had to be used like a conventional industrial weapon. Yet the proper course, negotiation,
appeared as out of reach as a capitulation by government. The
miners would not talk, the mine owners would not talk and the
government would not talk, at least not until the action was called
off. All this week of strike had achieved was to leave millions of
workers, whose regular wage left them with nothing to spare, a
week in arrears, and to threaten the security of their jobs and
pensions. If it continued, it risked not only bankruptcy – from
which in time the unions might recover – but a defeat of morale
that would destroy workers' faith in solidarity, collective bargaining
and the power of non-violent action.

But these were not arguments that could be aired in the midst of the strike. A decision that required persuasive explanation and the opportunity to debate had by its very nature to be imposed by ambush. The only choice open to the unions, having committed themselves to the strike in the first place, was to end it in a way that risked as much damage as would continuing it. They had come out in defence of the idea of solidarity. Their return to work could be seen only as its failure.

13

DAY 8, TUESDAY 11 MAY

May 11th Tuesday. School. By all appearances of today's papers the strike cannot last much longer. Everything is improving. There are many trains running – by slick volenteers – some of them university men in Oxford Bags etc. Walter Fourniss has joined up for the South Western Railway and I think that Vin & Don or Vin and Bruce, although only seventeen, are going to join up as special constables!! I wish we could do something to help. Did my music practice and homework, then took Spot for his night meander. Saw Newton and he came with me. Saw two others of the clique and Skinny came round and laughed at Nellie who was cutting the hedge. Quarrelled with A. over an equation.

Diary of Margaret Woods

THIS MORNING'S official bulletin from Eccleston Square was as upbeat as those of the previous seven days. Bulletin No. 16, handed out to the press as they arrived for their daily vigil, promised: 'A remarkable revelation of the cheerful determination of the rank and file to hold on for victory'. The intelligence summaries from which the bulletin was drawn spoke of the continuing 'great spirit' and 'wonderful enthusiasm'. Backing from non-strikers was reported to be growing rather than decreasing. In Dartford, 'the whole of the clubs in the area have placed their premises at our disposal free of charge'; in Worthing, where the support of the public was said to be 'above all praise', whist drives, dances, cricket matches and women's meetings were all reported. The bulletin was, however, a singular misrepresentation of the mood inside 32 Eccleston Square.

The longer the strike lasted, the better organized and more

confident the local strike committees became. At the start of the second week, many had at last negotiated all the obstacles and started to publish their own strike newssheets. A familiarity with the tactics of the police and the non-strikers was being established that strengthened the strike committees' ability to act. But at the same time, political resolve against the strike was strengthening, and its opponents too became more confident. Some union leaders feared the centre was about to lose control. Excusing the surrender afterwards, the General and Municipal Workers' Union's general secretary Charles Dukes pointed out: 'Every day that the strike proceeded the control and the authority of that dispute [were] passing out of the hands of responsible Executives in to the hands of men who had no authority, no control, and [were] wrecking the movement from one end to the other.' [1]

Nor was everything calm. The determination to break the strike on public transport led to varying degrees of violence wherever it was tried. Special constables were acquiring a rough reputation, and they were often accused of provoking or aggravating strikers and pickets. Brighton's[2] experience in the final days was typical of several towns and cities where, sometimes provoked by right-wing local newspapers, local authorities had decided to get public transport going again. In Brighton, a determined chief constable who had recently arrived in the town with a dubious record acquired quelling a riot at his previous posting in Luton, had decided to recruit mounted specials. A trio of local cavalry officers, two retired and one on leave from India, each raised an assorted troop of men from the farms and villages of the surrounding area, who were sworn in and issued with two batons, one short and one long, 'for use in charges'. They called themselves the Black and Tans after the regiment notorious for its brutal treatment of the Irish.

On this, the second Tuesday of the strike, they finally got their chance to perform. Early on, they paraded 'in blue uniforms, peaked caps and [with] stout ash sticks'. By mid-morning it was clear the plan was to get the trams running. A crowd of up to four thousand gathered, ignoring both the transport manager's appeal to leave and his warning that the police were at hand. The Chief Constable duly arrived by car and blew his whistle; the mounted police galloped round the corner and began forcing the crowd back. Among the crowd were women with children coming home from school for lunch. Bricks and bottles were thrown, the police charged. 'The crowd scattered like rabbits for shelter', an elderly man was knocked down, and another fell down a flight of stairs in his desperation to escape. Another man on his way with his wife to collect their child was stopped by a mounted special, who struck him with a shillelagh. 'They came through as if they were mad,' an eyewitness recalled, 'one special on horseback jumped over the wall into the recreation park where women & children were for safety ... & frightened the little children to death.' Local newspapers reported seventeen arrests and two serious injuries. A special lost an eye. Although the use of specials on horseback appears to have been unusual, similar scenes were reported from other towns and cities.

In London, the General Council were still reluctant to abandon the miners and endure again the accusations of betrayal and treachery. Not only was the news from the provinces reassuringly – perhaps alarmingly – confident, but there was no guarantee that eight days of strike would yet produce anything that could be hailed as any kind of victory. There was no clarity about the status of Samuel's memorandum, and Samuel himself could give no undertaking about the government's acceptance of his proposals. On the contrary, it had always been understood that he had no standing at all in Downing Street. All the General Council had for reassurance were the rumours, chance encounters and informal conversations through intermediaries that encouraged them to believe that Baldwin, at least, was anxious to settle. Hamilton Fyfe had a story about a nameless figure meeting an anonymous Downing Street secretary to establish for how long the government might be prepared to renew a subsidy. But the TUC had little confidence in assurances from the political wing of the Labour movement, whose leaders had condemned the principle of the strike. And there were as many rumours that Baldwin wanted to settle as there were saying that he could not settle without losing key members of his government. Among the rumours swirling like old newssheets around the Westminster gutters was the suggestion that the form of words agreed by Baldwin and the TUC before the strike began and subsequently repudiated by the full Cabinet had provoked threats of resignation from Churchill, Chamberlain and Birkenhead, together with as many as four other senior Tory figures.

The previous night's fleeting hope that the miners would accept the General Council's ruling had ebbed away. Whatever had been agreed at the outset of the strike, none of the union leaders present believed that the miners would accept that the General Council had the authority to impose terms on them. Previous experience had shown that the miners held tenaciously to any weapon they could find, and were inured by unemployment, past strikes and poverty wages to the hunger and hardship of a long dispute. They would not give their union colleagues cover for a retreat now. But if the TUC kept the strike on, it risked a slow crumbling, an undermining of their leadership and of the principles of trade unionism. The benefit would be felt only by the employers, who could exploit a weakened union movement, drive pay down further and fill jobs from the ranks of the non-unionized. Thomas, who throughout the strike had led the faction pushing for a settlement, reported that he had already got wind of difficulties in taking back strikers. 'Jimmy is wearing down,'[3] Citrine wrote in his diary, 'and today there was none of that customary forceful driving manner.' Towards the end of the morning, Thomas went back to Wimborne House and met again with the coal owners, represented by Lord Wimborne, and Lord Reading. Wimborne had already been discussing with the TUC's legal counsel details of what the coal owners were prepared to undertake. Curiously, at no point was lifting the miners' lockout raised in the discussions.

Lord Reading, according to Sitwell, had just learnt the startling news that the trade union leaders were to be arrested the following day. This was a development that had been rumoured all weekend: it had appeared that morning as a demand in one of the *Daily Mail*'s

more peremptory leaders, which was now being rushed out as a
leaflet. It was an acknowledged *Mail* tactic to get wind of, or be
briefed about, a forthcoming government announcement and then
to demand that it happened. Reading was a big beast on the
Conservative political scene, close to the Prime Minister and to
other senior Tories, and therefore well placed to have heard that
such a plan was afoot; moreover, the hardliners may have been
seeking an alternative to the restraint on trade union funds that had
been denied them. Yet although a case for the possibility of the
government considering the arrest of union leaders can be made
out, a stronger case against lies in the recent abandonment of
provocative legislation, as well as in influential reports from Conservative MPs who had been in their constituencies at the weekend
and found good humour and peaceableness. However much
Churchill, who had originally argued for arrests – even the King
had thought it a sound idea – may have wanted to carry the
proposal through, he had seen the danger inherent in his plan to
restrain trade union funds and it seems improbable that he would
have launched another even more aggressive action.

For whatever reason, Reading was determined to persuade
Thomas to set the case for a settlement before the TUC, and to
undertake to get the strike called off by the following morning. He
did not tell Thomas why it was so urgent; Thomas, who daily
feared arrest, may have guessed or imagined such a thing. If he did,
and if he had passed on his fear to the TUC, they would probably
have discounted it, well used as they were to Thomas's flights of
nervous fancy. Nor could a decision to settle be carried only by
him. However, others, including Bevin and the TUC chairman
Pugh, thought the end had to come, sooner rather than later. 'I
don't think it is right to go on asking the men to make sacrifices,'
Bevin said, 'if we can get justice in any other way.'

If the strike ended without significant gains, however, the union
movement might be even more damaged. The sense of betrayal
would end any prospect of useful trade union cooperation for a
generation. It risked, too, making industry the recruiting ground for

extremists; Communist literature was already sniffing betrayal and pointing to the failings of the national union leadership. After the strike, it would return to promote the case for shop stewards' committees and local trades councils, all the potentially subversive activities that weakened the centre and were so feared by the trade unions' leaders.

The negotiating committee now went back to Samuel to try to find a way of making his memorandum more acceptable to the miners by refining and expanding the details of wage negotiations, ensuring the lowest-paid would not suffer, re-establishing the principle of a national minimum and simplifying the Byzantine structure of district-level pay awards. They worked in a commit-ment that the industry would not recruit those who had only recently reached eighteen if unemployed miners were available, and specified that assistance would be given to miners who needed to move to find work. New housing would be built, or existing homes improved. Once again the miners were asked to reconsider.

WHILE ECCLESTON SQUARE wrestled with its options, in the High Court Mr Justice Astbury was delivering another damaging blow to the trade unions. Havelock Wilson, the general secretary of the National Sailors' and Firemen's Union, who had voted against the strike at the executives' conference on the eve of the dispute, sought an injunction to prevent some of his members being called out. It was against his union's rules to strike without a ballot, and there had been no ballot before the General Strike was called. The absence of democratic legitimacy for the action had been the cause of much comment among the right-wing press; now their criticisms were upheld. The judge, sitting in the Chancery Division of the High Court, granted the injunction, and also declared that the General Strike – on which he was not required to pronounce – was itself illegal. Sir John Astbury was a former Liberal MP, who on his retirement in 1929 would receive the unusual honour for a High Court judge of being made a privy councillor. The unions had been alarmed by Sir John Simon's declaration the previous week but,

eminent lawyer though he was, Simon had been speaking as a
Member of Parliament and a politician. Astbury, on the other hand,
had all the authority of the High Court behind him; furthermore,
to be a member of the High Court bench was assumed to elevate
the holder above considerations of politics and partiality. If Astbury
believed the strike was illegal, then trade unions whose funds were
already draining out in strike pay were now vulnerable to litigation
by employers for breach of contract and, potentially, by their own
members for breach of union rules.

The former Labour Attorney General Sir Henry Slesser this
time immediately questioned Astbury's ruling. He challenged
Astbury's view that a general strike was not an 'industrial dispute'
and therefore did not fall within the Trade Disputes Act of 1906
which gave trade unions immunity from damages. Astbury had
asserted that there could be no industrial dispute between the TUC
and the government. Slesser argued that superior authorities had
held that sympathy strikes were legal, and that an industrial dispute
could exist beyond the immediate employer–employee relationship.
But Slesser's case was drowned out by other developments. The
Conservative press, and even Liberal newspapers like the *Manchester
Guardian*, supported Astbury. Not until the following year, and
then only in an American academic publication, did a detailed
and authoritative refutation appear.

Astbury's ruling gave new life to the argument about the
purposes of the strike. In Manchester, as in many other cities,
the tramways were owned by the city, and their purpose was to
provide a service to the public. On Tuesday, the city's tramways
committee issued an appeal to the drivers, asking them to return to
work the following day. If the strike was not constitutional, in the
sense of seeking to coerce the government into changing its policy,
why were the tramway drivers striking? They had no dispute with
their employers. It could only be because it would cause maximum
inconvenience to the public. That was why they and other transport
workers were 'front line troops'. But, if the TUC's instructions to
its members were illegal, the *Manchester Guardian* commented the

following day, the drivers were under no legal or moral obligation to obey them. 'It is a perverted and almost incomprehensible sense of loyalty which now keeps them from work.' Finally, the ruling offered the government a way of threatening legislation to clarify the status of the strike, without needing to specify what that legislation would entail.

Without having received any specific explanation, many Londoners thought there was now a relaxing of tension, a sense of a corner turned. Settlement was in the air. Sir John Simon, although not recanting his opinion that the strike was illegal, presented to the Commons a reworked version of the Archbishop's appeal as a route to reopening negotiations. If there was still no real 'drift back to work', there was anecdotal evidence of small groups of workers returning. Maynard Keynes and Leonard Woolf were trying to get a strike edition of their weekly newspaper the *Nation* on to the streets. But Woolf had written an article arguing that the strike was not illegal, and the printers – 'a little clutch of the Government throttle', Virginia assumed – were refusing to print it. Later, however, another printer told her that all his men had come back to work and, as he needed something he could give them to do, he would be happy to take on the job. *The Times* declared that morning that 'no one suggests for a moment that any considerable number of men on strike are animated by revolutionary motives'. The *Brixton Free Press* thought that 'Every day, in every way, things are getting better and better.' It praised the government's handling of the situation and the patriotism of the citizenry, to which it attributed the turnaround. 'So splendidly have patriotic citizens come to the assistance of their country in the hour of peril within its own borders, so general has been the resentment against the attempt to paralyse the nation and to flout constitutional government, that the position of affairs is improving not only daily but hourly.' Fyfe noticed the *Gazette* had abandoned its revolutionary rhetoric about revolution in favour of inflated claims about the numbers going back to work.

And the position of the BBC was finally resolved. The Cabinet decided that it need not, after all, be commandeered. But the decision did not disperse the lingering shadow of censorship, as it had first seemed it might. Indeed, Reith had come to realize that it might have been better to be commandeered – to be, like the *Gazette*, an overt mouthpiece for propaganda, rather than living in the illusory half-light of an independence curtailed by the real or imagined threat of censorship. He wrote in his diary:

> The Cabinet decision is really a negative one. They want to be able to say that they did not commandeer us, but they know that they can trust us not to be really impartial ... I wanted the inconsistencies in our acts so far to be squared up, setting us right with the other side. Davidson, however, thought the Cabinet would only agree to a statement that we could do nothing to help the strike since it had been declared illegal. This does not seem to me straight.[4]

This was a new version of Reith's original position, and the position he argued to the Labour delegations who had pressed him for space on the airwaves. To them he had said that, with the strike *sub judice*, his hands were tied. Nor did it tally with the argument he put forward when he wrote an explanatory letter to his heads of department after the strike was over.

> There could be no question about our supporting the Government in general, particularly since the General Strike had been declared illegal in the High Court [which happened only on the penultimate day of the strike]. This being so, we were unable to permit anything which was contrary to the spirit of that judgement, and which might have prolonged or sought to justify the Strike ... But as it was we were able to give listeners authentic, impartial news of the situation to the best of our ability.[5]

But he admitted that the lack of clarity about the BBC's position had been 'embarrassing'. It had, however, been a justifiable sacrifice in the cause of promoting peace and harmony. Had the Company been commandeered, his confidential letter continued, they could not have 'initiated or emphasized statements likely to counteract a spirit of violence and hostility. We felt we might contribute, perhaps decisively, to the attitude of understanding without which goodwill could not be restored.' Reith put as fine a gloss on his actions as he could. He had established the idea of the BBC as a 'national institution, a national asset'. But in so doing he had accepted that it would always in the end owe allegiance to the government, and to the government's exclusive interpretation of what was right in the interests of the country. Before 1926 was out, he was fighting for the principle of controversiality in broadcasting, yet he restricted the BBC to a relationship with government – subsequently reinforced by its system of public funding – that was too intimate to allow it to be regarded as genuinely independent, one that neither individuals nor programmes could ever quite escape.

'From the above,' he concluded, 'you will realize that the position was one of extreme delicacy and embarrassment throughout. It was impossible to give the lead which we should have liked, but it is a satisfaction to find an almost universal appreciation and recognition of the services rendered, and it may be only ourselves who feel that we might have done more with a freer hand.'

At Eccleston Square that afternoon, Bevin's Strike Organization Committee had bowed to pressure and allowed local areas to call out the 'second row'. The engineering and shipbuilding unions were to stop work the following morning. No public announcement was made; newspapers called it a 'secret' move. The Plebs League, which thought it would have been much more effective to call out sanitary workers in the West End, suggested previous orders and counter-orders had left such confusion that it was the only way out. Kinder interpretations attributed the move to a wish – when the time came – to be seen to retreat from a position of strength. But in order to forestall argument about treason, no men in government or naval dockyards were to come out.

Although the Engineering Union had been severely affected by the collapse in exports – it had lost a hundred thousand members in only two years – it was still the largest single union in industries employing nearly half a million men. While the engineers and shipbuilders were still working, in some areas such as the Clyde the strike had barely made an impact. Together with the upbeat tone of the *British Worker*, and the BBC's announcement (even if it had earlier detected a tendency to drift back to work) that the strike was still solid, calling out the 'second row' boosted morale. But it also excited speculation about a fight to the finish that was soon to be disappointed. From contemporary accounts, it seems at least possible that there was a breakdown in communications inside Eccleston Square that matched the confusion outside it, and that the committee organizing the strike had failed to communicate with the committee negotiating a settlement.

In the early evening of Tuesday, the negotiating committee reported back to the General Council with the revised Samuel proposals. Samuel was to embody them in a letter to the TUC; the TUC would then formally 'withdraw' the General Strike and the government 'would arrange for a withdrawal of the lock-out notices' (it was not specified by what means). To Citrine, Samuel appeared to be reassuringly familiar with what was going on in Downing Street. He even confirmed reports of Baldwin's difficulties with his Cabinet. Thomas, perhaps influenced by his earlier encounter with Reading and Wimborne, was determined that Samuel's plan should be accepted. Bevin, who had not been at the earlier meeting of the General Council, bumped into George Hicks, another member of the negotiating committee, as he arrived at Eccleston Square. In the account Bevin later gave to his union, this was when he first learnt that the Samuel proposals had been accepted by the negotiating committee, and that this meant that the strike would end. Bevin urged hesitation. He was anxious about the 'demobilisation of our forces', and wanted to hear the miners' reaction.

At half past seven, the miners were invited in. Pugh, the chairman, 'tired, worn and a little bit sick of things', according to Bevin, 'did tell the miners they had to take it or leave it'. Ramsay

MacDonald, who sat as a silent observer through these long days of meetings, thought he was tactless, especially in dealing with Herbert Smith's accusation that they, the miners, had had the memorandum imposed upon them (a veiled reference to Thomas's role). 'Had I not known what had happened,' MacDonald admitted in his diary, 'it would have increased my suspicions. The scene was tense & sometimes the silent instants in the speeches were painful.'[6] Pugh's offhand manner was to become a major source of contention in the prolonged post-mortem that followed. Smith demanded to know why he had not been involved in the negotiations. Bevin urged them to take the document on its merits and see if it offered a solution. It took 'a good deal of persuasion' to get the miners even to go away and look at it. Subsequently, Smith insisted that he had offered to negotiate then and there on the document. 'I appealed to them,' he would say later, 'as I never appealed to anybody in my life to consider it. I was told that each union could manage its own business if the miners would accept the Samuel memorandum.'[7] In Citrine's account of the evening, Pugh went over the negotiations 'carefully and patiently', but Smith 'rose at once with a glint in his eye', condemned their efforts and demanded to know why a decision had to be taken in such a rush. 'Have you committed us to anything?' he demanded in a phrase laden with the aggressive suspicion that had swirled around all their encounters for the past week.

The miners retired next door to the boardroom of the Labour Party. The General Council was left behind; they knew they would not win the miners over. Bevin pushed for more details: was the document to be published? would the government accept it? would the lockout notices be withdrawn simultaneously with the return to work? He feared that, having fallen out with the miners, the TUC would then fail to win acceptance for the deal from the government. Since the government would not negotiate while the strike was on, it was quite impossible to be certain of its attitude. The permanent secretary at the Ministry of Labour, as well as Jones (through his political contacts) and other officials all maintained unofficial links with the TUC. None was authorized to do more than act as a sounding board. Nor did Citrine want to 'hand ourselves over, body and soul, to Baldwin'. Yet Bevin and the others, weary and unable to see an alternative, were persuaded that the answer to all his questions was yes. And Bevin found reassurance when, very late that night, Downing Street telephoned to know whether the TUC was to come to see the Prime Minister soon. 'I concluded that what we had been told of the Prime Minister being in possession of the information [i.e. Samuel's proposals] was correct.'

But Bevin counselled against seeing Baldwin that night. They were too tired – some of them had been drinking, Sidney Webb reported, and 'singing and telling stories' – and no plans had yet been made for getting the men back to work. Only later did Bevin discover a rather different scenario: that there had been no anxious Prime Minister waiting for confirmation of a plan of which he had been fully informed – rather, the phone call had been prompted by the TUC side after someone from the negotiating team (probably Thomas) had asked if they could see the PM. All Downing Street was anticipating, all Baldwin would accept, was unconditional surrender.

At around midnight, the miners returned from the deliberations. They rejected the proposals. If the TUC accepted them, it would be on their own authority. The miners' decision had been formally typed out (one of the few typed records of the whole week of negotiations). They handed it over and left. The remainder of the General Council relapsed into a bitter, perhaps guilty, character assassination. The miners were 'not big enough', not real trade unionists, 'they lived in villages and they thought in the mass', they had no understanding of the problems and responsibilities of running more general unions. 'They would never understand that all there would be left to sacrifice in a few days would be the broken-hearted best of our members.' Thomas spoke with emotion: tomorrow he would be 'going back to his own people'. Another member rose and paid inarticulate tribute to Thomas's fine work. 'Nobody has been more maligned than him and nobody has done more for the miners.'[8]

14

DAY 9, WEDNESDAY 12 MAY

May 12th. Wednesday. The strike has ended! Mother saw the sweep and he told her that news had come through by wireless. Mother said she could go into the High Road and sing God Save the King, three cheers for Mr Baldwin and the Government. I expect Dad and Mr Fourniss will be *so* peeved not to have been able to use their new batons but I expect they will be reserved for future household use!! I had better start being angelic henceforth. Took Gwen home on my saddle like I did yesterday. No accidents occurred today however, and we went along in fine style. Newton's scout evening. Took Spot out all the afternoon practically. Saw quite a lot of 49 'buses for the first time.

Diary of Margaret Woods

THE HEADLINE IN Beaverbrook's relentlessly hostile *Daily Express* on Wednesday morning was unusually acute. 'The Strike with a Broken Back,' it announced. Beneath the headline was a report that in the lobbies of the House of Commons the previous night, trade unionists had admitted that 'the organisation against it grows day by day'. The strike would end, several had predicted, this week.

As the government had gained confidence, the tone of its supporters in the press had mellowed. The *Daily Mirror*, which had now resumed printing as a broadsheet, showed Lady Mountbatten in high heels and furs 'lending a hand' in Hyde Park, and ran an editorial that explained to its readers, perhaps bewildered by the change in the paper's policy, that the strikers were not after all revolutionaries but men and women anxious to avoid trouble and get back to work. 'Workers have been led to take part in this attempt to stab the nation in the back by a subtle appeal to the motives of idealism in them.' Even the *Gazette* had calmed down. 'Order and Quiet throughout the Land,' it reported. 'The restraining influence of responsible Trade Union leaders [has] effectively suppressed tendencies to rowdyism,' another paper admitted. Confrontational aspects of the strike retreated in significance. An eighty-four-year old earl had signed up as a volunteer, but this merited only a tiny paragraph in the *Express*. The calling-out of the 'second row' of engineers and shipbuilders made little impact anywhere, and in some places appeared never to have happened. The headline 'Men Enthusiastically Obey Call' in the *British Worker* was contradicted by reports in the *Manchester Guardian* suggesting that only a fifth of them had come out; in some areas they had not even been called out.

In many cities, notably in the capital, there was extravagant military activity. In Brixton, the first contingent of 'tin hats' marched down the high street. 'All the men, of excellent physique, wore plain clothes but had armlets, steel helmets and truncheons. They marched in columns of four with correct military bearing and their progress was witnessed by large numbers of people.'[1] In central London, Virginia Woolf saw '5 or 6 armoured cars slowly going along Oxford Street; on each two soldiers sat in tin helmets, & one stood with his hand at the gun which was pointed straight ahead ready to fire'.[2]

At Eccleston Square, Samuel's final memorandum had been received, incorporating the last details of wage negotiation that had been inserted as an inducement to the miners. Samuel sent a covering letter to Pugh. It contained the ominously definitive passage: 'I have made it clear to your Committee from the outset that I have been acting entirely on my own initiative, have received no authority from the Government, and can give no assurances on their part.' Trying to create an undertaking where none existed, Pugh and Citrine replied: '[The committee] assume that during the resumed negotiations, the subsidy will be renewed and that the lock-out notices to the Miners will be immediately withdrawn.'

Only the coal owners and the government could enforce these conditions, and neither had taken part in the negotiations.

The miners refused to see Thomas again. Instead it was Bevin and other members of his Strike Organization Committee that took a taxi off to their headquarters in Russell Square for a final attempt to persuade them to negotiate. It was less a discussion than an appeal. The General Council had already decided to call off the strike, Bevin told them, and would see the Prime Minister at midday to tell him so. If the miners would not come in with them, not only were they unlikely ever to secure better terms, but it would make a future general strike impossible and split the industrial and political wings of the movement. He called for the miners, instead of demanding solidarity, to demonstrate that they too could make sacrifices in support of trade unions as a whole. The strike had cost Bevin's transport workers' union £360,000 in its first week. The men were worried about loss of pension rights and superannuation. He did not say it, but by implication there was no guarantee that, whatever the General Council wanted, the strike would last much longer.

The miners retired to consider. Bevin, and his committee chairman Purcell, told the General Council they would wait until 11.45, fifteen minutes before their meeting with Baldwin. If there was still no response, they would go to Downing Street anyway. When the miners' executive reappeared, it was to confirm what they had already guessed. Smith, a man of few words but capable of the occasional well turned phrase, dismissed Bevin and the whole of the TUC. They had 'been continually on the doormat of the Prime Minister' since the strike began; politicians had no part in an industrial war. 'There was more enthusiasm for the general strike amongst the rank and file than there was among the General Council.'

Back at Eccleston Square, the General Council waited with little hope for their ambassadors to return. Citrine rang Downing Street and asked for a room to be set aside where the Council could meet before seeing the Prime Minister. In the car on the way to No. 10, he and Thomas talked gloomily of the avalanche of recrimination that awaited them. As they passed Wellington Barracks they saw more exhibitions of military preparedness. Troops were practising with machine-guns. Others wore gas masks. Tanks were being overhauled. At Downing Street they met up with the TUC chairman Arthur Pugh, who asked bitterly, 'I wonder how long we are going to grovel on our hands and knees to the miners.' Bevin arrived from Russell Square. The miners would not go back to work, he confirmed; in fact, they would take no decision at all until they had had a delegates' conference the following Friday.

The Prime Minister had been expecting to hear from the unions since the previous evening. The Cabinet had not broken up until Citrine had told Downing Street, after midnight, that there would be no decision before the next day. Shortly before he met the miners, a note arrived for Baldwin from the Home Office, written by Joynson-Hicks and three other cabinet colleagues: 'I am writing ... to say that we are very nervous as to the risk of even appearing to enter into any negotiations with the TUC until there has been an unconditional withdrawal of the General Strike.'[3] The diehards were determined there was to be no backsliding by their peace-loving Prime Minister. In an extraordinary charade, before Baldwin would meet the General Council, the TUC delegation had to confirm to an official that they had come only to announce surrender. Bevin, seething with the offensive indignity of the encounter, recounted the scene to his own Council:

> When we went in, Sir Horace Wilson [permanent secretary at the Ministry of Labour] came to the door of the Cabinet room ... He said, 'Well then, Mr Pugh and Mr Thomas, what do you want to see the Prime Minister for?' They replied, 'We want to see him on the position.' The reply to this was, 'You know the Prime Minister will not see you before the strike is called off.' ... Thomas then said 'We have come to call the strike off.'[4]

The trade unionists had planned to announce formally that the strike was to be called off, to discuss briefly the likely problems of

the return to work and finally to agree arrangements for negotiations on the basis of the Samuel memorandum. At this point,
however, the miners, off stage, dealt the final blow to any semblance
of unity. By the time the TUC were ready to meet Baldwin, they
had announced to the press that they had rejected the Samuel
memorandum; even before the last chance to extract any concession
from the government could be grasped, the split in the movement
was being openly reported on the wires.

At No. 10, Baldwin invited Pugh to make the statement. The
Prime Minister looked 'haggard and drawn', Citrine thought. He
was escorted by a guard of cabinet colleagues which, although
without Churchill and Birkenhead who were attending the daily
Supply and Transport Committee meeting, included another tor-
mentor, Austen Chamberlain's half-brother Neville. Pugh, anxious,
rambled around the terrain of recent events, laying particular
emphasis on the encouragement Baldwin's broadcast had given
them to believe that negotiations could be reopened. Finally he
admitted: 'this General Strike is to be terminated forthwith'.
Baldwin repeated his words back to him. 'Immediately,' Pugh confirmed, adding somewhat incoherently the second part of the TUC's
agenda: 'It is merely a matter of the best way to get it done with
the least confusion.'

Baldwin promised to do all he could to get negotiations
restarted. Thomas appealed to him to promote a spirit of reconcili-
ation: 'The one thing we must not have is guerrilla warfare.' In
what Citrine called 'confident, almost aggressive, tones', Bevin
added: 'We have taken a great risk in calling the strike off. I want
to urge [that] it must not be regarded as an act of weakness but
rather one of strength.' Then, almost as an afterthought, he raised
the Samuel memorandum. 'I do not know whether I am overstep-
ping the bounds, but I would like you to give me an idea of
whether that means there is to be a resumption of the mining
negotiations with us, or whether all the negotiations have to be
carried on while the miners still remain out?'

This was the last gasp. If the strike had achieved its objective, the question would not have needed to be asked. The lockout would have been lifted, a guarantee of renewed subsidy granted. In the many hours spent on the expensively upholstered sofas at Bryanston Square, under the gaze of the Reynoldses and Gainsboroughs, the TUC had achieved nothing beyond an embroidered fig-leaf and a carefully formulated wish list. The nine days of solidarity and sacrifice by three million men and women would leave them not with the satisfaction of victory, nor even of a noble defeat, but only that most uncomfortable of results – a timid surrender.

It would have been small comfort that the exchanges revealed the degree of constraint under which Baldwin had been placed by his hawkish Cabinet. 'Well Mr Bevin, I cannot say more here at this meeting now. I did not know what points you were going to raise, or that anything would be said beyond the statement of Mr Pugh.' These were words for the record, the wherewithal to convey to his colleagues and to the wider world that there had been no negotiations to end the strike, that Baldwin's will to resist the pressure of an attack on the constitution had not for one moment faltered. The whole exchange was published later that day and appeared in the following day's newspapers; although without Baldwin's final comment – that they must cooperate to 'make this country a little better and a happier place than it has been in recent years'.

Outside No. 10, a crowd of press and interested spectators had gathered. First Jimmy Thomas came out, 'with the look of a man both bewildered and depressed. He walked in complete silence through the journalists and departed, no one venturing to ask him a question.' Then came other TUC leaders. 'They too all seemed very depressed,' newspaper reports later conceded. Finally a government official came out with Citrine and read the words: 'The General Strike is being terminated today.'

Citrine claimed later, struggling to explain how they had come to capitulate, that they were 'puzzled' by the government's attitude. They 'recognized that the position had been complicated by the miners' ... refusal to return to work', and that there was no mention of the lockout being withdrawn, but he felt as he and Tom Jones drafted the press statement that the government was trying 'to snatch the appearance of victory'. It was not just an appearance of victory: the government had won, and everyone knew it. Citrine did his best: he ensured that the BBC announcement would include the message that strikers should await the instructions of their unions before returning to work.

Pugh tried again to talk to Baldwin, pressing him to ensure the withdrawal of the lockout notices. Churchill, magnanimous in victory according to his credo, said: 'Thank God it is over, Mr Pugh.'

The TUC did their best with their failure. 'The Movement came out in order to ensure a fair deal for the miners. The G[eneral]. C[ouncil]. is satisfied that this can now be achieved.' But in the days that followed, they came to feel – or claimed to feel – that they had been tricked. They had understood, encouraged almost certainly by Thomas, that beneath the official denials of any authority, Samuel had been negotiating in the knowledge that nothing would be put on the table that was unacceptable to the government. In fact, because the miners refused to accept the memorandum, Baldwin was never tested. In the atmosphere created by the Archbishop's appeal, Samuel's moderate proposals, supported by an agreement to end not just the General Strike but the miners' strike too, could well have amounted to irresistible pressure on the government. However, a politician so instinctively reluctant to intervene in industry, and so constrained by his Cabinet from any appearance of weakness, could not have imposed an end to the lockout, and could only have reintroduced the subsidy on the guarantee of radical action to prevent it ever being needed again.

On other aspects, Baldwin was ready to act. Before the day was out, he met Lord Reading and invited him to chair the national wages board envisaged by Samuel as part of the settlement, lending support to the idea that he had both known of and supported the proposals, and had given thought to how they would be carried out. (The following day, though, Reading expressly denied that his appointment arose from the Samuel recommendations; indeed, he not only insisted it had been his own idea, but said he so disliked having to be bound by Samuel that he wanted to refuse the invitation.) However, as Reith had found, Baldwin was often content to allow people to believe he supported their argument without quite committing himself. His reluctance to pick a fight, his tendency to try to balance opposing forces, largely contributed to his reputation for weakness.

At the BBC Reith had been poised for a day and a night for this denouement. In his account of the fledgling newsroom's first breaking-news story, he was on air delivering the lunchtime bulletin. 'I had just begun to read the news, when I was told I was wanted urgently on the phone from Downing Street. So I broke off and said I would stop for the moment as it might be more important news was coming. Waterhouse [Baldwin's secretary] gave me a message which I went back to the microphone and read … It was rather wonderful to have been the first to give the news.' Reith had loved the challenge and the drama of the strike. 'It is great fun running a crisis.'[5] (Asa Briggs's account in his exhaustive *History of Broadcasting in the United Kingdom* is a little less dramatic. Intermediaries were involved; but intermediaries rarely featured in Reith's diaries.)

The news had been anticipated everywhere. Radio shops, around whose doors for the past nine days small knots of people had gathered to hear the latest, had their radio sets wired up for the benefit of the crowds in the street. Virginia Woolf, resolutely unimpressed by the BBC's efforts, wrote one last critical observation. In Tottenham Court Road she had heard on a furniture shop's wireless that the trade union leaders were in Downing Street. When she reached home, the announcer instructed listeners to stand by for important news. A little piano music was played. 'Then the solemn broadcaster assuming incredible pomp & gloom & speaking one word to the minute read out: Message from Downing Street. The TUC leaders have agreed that the Strike shall be withdrawn.'[6]

Soon afterwards *The Times*, in a rare afternoon edition, was on the streets. Samuel heard the news vendors' shouts as he walked away from Bryanston Square for the last time. A little later, Baldwin left Downing Street to make a statement in the Commons. A crowd had gathered outside, and when he emerged on the steps of No. 10 he was mobbed by about a hundred cameramen. The *Manchester Guardian* carried an eyewitness account. '"I say!" [Baldwin] exclaimed, and hesitated in surprise. He was about to get into his car when Mrs Winston Churchill came running out of No. 11, waving her hand and shouting "Hooray!". Mr Baldwin shook hands with her, and the people in the street raised a very hearty cheer for him, and there were shouts of "Good old Baldwin" ... people ran after the car shouting and waving all the way down to the House.'

Baldwin's reception in the Commons was a little rougher. 'We should resume our work in the spirit of co-operation, putting behind us all malice and all vindictiveness,' he appealed. But Tory backbenchers were reluctant to believe that the revolutionaries by whom they had been so genuinely frightened, had packed up and gone home without securing any commitment greater than this appeal for cooperation from a prime minister they considered so malleable. In his nightly report to the King, Baldwin explained the 'tremendous importance' Conservative MPs attached to appearing implacable in the face of an attack on the constitution. 'They found it difficult to believe the surrender was unconditional.'

What is the value of the Samuel document? wondered Mac-Donald. So did many others. Bevin, according to his biographer, was enraged by Baldwin's attitude and by a sense that he had been party to a catastrophic misunderstanding. It would be seen as suicide, he said. 'Thousands of men will be victimised as the result of this day's work.'[7] All afternoon and evening, the Eccleston Square phone lines were jammed by people experienced in industrial negotiation trying to fathom what had been the actual terms for ending the strike. The *British Worker* could add nothing: 'Strike Terminated Today,' said the headline in its first edition, and beneath it, 'Trade Union Congress General Council satisfied that

Miners will now get a fair deal'. But why? How? Inside, it published in full the Samuel memorandum; it asserted that 'the proposals, if approached and operated in a spirit of whole-hearted cooperation between all parties concerned should result in a more equitable and durable relationship than has hitherto existed in the mining industry'. *Should* result? There were no guarantees. Hamilton Fyfe saw a placard in a shop window, 'Peace with Honour'. But he was not convinced.

The strike was over. But neither government nor TUC believed that the *status quo ante* could be restored overnight. Both sides were aware that for the extremists, an unprecedented opportunity had arisen. Millions of men idle, many of them bewildered and angry that the strike had ended in defeat when they had been ready to continue the fight, were a recruiting ground for Communism that Lenin himself might have dreamed of creating. The government, always aware of what King Street aspired to and never quite confident that it lacked the resources to do it, prepared for serious unrest. Rather than start to demobilize the crisis centre in the Admiralty from which emergency operations had been run, they strengthened it.

'This morning they selected 50 toughs from the college,' wrote a Greenwich naval cadet, '& they sent 20 cars down from Scotland Yard for us before lunch, just before the strike ended. We were dressed in old clothes, white sweaters, uniform caps without badge & burberries & a prettier crowd you couldn't wish for. I took the precaution of laying a strong flat sponge inside my cap to protect the head.' Then the order was countermanded.

The news that the strike was off came as a thunderbolt to almost every strike committee and trades council in the country. In many places, planned activities continued: a huge march in Manchester began with the tramway men who had been instructed by the employers to return to work that morning. Several thousand more, marching four abreast, joined as they neared the city. Wearing war medals and carrying banners supporting the miners, they stretched back for half a mile towards the suburb of Hyde.

None had any idea of what the settlement comprised. The absence of normal newspapers had left a news blackout which, although not impenetrable, had been disorientingly effective. The strikers had listened to the BBC but discounted much of what was said. They knew from first-hand experience that it had been overrating and sometimes misrepresenting the extent of the drift back to work in town after town, and despite corrections telegrammed in, it never transmitted them. Even if it had reported the rumours that the national newspapers carried, they would have been dismissed as propaganda.

The local papers, as noted earlier, were extravagantly pro-government. The strikers' only trustworthy source of news beyond their own first-hand knowledge came from their local, very parochial, strike bulletins and from the *British Worker*, which had just started printing regional editions. But the *Worker*, mouthpiece for the TUC, had allowed whispers of negotiation or settlement into its columns only in order to deny them. The previous evening's edition, which would have reached the provinces the morning the strike ended, had declared, 'No Slacking', then asserted confidently: 'The number of strikers has not diminished: it is increasing. There are more workers out to-day than at any moment since the strike began.' On the same page came the announcement that the engineers were to join the strike.

Paralysed by the fear of a charge of betrayal, neither the TUC nor the political leadership had made any attempt to set out realistic aims for the strike, beyond the single vague objective of 'a fair deal for the miners'. Keeping the negotiations secret left no chance of preparing the strikers for the possibility of compromise in an atmosphere of relative calm. When the instructions to return to work reached them from the union head offices, at first it was assumed a great victory had been won. As the details emerged, the sense of shock and betrayal drove out any anxiety they may have been feeling about how to survive a long strike. And it was the emotions of the activists that were recorded, drowning out for ever the voices of ordinary men and women who, as the strike entered its second week with no prospect of movement on either side, must have been beginning to worry about pay and pensions and feeding the children.

Among the non-strikers, it was as if a shadow had been lifted. There was 'simple and uncalculating relief'; strangers stopped people in the street and banged on car windows to ask if they had heard the news. Hundreds of undergraduates who had come to London to protect life and property from the revolutionaries celebrated the strike's end by destroying some of that very property in drunken sprees. The West End was reminiscent of the night after the Oxford and Cambridge boat race.

Citrine, in the immediate aftermath of the day's events, defended the General Council's decision. 'We felt we could not continue longer with the certainty of our members remaining loyal.' Because the miners had rejected Samuel, it was impossible to test whether the lockout was to be lifted, and the appearance of defeat was unavoidable. He and Bevin had both anticipated the danger of the miners insisting on a veto and had tried to pull them inside the tent, prepared, however reluctantly, to accept a majority decision. But they had resisted to the end. 'They had neither the loyalty to the Congress, nor to their colleagues, nor the appreciation of the sacrifices of the movement, to enable them to rise above their restricted vision of their own coalfields.'

Any lingering confusion about the degree of defeat was swiftly dispersed by the manner of the large employers when the strikers tried to return to work. Little thought had been given to the difficulty of getting the strikers back in, and there was no time, as there would have been in a conventional industrial dispute, to negotiate the details. The scope of the potential disaster became immediately apparent. The railway employers, in particular, saw the strike's defeat as the opportunity to constrain trade union activity. The docks employers also intended to claw back recent concessions. Thomas, Bevin and the other union leaders once again took charge of their unions to negotiate the return. More tele-grams went out, contradicting the day's earlier order: the transport workers' strike was back on. In the evening, Bevin and other members of the General Council went back to Downing Street to demand that Baldwin intervene. Bevin, according to his record, told Baldwin and the Defence Minister who was also present: 'We have called off the strike against the constitution as you put it, but now we have called a constitutional strike to defend our wages and agreements.'

Baldwin told them he was planning to broadcast that night, and showed the script to Bevin. 'I told him it was very sentimental but not very effective.' At Bevin's request, Baldwin added in a call to employers and trade unions 'to meet forthwith'. Baldwin's sentimentalism was not entirely misplaced. In his valedictory broadcast that night, he said: 'Our business is not to triumph over those who have failed in a mistaken attempt'; and he promised to start a new round of coal negotiations immediately.

George V, who had been judiciously invisible throughout the strike, not even visiting the volunteers in Hyde Park as he had during the 1921 rail strike, issued a message from Buckingham Palace that showed the same influences, combining as it did a call for tolerance and forgiveness with praise for his people's steadiness that would set the tone for the way the country would understand the previous nine days:

> The Nation has just passed through a period of extreme anxiety ... at such a moment it is supremely important to bring together all my people to confront the difficult situation that still remains ... Let us forget whatever elements of bitterness the events of the past few days may have created, only remembering how steady and how orderly the country has remained, though severely tested, and forthwith address ourselves to the task of bringing into being a peace which will be lasting because, forgetting the past, it looks only to the future with the hopefulness of a united people.[8]

In a private letter to Baldwin he wrote more personal thanks: 'The success is largely due to your own untiring patience and wise determination to abide by what you believed to be in the best and truest interest of the people by whose suffrages you have been elected to govern.'

In the royal diary he wrote, even more complacently: 'Our old country can well be proud of itself, as during the last nine days there has been a strike in which 4 million men have been affected; not a shot has been fired & no one killed; it shows what a wonderful people we are.'

15

THE SONG OF TRIUMPH

The British and international bourgeoisie are singing their song of triumph over the defeat of the British general strike. It is a song that will be short-lived. The British general strike is not only the greatest revolutionary advance in Britain since the days of Chartism, and the sure prelude of the new revolutionary era, but its very defeat is a profound revolutionary lesson and stimulus.

> Rajani Palme Dutt, 'The Meaning of the General Strike',
> *Communist International*, no. 21, June 1926

May 13th Thursday. School. Cycling to school we saw ever so many 49 'buses – those going towards London packed full – those going to Streatham Hill nearly empty. Stayed to school dinner. Gwen managed to bag my beloved rubber in scripture – and I had made up my mind she wasn't going to have it. Alas. Came home and took Spot out on the common. Met Alan, Titch and George, the two latter having a holiday because it is Ascension day. Alan felt ill and mother packed him off to bed before tea. Did homework.

May 14th Friday. 'Buses and trams are running today driven by the original 'bus and trammen. Mr Fourniss told Dad that the attitude of the tramwaymen was glum, and that a little later they will wish that they hadn't struck more than they do now.

May 17th Monday. Everything seems normal now with 'buses, trams and trains running. The 'buses we saw were absolutely crowded. Did all my algebra during the morning and gave it in.

> Diary of Margaret Woods

WHO HAD WON, and who had lost?

Although the grim bearing of the TUC leaders leaving Downing Street carried its own message, as the General Strike ended, the
long battle to possess it began. Many took their line from the King
and the popular press: it was a victory only for the marvellous
sanity of the British nation. It was not the politicians and certainly
not the misguided workers who had triumphed, but a state of mind.
It was England! The government insisted it had not conceded an
inch, the trade unions claimed they had got enough of what they
had wanted when they first went on strike to make the outcome a
reasonable compromise. Baldwin's deeply held conviction about
his role as shepherd to the 'bewildered multitude of common folk'
left him unwilling to trumpet victory; the need to bring with him
a party still viscerally anti-trade union, unwilling to believe that
moderation had played an important role and braying for sacrificial
slaughter, required at least a gesture in the other direction. The
British Gazette shrieked, 'Surrender!' But some volunteers, now the
strike was over, refused to do jobs that trade unionists would be
doing if the employers would take them back. For the trade unions,
their very survival rested on proving they had not lost. But the
harder they defended the result, the more the pressure grew on
Baldwin to remind them that he and not they had won, and the
more emboldened the employers became in trying to prove it.

There was no question of ending the extensive powers the
government had taken under the state of emergency; 13 May was
the most dangerous moment since the start of the strike. The
damage went far beyond the broken windows and smashed bottles
in the gutters of the West End. The sense of sacrifice and common
purpose, either with the miners or with a nation struggling with
hardship and inconvenience, had been replaced with bewilderment
and uncertainty. People who expected to be able to get up in the
morning and catch the bus to work again found instead, because
the volunteers had been laid off, that there was even less public
transport than in the final days of the strike. Much more alarming
for the government was the fear of an uprising of some sort from

disaffected trade unionists, their bitterness played on by the small bands of Communists and Communist sympathizers who had played a disproportionately large role in organizing the strike, and who immediately it was settled, cried treachery. The General Strike had ended, but the red banner of Communism was still flying among the fallen.

The Communist-inspired National Minority Movement tried vigorously to fan the angry strikers into revolt against their leaders. 'Down with Compromise! Down with Hesitancy! All in for a General Strike and a General Settlement!' its leaflets cried. 'The Tory Government is attempting to smash the entire British Trade Union movement ... This fight is no longer a Miners' fight: it is a fight of the entire British Working Class; it is a fight for existence in the future.' In Salford, according to the daily Home Office police report, Communist headquarters were raided on 14 May and seven men arrested 'in the act of printing a pamphlet entitled "The Great Betrayal", in which they called on all workers to resume the general strike'. In Darlington, another briefing reported all the transport workers forming into a breakaway union to continue the strike. In Doncaster there was a riot when pickets stopped traffic and police intervened to clear the road. It was the second consecutive night of violent picketing; there were baton charges and eighty arrests. In Birkenhead and Salford the Chief Constable reported 'a nasty feeling against the volunteers', and said that the employers were 'trying to drive too hard a bargain'; there was a threat to call out electricity and sanitary workers if the corporation did not re-employ all the tram drivers. The Merseyside council of action was calling for the strike to continue. If the employers demanded new contracts, said the Cardiff Chief Constable, their position 'would be worse than during the strike'. He was taking on another fifty 'specials'.

As ever, the epicentre of concern was the area around the London docks, where strike activity was strictly controlled by the strike committee and Poplar council paid relatively generous rates of support to the strikers and their families – 15 shillings as opposed to 12 shillings elsewhere, in cash, with food vouchers as an extra. Government agents were working assiduously, scavenging for the scraps of trivia[1] that might or might not be a part of a larger puzzle. On the night of the 12th, the day the strike ended, the MP George Lansbury was reported by an MI5 agent to be in a car with three known Communists; later he was observed talking covertly to another small group of men. Outside the police station in Poplar in the East End the worst disturbances since the first night of the strike took place. The police charged the demonstrators, and there were 'many casualties'. Nearly a thousand men had gathered outside what was thought to be the local Communist headquarters, a building in Bow Road kept under constant guard. MI5 believed another building, near Charringtons Brewery in Mile End Road, was the London home of the Cheka, the Soviet secret police. 'In clearing the streets,' said an official report the following day, '14 people including the Mayor of Poplar were injured and treated at hospital.' There were ten arrests; all but one were bound over. On the 13th, after the earlier false alarms, three truckloads of naval cadets from Greenwich were driven in lorries to the Admiralty, 'dressed up as much like policemen as we could, with uniform boots and trousers, blue burberries, uniform caps & police badge in place of naval ones. They put 50 beds for us in a corridor at the Admiralty & we slept in our clothes with our boots on all ready like the fire brigade.' The following day, they went to Wellington Barracks to practise street fighting.[2]

Throughout the nine days, the nightmare that had haunted both government and TUC was that a 'revolutionary situation' of the sort that the Communist strike strategists envisaged might develop. Now the actions of each appeared perilously close to achieving it. The sense of betrayal and grievance was powerful; there was plenty of incendiary material for those interested in starting fires. Men and women who had been on strike for the miners were now on strike again, for themselves. A hundred thousand came out after the General Strike was called off. There were more people out on 13 May than at any time during the nine days. Employers argued that since their employees had broken their contracts of employment when they walked out on the 4th, they could not complain if they had to sign new contracts. Paradoxically, the attitude of employers, encouraged by an official government statement that there had been no undertaking to protect the strikers from victimization, gave the trade unions the opportunity to demonstrate their continuing strength. Unhappily for them, though, it served only to confirm how weakened they had become.

'Stick to your Unions ... Sign no individual agreements,' instructed the TUC – which, by neglecting its own undertaking to ensure that none would go back until all went back, had failed so completely to set an example. The railways, employers of a million or more in three different unions, had now experienced three national strikes and were determined to ensure that there would not be another for a long time. Every company refused to guarantee jobs. Felix Pole, general manager of the GWR, had run an energetic but largely unsuccessful campaign to persuade men to return to work during the strike; in each station he had had posted up Sir John Simon's opinion on the illegality of the strike, and the Astbury ruling; every striker received a letter reminding him that he had broken his contract. On Thursday the 13th, a new notice went up: 'The injury to trade is believed to be so serious that for some time full pre-strike services will not be required.' This gave the company justification for selecting those they would re-employ. The company would examine individually the position of men 'in positions of trust' – supervisory staff, whose support for the strike had been so effective at hobbling the volunteer effort – as well as anyone guilty of acts of violence or intimidation. And the guaranteed working week was suspended. Jimmy Thomas told Citrine he had never seen the managers in such a 'resentful and belligerent' mood.

Bevin was facing similar problems in the Port of London, where the national agreement for which he had fought so hard in 1921 was at stake. It was little better on his home territory. At Bristol docks, 670 blacklegs had been taken on, and they were still registering for work – 'four abreast', he wrote – as he negotiated to replace them with his members. Other unions offered support. The General Workers' Union sent out instructions that no one was to go back until everyone went back.

But before agreements were reinstated, employers in both railways and docks forced the unions to concede that the strike had been illegal. The final deal struck by the railmen stated: 'in calling a strike they committed a wrongful act against the Companies and agree that the Companies do not, by reinstatement, surrender their legal rights to claim damages'.[3] The railmen also undertook never again to call a lightning strike, nor to encourage senior staff to strike, and to allow the companies to move people as necessary. The settlement did not include those 'guilty of violence or intimidation'. And the rail companies, not the courts, would judge who they were. The rail unions were on parole; further trouble, and their licence would be revoked. In the autumn, because of slack trade and the ongoing miners' strike, nearly a quarter of the NUR's members, forty-five thousand, were still waiting to be taken back, families forced on to outdoor relief, children fed by charities and sympathetic local authorities. The Railway Clerks' Association, many of whose members were in senior positions, suffered particular hostility. It took five years' obstruction of railway bills by the union's MPs in the Commons to force the reinstatement of their members. Not until 1931 did the last clerk go back.[4]

Nonetheless, by the end of the week some semblance of normality had returned. On the 14th, when the deal was signed, Ramsay MacDonald reported: 'Thomas rang me & spoke through tears. He had been photographed with the railway managers & feels that the old happy world has returned.'[5]

As BEVIN had predicted, thousands of men were victimized. It might have been worse, had Labour, and Baldwin, not forced the issue. Harold Laski wrote to Tom Jones, and probably MacDonald too, of the dangers of a Carthaginian surrender, of the government and employers allowing neither 'house nor crop to rise again'. The TUC too appealed to MacDonald, who immediately prompted a debate on the terms of the return to work in the Commons, which took place on the evening of the 13th. But it was Thomas who, by his eloquence and his authentic rage, spoke to most effect in the Labour cause. Where MacDonald, thought Tom Jones as he watched from the officials' box beside the government front bench, was every inch the aristocrat, 'a little histrionic and patronising to the Party behind him', Thomas was 'the genuine article, and much more effective, because the House is made to feel that he is voicing with conviction the views of vast multitudes of working men'.

Once again, the voice of reassurance was Baldwin's. His speech had been first drafted by Birkenhead, perhaps for his legal expertise, but perhaps also to establish that he too was now committed to conciliation. Baldwin rewrote it with care and delivered it with an emphasis that the employers could not ignore. He warned that he would countenance no attempt to use the strike to drive down wages or change conditions. 'I have always urged that the occasion calls neither for malice, nor for recrimination, nor for triumph.' And, after a declaration of his support for the principles of trade unionism, he ended, perhaps with personal feeling as well as anxiety about the danger of unrest: 'We know that in all these great organisations there are some who are of little help. At a time like this there are some who like fishing in troubled waters. Let us get the workers calm as soon as we can, lest their work spoils the work of half a century.'

That morning, in a rare tribute, the Cabinet that had caused Baldwin such difficulty moved a motion of thanks for leading the nation to success. The Cabinet's new appreciation of Baldwin may have owed something to the newspaper coverage. When he won the last election on the back of the *Daily Mail*'s publication of the Zinoviev letter, Beaverbrook jeeringly telegrammed his older rival Rothermere: 'Congratulations. Now you have to live with him.'[6] After the end of the strike, the *Mail* was calling Baldwin 'one of our greatest Prime Ministers'. In a leader it declared: 'the country has come through deep waters and it has come through in triumph, setting such an example to the world as has not been seen since the immortal hours of the War. It has fought and defeated the worst forms of human tyranny. This is a moment when we can lift up our head and our hearts.'

It is not easy to judge how far Baldwin reflected and how far he created the national mood, but his great political asset, as ever, was his personification of Englishness. Certainly his admirers, who now wholeheartedly included Tom Jones, believed his style had been 'the chief asset in keeping the government steadfast'.

It was easy to elide praise of the national spirit with praise for Baldwin and his low-key, dogged stoicism and the conscious appeal of his speeches to the spirit of Englishness. The BBC, in what Reith described as a 'little thing of our own', thanked 'Almighty God who has led us through this supreme test with National health unimpaired ... the Nation's happy escape has been in a large measure due to the personal trust in the Prime Minister, not misplaced'. The *Daily Mirror*, reminding its readers again that badness was foreign, and foreignness, bad, said: 'The unconquerable spirit of our people has been aroused again in self-defence – as it was against the foreign foe in 1914.' *The Times* thought that, in 'a fundamental struggle between right and wrong ... victory was won ... by the splendid courage and self-sacrifice of the nation itself'.

But some newspapers did distinguish between Baldwin and the nation: sections of the right-wing press remained suspicious of the degree of negotiation that had taken place, and thought it not quite enough of a surrender. It was considered necessary, in order to stifle these whispers, to publish the carefully worded exchange of letters between the Labour Minister Steel-Maitland and Herbert Samuel that had taken place before Samuel's talks with the trade unions began. The government, Steel-Maitland had written, hinting that it would act swiftly to prevent such a strike ever happening again, 'cannot enter upon negotiations unless the strike is so unreservedly concluded that there is not even an implication of such a bargain upon their side as would embarrass them in any legislation'. Samuel had responded: 'I have made it perfectly clear that I have been acting entirely on my own initiative, without any kind of authorisation from the Government.'[7]

The *British Gazette* claimed by the end of the strike that it was the world's largest-circulation newspaper, with well over a million copies printed each night. Churchill, at a meeting on Day 9, had suggested to the newspaper proprietors that the paper continue for as long as the emergency lasted.

The idea was swiftly rejected. The *Gazette* had become a byword for profligacy: there were accusations that it had been delivered, sometimes in twos, where none had been ordered, and sometimes whole bundles had been tossed on to street corners; in Durham, it was reported to have been dropped from aeroplanes. London, Geoffrey Dawson alleged, 'was soon littered with large bundles of Gazettes that, so far from being read, were never even untied'. Its content was universally attacked, most picturesquely by Lloyd George who thought it 'a first-class indiscretion clothed in the tawdry garb of third-rate journalism'; the *New Statesman* described it as 'a disgrace alike to the British Government and to British journalism ... it made no pretence of impartiality; it exaggerated, distorted and suppressed news, speeches and opinions for propagandist purposes'. Davidson, who was proud of the *Gazette*, if worn out by Churchill, had seen it as a fair compromise. 'Winston is really a most remarkable creature. His energy was boundless and he ran [the *Gazette*] entirely on his own lines. Whether it was right or wrong he desired to produce a newspaper rather than a news-sheet. He in fact conceived that the British Gazette should be a better newspaper than any of the great journals whose operations had been temporarily suspended.'[8]

The *British Worker*, reduced to four pages by the depredations of the *Gazette*, kept going as the mouthpiece for the TUC until Monday the 17th. For the final few days, Hamilton Fyfe was allowed, as he had always wished, to include more general news. Its purpose, now the strike was over, was to undermine the government's insistence that it had not negotiated, with a counter-assertion that both sides understood that Samuel represented 'well-informed public opinion'. It also challenged the idea that 'the nation' had somehow been the exclusive property of the non-strikers, and produced evidence to show that the nation had actually been with the workers more than with the government. Most newspapers remarked on the good behaviour of the strikers and blamed only a 'group of fanatics' or, more sedately, a 'sectional organisation', for taking advantage of their goodwill. The *British Worker*, however, attacked the 'poison gas' of misrepresentation, and pointed to examples of middle-class support – the donations that arrived at Eccleston Square and the contributions to collections at rallies and open-air meetings. There was other evidence: some newspapers carried sympathetic accounts of the conditions in which miners worked and their families lived. Some protested, as did the *Daily Mirror* – which within ten years had gone over to the Labour cause – at the harshness of sentences when the law was infringed, like the birching of children for minor offences. There was general concern about the depths of poverty and hunger to which unemployment had reduced some people. One story, repeated in various forms during the strike, involved variously the police or a whip-round in court paying the fine imposed on a child who had stolen some bread. In some accounts, the mother fainted from hunger.

As well as the nation's conscience, there was another factor: the first, shared, experience of total war that on one side had started a slow erosion of deference, and on the other had fostered a more genuine respect. The *Manchester Guardian* thought the 'comradeship which still persists in the minds of both strikers and volunteers, was a big factor in the unparalleled pacific character of this great conflict ... it is only men too old to have been in the war who now talk of "teaching the workmen the lesson they deserve"'. There was 'a common trench language' that united men who 'knew all about arms and bloodshed' and kept the fools on both sides in check. Hamilton Fyfe, in his book on the strike, described a letter he had had from a 'middle-class woman' who said she saw the strikers not as enemies but as the young men who had answered the nation's call to arms barely ten years earlier; in the faces of the pickets she saw 'bloodstained Tommies keeping the enemy out of my home'. The attempt to suggest that veterans would not strike led to marches of men wearing their war medals, and declarations of patriotism in speeches – one strike committee, in Widnes, sang 'God Save the King' at the end of its meetings. The equality of sacrifice experienced during the war years was a faint but recurring refrain throughout the strike.

Still, it was not by what the nation had in common, but by its divisions, that many at first defined the strike. The idea of the moneyed and educated driving tube trains and working as porters was so quaint, so amusing, and yet so noble. To those who wanted to see it from this perspective the strike illustrated the unbroachable divisions of class in England. Some newspapers asserted that the volunteers had been more efficient than the normal workforce, although without commenting on the possible impact of diet and housing on their performance. Osbert Sitwell, ferried back and forth in his brother's Rolls Royce between the great houses of Mayfair in his campaign to find a just solution, paused in his breathlessly solipsistic account[9] only to describe a conversation with his chauffeur in which it was discovered that the young man customarily breakfasted on Fuller's chocolate cake. For Sitwell, whose chef was only one of life's many essentials, no more needed to be said. The workers were another country.

Geoffrey Dawson of *The Times* cherished the familial unity of undergraduates and city bankers against the other world outside – decent chaps in normal times, but men, not masters. Of the literary diarists, Arnold Bennett continued to believe the strike had been a 'political crime'. On the day it ended, he wrote: 'The general strike now seems pitiful, foolish – a pathetic attempt of underdogs who hadn't a chance when the over-dogs really set themselves to win. Everybody, nearly, among the over-dogs seems to have joined in with grim enthusiasm.'[10] Virginia Woolf worried that 'Labour was being diddled again' and about whether, in the future, her pages on the strike would look dull. 'Excitements about what are called real things are always unutterably transitory.'[11]

The TUC's last hope that they could claim to have secured some kind of victory, to have made possible the resumption of negotiations and the continuation of subsidy, lay beyond their control, with the miners and the government. On the Friday, two days after the General Strike ended, the government published proposals to end the miners' strike. Less generous than Samuel's they were nonetheless close enough for the TUC to claim a degree of influence. That any government proposals emerged at all was an achievement in itself: after the publication of the original Samuel Commission report back in March, the government had refused to recognize that it had a role in settling the dispute. Now it was putting forward concrete proposals. It would legislate for the amalgamation of pits, introduce a welfare levy on profits, restrict recruitment to unemployed miners and introduce a national wages board. To settle the immediate dispute, there would be a subsidy, but only of £3 million – enough for about six weeks rather than the three months the miners wanted. Then there would be pay cuts, but how and where would be determined by the new wages board. It was hazy about one of the miners' central objectives, the maintenance of a national minimum at all levels.

In most of their details, these were plans Baldwin had had in mind before the subsidy ran out at the end of April but had held back from offering in the hope that the industry would sort itself out. The miners, though, who had been making slightly warmer noises about the memorandum that they had rejected when the strike was called off, again rejected Baldwin's proposals and held to their slogan, 'Not a penny off the pay, not a minute on the day.' The Mine Owners' Association responded in the manner of the other employers in the wake of the General Strike, telling Baldwin not to meddle. It would be 'impossible to continue the conduct of the industry under private enterprise unless it is accorded the same freedom from political interference that is enjoyed by other industries'.¹² Baldwin now reminded the miners that the proposal was on the table for only another month. Then in June, in a move that destroyed any notion of an impartial government and any prospect for the Samuel report, he introduced legislation suspending the seven-hour day in the mines. As successive inquiries had established, the only way that the miners could earn a living wage out of the profits of the coal industry was through rationalization, reorganization and investment. The owners, dominated by the short-termists, were too opposed in principle, and too fragmented in practice, to bring about such a transformation. Government had to find a way of intervening; but it was beyond the Conservative Party to encompass an idea that was the antithesis of its instincts. It wanted to end the miners' strike, if only because of the part it played in perpetuating social unrest. But it could not take the powers that alone might have achieved an acceptable settlement.

The miners' intransigence had not advanced their cause. It took six more months before they finally settled, on worse terms than they might have achieved before the General Strike began. Their leaders were sustained by political belief, the ordinary members by the unacceptability of the wage offer and the everyday reality of living in poverty. So terrible were the conditions in which they worked, many were reported to be in better health at the end of the strike despite the poverty. As the year ground on and Cook and Herbert Smith prepared to sue for peace, delegate conferences repeatedly rejected their proposals and elected to stick it out. Efforts by other union leaders to try to mediate were stiffly rejected. Then the miners, still wanting everyone to fall in step with them, asked for an embargo on coal imports. Neither Thomas nor Bevin could tolerate the damage this would do to small sectors of their unions, nor the risk that it would lead to a lockout that would further deplete their strike funds. Bevin also demanded, bitterly, a guarantee that striking miners would not, in any eventuality, come in and blackleg. So much for solidarity. The miners' strike wore on. Not until December, when winter closed in, did cold and hunger drive them back to work, in dribs and drabs, on terms of abject surrender: district pay awards, less money and longer hours had all to be conceded.

Ordinary strikers' memories of the strike were coloured by the excitement of novelty, and righteous indignation about the way it had ended: in a feeling of betrayal that only accentuated their sense of the nobility of their sacrifice during those nine days. This Clydesider's memory is typical: 'I've never seen it before or since, and as a young man it's always recorded in my memory as being the most outstanding example of how unity in action can bring a government to its knees.'[13] But of course, the government, far from having been brought to its knees on 12 May, had been incomparably strengthened. And Britain has never had another general strike.

THE INVENTION OF THE LEFT

The strike reflected the growing discontent of the workers with the whole structure and policy of the industrial system, and their determination to resist the traditional idea, that bad trade can be made good, economic vitality and progress attained and industry placed in a healthy condition by the mere expedient of degrading the standard of life of the working people.

Arthur Pugh, chairman, TUC Congress, September 1926

The severity of a storm is shown by the wreckage it leaves after it. It was the confusion of the strike's aftermath that made us realise how vast a thing it had been.

Daily News, Friday 14 May 1926

WITHIN A MONTH of the end of the General Strike, the government was seeking to fan the embers of the Communist threat; at the same time, Communists themselves were revealing their despair at the outcome of the strike they had thought would provoke a revolution. In June, documents from the 1925 plundering of Communist headquarters were released by the government in an official Blue Book. The Communists, commented *The Times*, 'constitute a grave warning to every party in the country'. The *Daily Herald* disagreed. '[The Blue Book] may enlighten some who have fondly imagined that British Communists were the Left Wing of Labour. It shows they are actively hostile to Labour and will stick at nothing to injure it.'

At almost the same time, Rajani Palme Dutt, the cosmopolitan

Oxford classicist turned revolutionary, mentor and political partner of Harry Pollitt, future general secretary of the Communist Party, attempted to reinvent the strike in a long analysis that appeared in June's *Communist International.* In 'The Meaning of the General Strike' Palme Dutt, who often set the pace for Communist argument in Britain, abandoned all ideas of working within existing Labour structures and tore into the trade unions and their mouthpiece, the *British Worker,* for their pusillanimous conduct of what might have been, he declared, the final battle in the class war. 'The bravest fighters of the working class, who were going to prison in hundreds, were without honour in the Labour organ,' he wrote – accurately, for the *British Worker* carried no reports of court cases. And then, with the shrewdness of an outsider, he identified the hidden appeal of the paper's seemingly artless elevation of the humdrum: 'Instead [it] was publishing news of jolly billiard matches between police and strikers in some remote village, or advising strikers to stay at home and amuse the children.'[1]

Palme Dutt's long philippic embraced the High Court and the trade unions as well as the *Daily Mail,* reformism and pacifism. The workers had been tricked by the fantasy of a middle way, but now the 'trappings of middle-class power' were ruthlessly exposed. The bourgeoisie had always understood that the strike was a political struggle, and when it began it called in all the forces of the state for support; only the trade unions had clung to the delusion that this was just a rather large industrial dispute. For Palme Dutt, the experience of 1926 demonstrated that the only way to win power for the working class was through the unifying, centralized and, above all, uncompromising Communist Party. In the immediate aftermath, the few thousand in Britain who wanted a revolution signed up; the millions of others who did not, began to realize that Labour was not after all such a threat to the existing order. Palme Dutt's article marked the beginning of the rebuilding of Labour's credibility among a middle-class electorate; this was an unmistakable signal that the Labour Party would be safe from Communism for the foreseeable future. Equally, when Labour failed again only

five years later, the Communist analysis became the more persuasive for having at first gone unheeded.

History is written by the victors, Nehru said. Communist
writers in 1926 set out to make sure that history would see the
workers, and their true representatives, the Communists, as the true
victors of the General Strike. A series of angry outpourings that
took their line from Palme Dutt's indictment of the trade union
and Labour leadership, and lauded the commitment and the collective power of the masses, were soon in print. Written to staunch the
flow of left-wing morale and to elevate the virtues of the workers
at the expense of their leaders, these were based on more extensive
research than attempted by other participants, most of whom were
too relieved that the experience of a general strike was behind
them to revisit it so soon. Before the end of the year, the Communist-
controlled Labour Research Department at the TUC would publish
two slim but detailed volumes, one by Robin Page Arnot giving
documentary support to the Palme Dutt thesis of betrayal, the
other by Emile Burns on the working of trades councils during the
nine days, a work that the author hoped would be useful in a future
general strike. '"Never again",' said Burns in his introduction, 'is
the despairing prayer of individuals who do not like the course of
events, rather than a serious judgement of what the course of events
is likely to be.' His research into what had actually happened, he
stated, would enable trades councils 'to deal effectively with any
similar emergencies which may arise in the future'.[2]

Communist polemicists did not spare the Miners' Federation
secretary Arthur Cook, even though the miners had yet to capitulate to the owners' demands. The most radical of the trade union
leaders, Cook was attacked for failing twice over: first he had not
managed to sustain the TUC's resolve to continue the General
Strike; then, he had not even attempted to re-ignite it by exploiting
the anger and sense of betrayal among ordinary union members. In
his own defence, Cook too wrote an account of the strike, *The Nine
Days*, passing the buck to the TUC.

The urbane Hamilton Fyfe was chief apologist for the Labour

movement. In a defensive little volume he settled old scores with the print unions, whom he blamed for obstructing him at every turn. He had felt, he said, like the Russian commander of a revolutionary unit ordered to capture a strongpoint. Every hundred yards or so of their advance the men stopped and went into a huddle, before turning and continuing. When the mission had eventually been accomplished, the commander asked what had happened. 'They were voting on whether to go on or not,' he was told. Yet for all his dislike for the curious trade union combination of excessive democracy allied with bureaucratic nit-picking, Fyfe remained obedient to the censors' strictures on correct nomenclature, and called his account *Behind the Scenes of the Great* [not the 'General'] *Strike*. He candidly acknowledged the 'bitter' feeling against the General Council and in particular against Jimmy Thomas, but placed the blame firmly on the miners' leaders, 'who wouldn't agree to anything'. On the front cover, he promised: 'For every 100 copies sold the Author gives a child's keep for two weeks to the Miners' Fund.' Tiptoeing along the line between justifying the TUC's decision to end the strike, and celebrating the solidarity of the workers in their 'quiet, dignified withdrawal of labour ... [their] splendid demonstration of comradeship', he concluded: 'After it *nothing can ever be the same again*.'[3] But he did not say what would be different, or in what way.

The TUC delayed entertaining its critics until the miners were back at work in the new year. But if it hoped tempers would cool during the long wait, it had underestimated its members' mood. In January 1927, at an angry and acrimonious post-mortem, the miners led an attack that was echoed among ordinary delegates from other trade unions. But in the final vote they had little support. Arthur Pugh, who had been at the centre of the negotiations throughout, defended the conduct of the strike, ticking off its achievements like a boy scout assembling his certificates: these achievements, he explained, had entitled all trade unionists to full membership of the ruling classes. Trade unions, he asserted without quite proving it, had been shown to be an indispensable part of the constitution, as indispensable as Parliament and the law courts; respecters of democracy and, by their responsible exercise of their own power, its protectors. The trade union movement was not political in the negative sense that the government had implied. It did not want to override the expression of the will of the people. Nonetheless, Pugh argued, trying to lift his members' heads beyond defeat, it was time the TUC started to think about politics, about economics and economic democracy and about the part workers should play.

As for the movement's industrial muscle, it was Citrine who acknowledged the new limits they now recognized. 'The theory of the General Strike has never been thought out. The machinery of the trade unions was unfortunately not adapted to it. Their rules had to be broken for the executives to give power to the General Council to declare the strike ... it was full of imperfections in concept and method.'[4] Citrine argued that the cost of the strike to the nation – put at £400 million by Citrine – and to the government – a further £80 million – left the trade union movement the real victors; at least the sheer economic impact of their action might deter future governments from pursuing such an expensive vendetta again.

But if a case could be made out in defence of the General Strike, there was no enthusiasm to repeat the experiment. The terms of the return to work forced the union leaders to lay aside the strike as a weapon. On the strength of Simon and Astbury, the employers now held over them the threat of legal action to recover damages. To strike could bankrupt the unions. There would be fewer stoppages in 1927 than at any time since 1900. Instead, with perceptions sharpened by the threat of new legislation attacking trade union rights, thoughts turned to negotiation and the development of what Citrine called 'a sense of responsibility'.

There were plenty of reasons beyond the failure of the General Strike for the unions to think again about their role, and how they were to pursue it. A frightening slide in membership followed sharply on defeat. Bevin's Transport Workers' Union lost a tenth of its members; most others experienced falls, and between 1926 and

1929 the number of people in unions affiliated to the TUC fell by 700,000. The effect of declining numbers broadly coincided with Baldwin's surrender to the old school over trade union legislation, and gave the unions a further reason to develop an interest in cooperation. This culminated in the Mond–Turner talks, led by Sir Alfred Mond of ICI and Ben Turner, then Chairman of the TUC, and the establishment, in 1929, of a national industry council, whose purpose was to discuss problems of industrial restructuring and unemployment. It was the first attempt to recognize the contribution to policy-making that could come from organized labour. That it was a casualty of economic crisis and slump in the early 1930s did not invalidate the intentions behind it. In the event, a national industry council that had no political power was doomed to ineffectiveness.

The nation's gratitude to Baldwin for leading it through the strike was short-lived; his own party was inclined to believe he should have been tougher; many non-Conservatives thought that his obduracy had provoked the strike. In June, after his proposals adapting the Samuel memorandum were rejected by the miners, he appeared to lapse again into inertia. All the public saw was his repeal of the seven-hour day Act, followed by the Trade Disputes Act that ended the automatic political levy imposed on union members, which was vital to the Labour Party's finances. It also, in purporting to clarify the law on sympathy strikes, laid over it a heavy cloak of obfuscation that could be interpreted to mean that all but the most narrowly drawn strikes were illegal. This move appeared vindictive even to some Conservatives, and played a large part in reviving Labour in the perception of the electorate, while the Act itself was badly drafted and had little real impact before its triumphant repeal by the first majority Labour government in 1946.

Solidarity of the working class against the solidarity of the nation? Citrine had wondered, in 1925, what choice union members would make if a general strike was portrayed as a challenge to the constitution. He feared that the constitution might just prove to have a greater appeal than class identity. Instead, it seemed that the final victory of the General Strike was to show that it was not necessary to make that choice: it was possible to be both English and working-class Socialist. Labour, and the trade union movement, had proved they were not the pawns of Moscow, in the nightmare grip of an alien force. If England was the country of the establishment, open only to those who wore the club tie and scrupulously observed the establishment's rules, then the Labour Party and the unions had shown they were English. They belonged.

Only when the miners' strike was formally over did the government give up the emergency powers it had taken on 1 May and admit that the crisis had ended without ever reaching anything near the danger pitch that had been so luridly prophesied in the months before the General Strike. Afterwards, no one could understand why they had been quite so scared. 'I hope the historian of the future,' wrote the intelligent and thoughtful scion of one of England's noble families, Lord Eustace Percy, 'will not under-rate the reality of that trend of English thought of the Twenties, just because some contemporaries were needlessly scared by it.'[5] To many people, no longer afraid – or not nearly as afraid as they had been – and warmed by the self-congratulatory outpourings that greeted the end of the strike, the miners soon came to look more pitiful than powerful, and the men and women who had gone on strike in such a disciplined and generous manner seemed more like heroes than incipient revolutionaries. 'It was Tom Brown's last stand,' was A. J. P. Taylor's verdict on the volunteer effort; but even blurred by nostalgia, the undergraduate bus drivers and the temporary dockhands looked a little misguided, and at worst more like the bully Flashman than the eponymous hero of the schoolboy tale. Baldwin and his government, who had briefly appeared as saviours of England and of the English way of life, were now seen to have been rather hysterical and mean-spirited. Graham Greene, for one, who was working on *The Times* in 1926, subsequently found his past a mild embarrassment. The following year, George Orwell began his tramp from the East End of London to Wigan Pier, seeking to escape 'from every form of man's dominion over man'.[6]

Orwell had been influenced by the five years he had spent as a colonial servant in Burma. Other men and women, too, began to see more clearly that there were millions of people at home oppressed by their economic situation and by the lack of educational opportunities.

A decade had elapsed since the Russian Revolution, and nine years since the end of the Great War. The world was not stable, but it was becoming unstable in a familiar way. The fading newsreel of the 'Asiatic hordes' overturning a regime connected by birth to all the crowned heads of Europe was no longer quite so terrifying; the Bolsheviks were now just 'Bolshies', and Bolshie-bashing was evolving from something far too alarming to laugh about into little more than a comic turn. Now there were new preoccupations, nearer to home. For many, victory and the peace were bearing the prizes of comfort and new freedoms, better housing, wireless, cinema, travel and motor-cars, an unheard-of liberty for women to work, to enjoy sex with some confidence in birth control, even to vote at twenty-one. The fears that had inspired a thousand headlines and sold hundreds of millions of newspapers were dissipating. The worst had happened, and it had not after all been so bad. Sir Philip Gibbs's middle-class hero preparing to defend all that was most dear to him became P. G. Wodehouse's Spode in his absurd shorts, living on a secret income from a Bond Street lingerie shop.

THE SECURITY OF the nation is the first purpose of government. From the moment the Czar's grip on power faltered, the ruling classes everywhere trembled. In Britain, for the first time the fear was magnified and projected through mass-circulation newspapers which had found a running story, a Daily Scare, that their readers wanted to know about, was easy to present in simplistic terms of good and evil, and significant enough to allow them to disguise the trivia of daily developments with demands for government intervention. Baldwin's political career, which had seemed to have no particular destination, was made by these slowly evolving events. His steady, reassuring figure and his ability to represent so truthfully the England that the mass-circulation papers were addressing, offered the appearance of safety to a scared people. The louder the newspapers shouted about the Reds, and the more his Home Secretary Joynson-Hicks failed either to contradict or to deny stories that he knew to be inaccurate, the more important the avuncular, pipe-smoking, risk-averse Baldwin appeared. Neither Baldwin nor the Conservative government caused the General Strike; but, like the newspapers, they played a large part in creating the climate in which it could happen, even against the wishes of most of the Labour movement's leaders; and by their handling of the final negotiations they precipitated a crisis that almost no one wanted. The months of foreplay, the alarmist headlines, raids, arrests and trials, made some climax, some denoument, politically inevitable. Something had to be done. The General Strike was it.

To an extent, the strike was also the resolution of a family argument on the left about the relationship between industrial and political power, and the pace of reform and the allure of revolution. It suited Conservative political purposes to portray it as a challenge to the state itself; some Conservatives genuinely believed it. When, some years later, Citrine sat next to Churchill at a lunch with the ubiquitous political hosts Lord and Lady Wimborne, Citrine asked him if he had really believed everything he had said about an attack on the constitution, Churchill had strongly insisted that he had. 'I saw red,' he told the TUC's general secretary.[7] That, of course, was the problem. Conservatives saw red everywhere. Concerned about what would be the most effective response to the challenge of Labour and the universal franchise, many failed to distinguish between the TUC General Council and the Communist Party.[8]

The hysterical anti-Communism of the first half of the 1920s made it harder but also more pressing to accommodate legitimate demands. For all his hostility to state intervention, Baldwin presided over the introduction of a central electricity grid, which was to be run by a national board appointed by ministers – broadly the structure adopted by the Attlee government when finally nationalization arrived in 1945. The leading diehards were also anxious to remove popular grievances. Churchill – who during Baldwin's summer holiday had nearly succeeded in settling the miners' strike by doing what Baldwin would not and frightening the owners into submission – and in particular Neville Chamberlain, Minister of Health, brought in progressive social legislation introducing the principle of contributory pensions as an extension of national health insurance, as well as helping people to buy their own homes. It was Chamberlain who pursued reform most vigorously. 'Unless we leave our mark as social reformers,' he wrote to his sister, 'the country will take it out on us hereafter.'[9]

The Conservative right was still not quite ready to abandon the Red Menace. A triumph had been won over the reds in the unions, but Churchill, Joynson-Hicks and both Austen and Neville Chamberlain still feared the power of ideological and imperial subversion inherent in the Soviet Union, particularly since Communism was now overtly challenging Britain's Empire in the Far East and India. The right still believed that the real target remained the Empire's heart, England, and that there were agents at work who continued to try to subvert the constitution. The *Daily Mail*, most ardent defender of Empire, enthusiastically supported their cause. On 12 May 1927 – by curious coincidence, the anniversary of the end of the General Strike – the offices of Arcos, an Anglo-Russian trading company, were raided, allegedly in pursuit of an unidentified secret document. Hundreds of papers and other material were seized once again. This was proof, it was claimed, that there was indeed a network of agents operating behind the façade of a legitimate company. Subsequently the documents seemed of questionable value, and Baldwin, who had been no enthusiast for the raid, fumbled when challenged in the Commons. But it could hardly be admitted that such a raid, involving large numbers of police, had in fact led up a political cul de sac. Less than a fortnight later, trade and diplomatic links with the Soviet Union were broken. Many of the Arcos documents for which at the time so much was claimed remain uncatalogued to this day.

The Arcos raid marked the end of the active stoking of a

climate of fear. But its effects lingered. The experience of the strike had still not resolved the conflicting ambitions of Labour's component parts. While trade unionists' lingering faith in direct-action strategies, as Beatrice Webb foretold, was finally destroyed, the Independent Labour Party radicals were inclined to see the strike's denouement as one more reason for an uncompromisingly left-wing political agenda. Ramsay MacDonald, although reassured by a series of by-election successes, talked anxiously of the 'Buffalo Bill whoops' made by the ILP MPs, whose ideas kept frightening the voters back towards what seemed to be an alarmingly resurgent, and challengingly creative, Liberal Party. The Conservatives did not win a single by-election after the strike; Labour won thirteen. But the Liberals, reunited in the autumn of 1926 under Lloyd George, for a time seemed in a position to keep the untidy compromises of three-party politics alive.

It was an uncertain period: the Labour Party attracted a number of talented but eccentric figures, like its wealthy benefactor Sir Ernest Benn who was moved by the strike (which came a year before the birth of his nephew Tony) to write down his own thoughts on what the Labour leader should be doing. 'If I were Labour leader,' said Sir Ernest, 'I would declare socialism is "a snare and a delusion"; everywhere there is socialism there is a low standard of living.'[10] But whatever Sir Ernest envisaged, it was not a Labour party. Nor were Oswald Mosley's ambitions reassuring, however much MacDonald delighted in the extravagant company of the aristocratic Labour MP and his wife Lady Cynthia, daughter of the former Foreign Secretary Lord Curzon. MacDonald feared that if his party failed to win power at the next election it might never hold office again. But he had to struggle continually to maintain the careful, pragmatic gradualism he believed was essential to win middle-class support, particularly after Lloyd George boldly tried to outflank him on the left with a radical plan to reduce unemployment by three-quarters.

Paradoxically, and unreflected in the mirror of the popular press, democratic politics were about to meet – and fail – a further great challenge, the challenge of economic collapse at home and the rise of Fascism abroad. In the 1930s the real political debate, excluded from a consensus-bound Westminster, began to be heard outside, and Communism, once the stuff of social exclusion, achieved a wider support than at any time before or since. The first surge in Communist support came in the immediate aftermath of the strike. The following year membership fell back sharply. But slowly Communism began to achieve a disreputable kind of respectability that reached beyond the politically aware working classes, to the middle and upper classes whose social consciences were first aroused by the plight of the miners and the inadequacy of the response of both the trade unions and the politicians. Over the next fifteen years, this movement grew into a cross-class alliance and shaped a generation of politicians and intellectuals, of right as well as left: democratic politicians like the Labour Chancellor Denis Healey and double agents such as Kim Philby and Donald Maclean who defected to Moscow in the 1960s.

There was no national coal strike in Britain for almost fifty years, and then there were two in quick sucession. In 1972, victory for what had become the National Union of Mineworkers was followed by a second national strike that lasted from the end of 1973 and into 1974; after the introduction of a three-day week to conserve power, and amid injunctions to clean your teeth in the dark and bath with a friend, Edward Heath called a snap election, which he lost. It seemed once more that the balance of power might tilt away from the state and towards trade unions. A half century after its defeat, the General Strike became a source of emotional inspiration, an object lesson in the betrayal of the working classes by their political leaders. Trade union membership soared until by 1980, its apogee, more than twelve million people, or nearly half the workforce, were in unions affiliated to the TUC. A relatively small but energetic group of them sought to prevent what they feared would be a second betrayal by political and industrial leaders, by consolidating their numerical strength through control of the political wing of the movement.

In 1979 the Labour government fell and was out of office for eighteen years. Fired by prolonged depression, unemployment, and an end to the upward surge in pay rates, industrial disputes flared until in 1984 another climax was reached. Margaret Thatcher, buoyed by the recapture of the Falklands from Argentina, branded the NUM's leader Arthur Scargill 'the enemy within' and fought a ruthlessly well prepared campaign that echoed many of the features of the miners' lockout of 1926. Coal stocks were high, the police were prepared; and public opinion, although always sympathetic to the miners, regarded with alarm Arthur Scargill's luridly portrayed zealotry. The miners were protesting at plans to impose sixty-four thousand redundancies and close dozens of pits in order to reduce capacity by 25 million tonnes in an industry that received over a billion pounds' worth of subsidy a year. This time – and almost certainly in explicit recognition of the 'betrayal' of 1926 – the NUM refused to solicit support from the TUC in any way. As in the 1920s, the strike dragged on, supported, despite a lack of enthusiasm for it in the first place, by the courage and solidarity of miners' communities. Its final defeat gave a new edge to the Conservatives' determination to rescind trade union privileges. In many areas of trade union law, the clock was wound back by nearly sixty years.

Three years later, Thatcher won a third election victory the scale of which could only be explained by wide support among trade unionists. The lesson that Labour took from its defeat then, and again in 1992, was the same that MacDonald had taken in 1926. Most voters, and most trade unionists, were inherently conservative. Only a party that recognized Socialism's limited appeal – and acknowledged the limitations of Socialism – would triumph at the ballot box. New Labour is the party Ramsay MacDonald dreamt of creating.

Notes

CHAPTER 1

1 Quoted in Alan Bullock, *The Life and Times of Ernest Bevin*, vol. 1, Heinemann, 1960, p. 252.
2 PRO HO144/4684, p. 33.
3 PRO KV2/1186.
4 Churchill, 'The Aftermath', quoted in Robert Rhodes James, *Churchill: A Study in Failure 1900–1939*, Penguin Books, 1981.
5 *Beatrice Webb's Diaries 1924–1932*, ed. Margaret Cole, Longmans, Green & Co., 1956, 19 Sept. 1925.
6 Figures from D. Butler and G. Butler, *Twentieth-Century British Political Facts*, Palgrave, 2000.
7 Cole, *Beatrice Webb's Diaries*, 28 July 1927.
8 Bullock, *Bevin*, p. 137.
9 Ibid., pp. 132–3.
10 Sankey Commission on miners' housing quoted in Charles Loch Mowat, *Britain between the Wars 1918–1940*, p. 33.
11 Max Goldberg, interviewed for the South Wales coalfield project.
12 Jim Evans, interviewed for the South Wales coalfield project.
13 Used in the title of an admiring pamphlet about A. J. Cook by Paul Foot, *Agitator of the Worst Kind: Portrait of Miners' Leader A. J. Cook*, Bookmarks, 1986.
14 *Thomas Jones: Whitehall Diary*, vol. 1, *1916–1925*, ed. Keith Middlemas, Oxford University Press, 1969, 17 January 1920.
15 Cole, *Beatrice Webb's Diaries*, 8 May 1927.
16 Middlemas, *Jones*, vol. 1, 19 January 1920.
17 The best short account of the negotiations is in Mowat, *Britain between the Wars*.
18 Quoted in R. Palme Dutt, 'The Meaning of the General Strike', *Communist International*, June 1926.
19 Middlemas, *Jones*, vol. 1, 4 April 1921.

20 Sir Philip Gibbs, *Middle of the Road*, London, 1922, quoted in Mowat, *Britain between the Wars*.

21 'Strike Strategy in Britain', PRO HO144/4684.

22 Bullock, *Bevin*, p. 252.

23 Figures from Butler and Butler, *British Political Facts*, and Mowat, *Britain between the Wars*.

24 Robert Rhodes James, *Memoirs of a Conservative*, Weidenfeld & Nicolson, 1969.

25 Middlemas, *Jones*, vol. 1, 28 May 1923.

26 'The Davidson memorandum', quoted in Keith Middlemas and John Barnes, *Baldwin*, Weidenfeld & Nicolson, 1969 (and many other places).

27 Royal Archives K1894, 2 quoted in Harold Nicolson, *King George V*, Constable, 1952, p. 380.

28 Quoted in Kenneth Rose, *King George V*, Phoenix Press, 1983.

29 Harold Nicolson, *Curzon: The Last Phase*, 1934.

30 Harold Nicolson to Kenneth Rose, quoted in Rose, *George V*.

31 Quoted in ibid., p. 340.

32 These and other quotations from Fascist literature come from PRO KV3/57.

33 *Hansard*, 17 April 1923.

34 Speech in Edinburgh quoted in Middlemas and Barnes, *Baldwin*, p. 170.

35 See Philip Williamson, *Stanley Baldwin*, Cambridge University Press, 1999, for an interesting discussion of these ideas.

36 See Middlemas and Barnes, *Baldwin*, note to p. 168.

37 Roy Jenkins, *Asquith*, HarperCollins, 1988.

38 See Middlemas and Barnes, *Baldwin*, p. 260.

CHAPTER 2

1 Osbert Sitwell, *Laughter in the Next Room*, Macmillan, 1958.

2 In Kenneth Rose, *King George V*, Phoenix Press, 1983.

3 Quoted in David Marquand, *Ramsay MacDonald*, Richard Cohen Books, 1977, p. 304.

4 Ibid., p. 246.

5 *The Diary of Beatrice Webb*, ed. Norman and Jeanne MacKenzie, vol. 4, Virago, 1985, p. 16.

6 Baldwin papers, quoted in Keith Middlemas and John Barnes, *Baldwin*, Weidenfeld & Nicolson, 1969.

7 Alan Bullock, *The Life and Times of Ernest Bevin*, vol. 1, Heinemann, 1960, p. 236.

8 All from David Marquand, *Ramsay Macdonald*, Richard Cohen Books, 1997, who was quoting from Richard W. Lyman, *The First Labour Government*, 1924.

9 Quoted in, Middlemas and Barnes, *Baldwin*, p. 274; John Ramsden, *A History of the Conservative Party: The Age of Balfour and Baldwin, 1902–1940*, Longman, 1978, also explains Baldwin's motives thus.

10 Robert Rhodes James, *Memoirs of a Conservative*, Weidenfeld & Nicolson, 1969.

11 Ibid., p. 199.

12 Quoted in Robert Skidelsky, *John Maynard Keynes*, vol. 2, *The Economist as Saviour 1920–1937*, Macmillan, 1992, p. 198.

13 From *The Economic Consequences of Mr Churchill*, quoted in ibid., p. 204.

14 Quoted in Bullock, *Bevin*, vol. 1, p. 274.

15 Quoted in ibid., p. 277. Baldwin later denied he had said it.

16 Walter Citrine, *Men and Work*, Hutchinson, 1964, p. 142.

17 Quoted in Middlemas and Barnes, *Baldwin*.

18 Quoted in R. Palme Dutt, 'The Meaning of the General Strike', *Communist International*, June 1926.

19 An ILP audience in August 1925. Quoted in Marquand, *MacDonald*, Jonathan Cape, p. 424.

CHAPTER 3

1 PRO KV3/25. But it could be forged! There are several more in the archives.

2 PRO HO144/4684.

3 Ibid.

4 http://archive.workersliberty.org/wlmags/wl50/history2.htm.

5 Sir Wyndham Childs, *Episodes and Reflections*, Cassell, 1930.

6 Robert Benewick, *The Fascist Movement in Britain*, Penguin Press, 1972.

7 See ibid., p. 38.

8 The incident is described in Gordon Brown, *Maxton*, Mainstream Publishing, 1986.

9 PRO HO144/22372.

10 ADM1/8657/48, 23 Dec 1924; HO45/25439.

11 Labour Party Conference record, Liverpool, 1925.

12 PRO HO144/6682.

13 Alan Bullock, *The Life and Times of Ernest Bevin*, vol. 1, Heinemann, 1960, p. 283.

14 See PRO KV3/11.

15 PRO HO144/6682, cutting from *Daily Mail*, 23 Sept. 1925.
16 *Beatrice Webb's Diaries 1924–1932*, ed. Margaret Cole, Longmans, Green & Co., 1956.
17 Bullock, *Bevin*, p. 280.
18 *Manchester Guardian*, 6 Oct. 1925.
19 Quoted in Asa Briggs, *The History of Broadcasting in the United Kingdom*, vol. 1, *The Birth of Broadcasting*, Oxford University Press, 1961, p. 367.
20 PRO HO45/12336.
21 PRO KV3/58.
22 Quoted in R. I. Hills, *The General Strike in York*, Borthwick Papers, no. 57.
23 Robert Graves and Alan Hodge, *The Long Week-end: A Social History of Britain 1918–1939*, Four Square, 1961, p. 148.
24 *Hansard*, 1 Dec. 1925, col. 2086.
25 Quoted in Margaret Morris, *The General Strike*, Journeyman Press, 1980, p. 381.
26 Robert Rhodes James, *Memoirs of a Conservative: J. C. C. Davidson's Memoirs and Papers, 1910–1937*, Weidenfeld & Nicolson, 1969, p. 179.
27 Ibid., p. 180.
28 Paul and Carol Carter, *The Miners of Kilsyth in the 1926 General Strike*, Our History series, Communist Party of Great Britain, 1976.

CHAPTER 4

1 Walter Citrine, *Men and Work*, Hutchinson, 1964, p. 138.
2 Ibid., p. 147.
3 *Thomas Jones: Whitehall Diary*, vol. 2, ed. Keith Middlemas, Oxford University Press, 1969.
4 *Hansard*, 2 Feb. 1926, col. 8.
5 *Hansard*, 4 Feb. 1926, col. 511.
6 Document D29 in Robin Page Arnot, *The General Strike, May 1926*, EP Publishing, 1975.
7 Citrine, *Men and Work*, p. 133.
8 Page Arnot, *General Strike*.
9 Middlemas, *Jones*, vol. 2, p. 18.
10 Robert Rhodes James, *Memoirs of a Conservative*, Weidenfeld & Nicolson, 1969.
11 Middlemas, *Jones*, vol. 2, p. 12. Jones's contemporaneous insider's account is sharp and funny.

12 See Asa Briggs, *The History of Broadcasting in the United Kingdom*, vol. 1, *The Birth of Broadcasting*, Oxford University Press, 1961.

13 Middlemas, *Jones*, vol. 2, p. 19.

CHAPTER 5

1 Bevin's statement to his officers, 27 May 1926. Quoted in Alan Bullock, *The Life and Times of Ernest Bevin*, Heinemann, 1960, p. 300.

2 TUC, 'The Mining Situation', report of Conference of Executives of Affiliated Unions. Quoted in ibid., p. 302.

3 Walter Citrine, *Men and Work*, Hutchinson, 1964, p. 156.

4 Ibid., p. 158.

5 Imperial War Museum, Rear-Admiral J. Howson's midshipman's journal, 2075 PP/MCR/375.

6 C. R. Potts, *The GWR and the General Strike*, Oakwood Press, 1996.

7 TUC, Report of Conference of Executives of Affiliated Unions, 29 Apr.–1 May 1926.

8 Pollitt papers, Museum of Labour History, Manchester.

9 TUC, Report of Conference of Executives of Affiliated Unions, 29 Apr.–1 May 1926.

10 'The Mining Situation', report of Conference of Executives of Affiliated Unions, 29 Apr.–1 May.

11 Ramsay MacDonald, diary, quoted in David Marquand, *Ramsay MacDonald*, Richard Cohen Books, 1997.

12 *Manchester Guardian*, 3 May 1926, quoted in *The Guardian Book of the General Strike*, ed. R. H. Haigh, D. S. Morris and A. R. Peters, Wildwood House, 1988.

13 Paul and Carol Carter, *The Miners of Kilsyth in the 1926 General Strike*, Our History series, Communist Party of Great Britain, 1976.

14 *Thomas Jones: Whitehall Diary*, vol. 2, *1926–1930*, ed. Keith Middlemas, Oxford University Press, 1969, p. 27.

15 *Beatrice Webb's Diaries 1924–1932*, ed. Margaret Cole, Longmans, Green & Co., 1956.

16 *The Reith Diaries*, ed. Charles Stuart, Collins, 1975.

17 Haigh, Morris and Peters, *Guardian Book*, p. 15.

Chapter 6

1 *Hansard*, 3 May 1926, col. 81.
2 Hamilton Fyfe, *Behind the Scenes of the Great Strike*, Labour Publishing Co., 1926.
3 Robert Rhodes James, *Memoirs of a Conservative*, Weidenfeld & Nicolson, 1969, p. 231.
4 *Hansard*, 3 May 1926, col. 73.
5 C. R. Potts, *The GWR and the General Strike*, Oakwood Press, 1996, where many of the communications are reproduced.
6 Robin Page Arnot, *The General Strike, May 1926*, EP Publishing, 1975, p. 175.
7 R. W. Postgate, Ellen Wilkinson MP and J. F. Horrabin, *A Workers' History of the Great Strike*, Plebs League, 1927.
8 Citrine papers, quoted in Robert Taylor, *The TUC from the General Strike to the New Unionism*, Palgrave, 2000.
9 *The Journal of Arnold Bennett*, vol. 3, *1921–1928*, Doubleday, 1933.
10 *Beatrice Webb's Diaries 1924–1932*, ed. Margaret Cole, Longmans, Green & Co., 1956.
11 D. R. Davies, *In Search of Myself*, London, 1961, quoted in Margaret Morris, *The General Strike*, Journeyman Press, 1980, in the essays by Stuart Mews, *The Churches*.
12 Quoted in Rhodes James, *Memoirs*, p. 193.
13 From Potts, *The GWR*. The Clinker diary is in the collection of Brunel University.
14 Fyfe, *Behind the Scenes*, p. 25.
15 See Asa Briggs, *The History of Broadcasting in the United Kingdom*, vol. 1, *The Birth of Broadcasting*, Oxford University Press, 1961, for the full account of the BBC in the General Strike.
16 See Geoffrey Dawson, *Strike Nights at Printing House Square*, privately published, 1926, for a full account.

Chapter 7

1 *Brixton Free Press*, no. 1, Wed. 5 May 1926. British Newspaper Library.
2 Ibid.
3 Recounted in Francis Wheen, *The Soul of Indiscretion: Tom Driberg*, Fourth Estate, 2001.
4 Walter Citrine, *Men and Work*, Hutchinson, 1964, p. 179.

5 'BW', in *Sheetmetal Workers' Quarterly*, Oct. 1926, quoted in R. W. Postgate, Ellen Wilkinson MP and J. F. Horrabin, *A Workers' History of the Great Strike*, Plebs League, 1927, pp. 34–5.

6 See Paul and Carol Carter, *The Miners of Kilsyth in the 1926 General Strike*, Communist Party of Great Britain, 1976.

7 This account is taken from Emile Burns, *The General Strike 1926 – Trades Councils in Action*, Lawrence & Wishart, 1975 (first published, 1926).

8 Quoted in Asa Briggs, *The History of Broadcasting in the United Kingdom*, vol. 1, *The Birth of Broadcasting*, Oxford University Press, 1961.

9 *The Diary of Virginia Woolf*, ed. A. E. Bell, vol. 3, *1925–1930*, Hogarth Press, 1980, p. 77.

10 *British Gazette*, no. 1. British Newspaper Library.

11 Quoted in Kenneth Rose, *King George V*, Phoenix Press, 1983.

12 *The Journal of Arnold Bennett*, vol. 3, *1921–1928*, Doubleday, 1933, p. 148.

13 Bell, *Woolf*, p. 77.

14 Margaret Morris, *The General Strike*, Journeyman Press, 1980, in Stuart Mews, *The Churches*, on whose excellent chapter much of this relies.

15 See Geoffrey Dawson, *Strike Nights at Printing House Square*, privately published, 1926.

16 PRO KV4/246, official diary of MI(B).

17 Ibid., 'MI5 and the Strike'.

CHAPTER 8

1 Viscount Samuel, *Memoirs*, Cresset Press, 1945, p. 187.

2 Birmingham Public Libraries, Social Sciences Department, *General Strike 1926, the 'Nine Days in Birmingham'*. Excellent local account.

3 *The Diary of Virginia Woolf*, ed. A. E. Bell, vol. 3, *1925–1930*, Hogarth Press, 1980, p. 78.

4 This account relies on R. I. Hills, *The General Strike in York*, Borthwick Papers no. 57.

5 PRO KV4/246.

6 *Brixton Free Press*, 6 May 1926. British Newspaper Library.

7 Quoted in J. H. Porter, *Devon and the General Strike*. British Library.

8 *The Reith Diaries*, ed. Charles Stuart, Collins, 1975, p. 93.

9 Quoted in Asa Briggs, *The History of Broadcasting in the United Kingdom*, vol. 1, *The Birth of Broadcasting*, Oxford University Press, 1961, p. 363.

CHAPTER 9

1 From R. I. Hills, *The General Strike in York*, Borthwick Papers no. 57.
2 Walter Citrine, *Men and Work*, Hutchinson, 1964, p. 184.
3 TUC Intelligence Dept, 8 May 1926, Food Supply Arrangements. See excellent website: www.unionhistory.info.
4 *Thomas Jones: Whitehall Diary*, vol. 2, ed. Keith Middlemas, Oxford University Press, 1969, p. 41.
5 *The Reith Diaries*, ed. Charles Stuart, Collins, 1975, p. 94.
6 *Into the Wind*, p. 109, quoted in Asa Briggs, *The History of Broadcasting in the United Kingdom*, vol. 1, *The Birth of Broadcasting*, Oxford University Press, 1961, p. 379.
7 Quoted in Julian Symons, *The General Strike: A Historical Portrait*, first published London 1957; Cresset, 1987.
8 Robert Rhodes James, *Memoirs of a Conservative*, Weidenfeld & Nicolson 1969, p. 248.
9 Quoted in Briggs, *History of Broadcasting*, vol. 1, p. 379.
10 Ibid.
11 *The Diary of Virginia Woolf*, ed. A. E. Bell, vol. 3, *1925–1930*, Hogarth Press, 1980, p. 80.
12 Hamilton Fyfe, *Behind the Scenes of the Great Strike*, Labour Publishing Co., 1926.
13 See PRO KV4/246.
14 Geoffrey Dawson, *Strike Nights at Printing House Square*, privately published, 1926.
15 Ibid., p. 33.

CHAPTER 10

1 *Thomas Jones: Whitehall Diary*, vol. 1, ed. Keith Middlemas, Oxford University Press, 1969.
2 *British Worker*, Sunday 9 May 1926.
3 PRO KV4/246.
4 See Margaret Morris, *The General Strike*, Journeyman Press, 1980.
5 Quoted in Hugh Thomas, *John Strachey*, Eyre Methuen, 1973, pp. 57–8.
6 I am indebted for this account to J. H. Porter, *Devon and the General Strike*, British Library.
7 Middlemas, *Jones*, vol. 2, p. 44.

8	Robert Rhodes James, *Memoirs of a Conservative*, Weidenfeld & Nicolson, 1969, p. 244.

9	Quoted in Robert Rhodes James, *Churchill: A Study in Failure, 1900–1939*, Weidenfeld & Nicolson, 1970; Penguin Books, 1981, p. 223.

10	Harold Nicolson, *King George V*, Constable, 1952, p. 418.

11	C. H. Drage's diary, 10935 PP/MCR/99. Imperial War Museum.

12	Cmr H. G. D. de Chair, letter, Imperial War Museum, 7866 P314.

13	Walter Citrine, *Men and Work*, Hutchinson, 1964, p. 186.

14	Osbert Sitwell, *Laughter in the Next Room*, Macmillan, 1958, p. 236.

15	Ibid., p. 242.

16	This account is largely taken from *The Reith Diaries*, ed. Charles Stuart, Collins, 1975, pp. 94–5.

17	Robert Rhodes James, *Memoirs of a Conservative*, Weidenfeld and Nicolson, 1969.

CHAPTER 11

1	Quoted in Margaret Morris, *The General Strike*, Journeyman Press, 1980, in the specially written essay by Stuart Mews, *The Churches*, p. 328.

2	Quoted in Hamilton Fyfe, *Behind the Scenes of the Great Strike*, Labour Publishing Co., 1926, p. 63.

3	Quoted in ibid., p. 75.

4	R. W. Postgate, Ellen Wilkinson MP and J. F. Horrabin, *A Workers' History of the Great Strike*, Plebs League, 1927.

5	Newcastle edition of the *British Worker*, 11 May (issue 1).

6	*Brixton Free Press*, Monday 10 May 1926.

7	Fyfe, *Behind the Scenes*, p. 60.

8	*Spectator*, 8 May, 1926.

9	Mrs J. Evans Audio Recording 172, South Wales coalfields project, University of Wales, Swansea.

10	*Preston Strike News*, no. 4.

11	Osbert Sitwell, *Laughter in the Next Room*, Macmillan, 1958, p. 245.

12	This paragraph and the one that follows rely heavily on Walter Citrine, *Men and Work*, Hutchinson, 1964.

13	PRO KV4/246.

14	*The Guardian Book of the General Strike*, ed. R. H. Haigh, D. S. Morris and A. R. Peters, Wildwood House, 1988, p. 87.

15	*The Journal of Arnold Bennett*, vol. 3, *1921–1928*, Doubleday, 1933.

16	*British Independent*, 11 May 1926.

Chapter 12

1 C. R. Potts, *The GWR and the General Strike*, Oakwood Press, 1996.
2 Kensington Strike Committee, quoted in R. W. Postgate, Ellen Wilkinson MP and J. F. Horrabin, *A Workers' History of the Great Strike*, Plebs League, 1927.
3 TUC leaflet reprinted in Potts, *The GWR*.
4 See Potts, *The GWR*.
5 R. S. Joby, *The Railwaymen*, David and Charles, 1984.
6 *The Diary of Virginia Woolf*, vol. 3, *1925–1930*, Hogarth Press, 1980, p. 82.
7 PRO KV4/246, 'P' reports.
8 Postgate, Wilkinson and Horrabin, *Workers' History*.
9 *Thomas Jones: Whitehall Diary*, vol. 2, ed. Keith Middlemas, Oxford University Press, 1969, p. 45.
10 Hamilton Fyfe, *Behind the Scenes of the Great Strike*, Labour Publishing Co., 1926, p. 68.
11 Quoted in Kenneth Rose, *King George V*, Phoenix Press, 1983, p. 341.
12 Viscount Samuel, *Memoirs*, Cresset Press, 1945.
13 Walter Citrine, *Men and Work*, Hutchinson, 1964, p. 194.
14 *British Worker*, 11 May 1926.
15 *Beatrice Webb's Diaries 1924–1932*, ed. Margaret Cole, Longmans, Green & Co., 1956, p. 100.
16 These and all the TUC intelligence committee reports are available on the TUC's excellent http://www.unionhistory.info website.
17 *The Reith Diaries*, ed. Charles Stuart, Collins, 1975, p. 96.

Chapter 13

1 Quoted in Julian Symons, *The General Strike*, first published London 1957; Cresset Library, 1987, p. 211.
2 This account is taken from *Who Were the Guilty? General Strike Brighton 1926*, Brighton Labour History Press, 1976.
3 Walter Citrine, *Men and Work*, Hutchinson, 1964, p. 197.
4 *The Reith Diaries*, ed. Charles Stuart, Collins, 1975, p. 96.
5 Asa Briggs, *The History of Broadcasting in the United Kingdom*, vol. 1, Oxford University Press, 1961, p. 365.
6 Quoted in David Marquand, *Ramsay MacDonald*, Richard Cohen Books, 1977, p. 439.

7 Quoted in Alan Bullock, *The Life and Times of Ernest Bevin*, Heinemann, 1960, pp. 330–1.

8 This account leans heavily on Walter Citrine, *Men and Work*, Hutchinson, 1964, and Bullock, *Bevin*, as well as Viscount Samuel, *Memoirs*, Cresset Press, 1945; and *Thomas Jones: Whitehall Diary*, vol. 2, ed. Keith Middlemas, Oxford University Press, 1969.

CHAPTER 14

1 *Brixton Free Press*, 12 May 1926.

2 *The Diary of Virginia Woolf*, ed. A. E. Bell, vol. 3, *1925–1930*, Hogarth Press, 1980, p. 84.

3 *Thomas Jones: Whitehall Diary*, vol. 2, ed. Keith Middlemas, Oxford University Press, 1969, p. 48.

4 Alan Bullock, *The Life and Times of Ernest Bevin*, vol. 1, Heinemann, 1960, p. 334.

5 *The Reith Diaries*, ed. Charles Stuart, Collins, 1975, p. 97.

6 Bell, *Woolf*, vol. 3, p. 84.

7 Bullock, *Bevin*, p. 337.

8 Quoted in Harold Nicolson, *King George V*, Constable, 1952, p. 420.

CHAPTER 15

1 PRO KV4/246.

2 Cmr. H. G. D. de Chair, letter, Imperial War Museum 7866 P314.

3 Reprinted in C. R. Potts, *The GWR and the General Strike*, Oakwood Press, 1996.

4 See *Single or Return? The Official History of the TSSA*, www.tssa.org.uk.

5 Quoted in David Marquand, *Ramsay MacDonald*, Richard Cohen Books, 1997, p. 440, diary entry for 14 May.

6 S. J. Taylor, *The Great Outsiders, Northcliffe, Rothermere and the Daily Mail*, Phoenix Giant, 1996, p. 249.

7 Quoted in Robin Page Arnot, *The General Strike, May 1926*, EP Publishing, 1975, p. 240.

8 Robert Rhodes James, *Memoirs of a Conservative*, Weidenfeld & Nicolson, 1969, p. 245.

9 Osbert Sitwell, *Laughter in the Next Room*, Macmillan, 1958.

10 *The Journal of Arnold Bennett*, vol. 3, *1921–1928*, Doubleday, 1933, p. 151.

11 *The Diary of Virginia Woolf*, ed. A. E. Bell, vol. 3, *1925–1930*, Hogarth
   Press, 1980, p. 84.
12 Quoted in Charles Loch Mowat, *Britain between the Wars*, Methuen,
   1955, 1968, p. 332.
13 Glasgow Digital Library, Red Clyde on www.strath.ac.uk/redclyde.

Chapter 16

1 *Communist International*, no. 21, June 1926.
2 Emile Burns, *The General Strike 1926 – Trades Councils in Action*,
   Lawrence & Wishart, 1975.
3 Hamilton Fyfe, *Behind the Scenes of the Great Strike*, Labour Publishing
   Co., 1926.
4 Walter Citrine, *Men and Work*, Hutchinson, 1964, p. 217.
5 Lord Eustace Percy, quoted in Keith Middlemas and John Barnes,
   Baldwin, Weidenfeld & Nicolson, 1969, p. 392.
6 See D. J. Taylor, *Orwell: The Life*, Chatto & Windus, 2003.
7 Citrine, *Men and Work*, p. 216.
8 See Keith Middlemas, *Politics in Industrial Society*, André Deutsch, 1979,
   for an interesting discussion of these points. Also Maurice Cowling, *The
   Impact of Labour*, Cambridge University Press, 1971.
9 From Middlemas and Barnes, *Baldwin*, p. 284.
10 *If I Were Labour Leader*, written and published by Sir Ernest Benn,
   London, 1926.

Bibliography

MUSEUMS, LIBRARIES AND OTHER SOURCES

In the helpful Museum of Labour History in Manchester the following are available:

Birmingham Public Libraries, Social Sciences Department: *General Strike 1926, the 'Nine Days in Birmingham'*
Brighton Labour History Press 1976: *Who were the Guilty? General Strike Brighton 1926*
R. I. Hills, *The General Strike in York*, Borthwick Papers no. 57

The Museum also has full sets of TUC and Labour Party conference records, and Harry Pollitt's papers.

Another local history, available at the British Library, is:

Goodhart, A. L., *The Legality of the General Strike in England*, Yale Law Journal, 1927

The British Newspaper Library at Colindale, north London, has full sets of the *British Gazette*, the *British Worker* and many local newssheets.

The Imperial War Museum kindly made available the following accounts from its archive:

Rear-Admiral J. Howson's midshipman's journal, 2075 PP/MCR/375
C. H. Drage's diary, 10935 PP/MCR/99
Commander H. G. D. de Chair's letters 7866 P314

The National Archives: Public Record Office (Kew)

There are countless files relating to the General Strike and more are becoming available all the time. The following are some of the most useful:

ADM1/8657/48   Communist attempts to introduce propaganda into HM ships by means of newspaper boys delivering papers on board ships in harbour

CAB 27/332   Whitehall Departmental situation reports

HMSO Cmd 2682   Documents seized in raid on Communist headquarters, 1925

HO45/25439   DISTURBANCES   Communist activity within the National Sailors' Union

HO144/4684   DISTURBANCES   Activities of the Communist Party of Great Britain. The relative responsibilities of Attorney General and Home Secretary in instituting political prosecutions

HO144/6682   DISTURBANCES   Communist Party activities

HO45/12336   DISTURBANCES   Organization for the Maintenance of Supply (OMS)

HO144/22372   DISTURBANCES   Communist propaganda to incite His Majesty's Forces to mutiny

KV2/1186   Campbell prosecution

KV3/25   Documents seized in police raid on Communist Party headquarters in 1925

KV3/57   Activities of the British Fascist Organization in the UK (excluding the British Union of Fascists)

KV4/246   Summary of events and action taken by Military Security Intelligence and MI5 and its emergency section, known as MI(B), during the 1926 General Strike

Websites

www.unionhistory.info   excellent TUC website with documents, timelines etc.

www.strath.ac.uk/redclyde   oral history

www.tssa.org.uk   for *Single or Return? The Official History of the TSSA* [Transport Salaried Staffs' Association]

www.workersliberty.org   what the Communists are thinking now

General

Beckett, F., *Enemy Within: The Rise and Fall of the British Communist Party*, Merlin Press, 1995

Benewick, R., *The Fascist Movement in Britain*, Penguin Press, 1972

Blake, R., *The Conservative Party from Peel to Churchill*, Fontana/Collins, 1972

Briggs, A., *The History of Broadcasting in the United Kingdom*, vol. 1, *The Birth of Broadcasting*, Oxford University Press, 1961

Burns, E., *The General Strike 1926 – Trades Councils in Action*, Lawrence & Wishart, 1975

Butler, D., and Butler, G., *Twentieth-Century British Political Facts 1900–2000*, Palgrave, 2000

Carter, C., and Carter, P., *The Miners of Kilsyth in the 1926 General Strike*, Our History series, CPGB, 1976

Coates, D., *The Labour Party and the Struggle for Socialism*, Cambridge University Press, 1975

Colls, R ., *Identity of England*, Oxford University Press, 2004

Cowling, M., *The Impact of Labour 1920–1924: The Beginning of Modern British Politics*, Cambridge University Press, 1971

Dawson, G., *Strike Nights at Printing House Square*, privately published, 1926

Fyfe, H., *Behind the Scenes of the Great Strike*, Labour Publishing Co., 1926

Graves, R., and Hodge, A., *The Long Week-end: A Social History of Britain 1918–1939*, Four Square, 1961

Haigh, R. H., Morris, D. S., and Peters, A. R., eds, *The Guardian Book of the General Strike*, Wildwood House, 1988

Harmer, H., *The Longman Companion to the Labour Party 1900–1998*, Longman, 1999

Martin, K., *The British Public and the General Strike*, Hogarth Press, 1926

Middlemas, K., *Politics in Industrial Society*, André Deutsch, 1979

Morris, M., *The General Strike*, Journeyman Press, 1980

Mowat, C. L., *Britain between the Wars 1918–1940*, Methuen, 1955

Mowat, C. L., *The General Strike, 1926*, Archive Series, Edward Arnold, London, 1969

Norton, P., and Aughey, A., *Conservatives and Conservatism*, Temple Smith, 1981

Orwell, G., *Essays*, Penguin Classics, 2000

Page Arnot, R., *The General Strike, May 1926: Its Origin and History*, EP Publishing, 1975

Pelling, H., *A History of British Trade Unionism*, Penguin Books, 1976

Pelling, H., *A Short History of the Labour Party*, 7th edn, Macmillan, 1982

Pimlott, B., and Cook, C., *Trade Unions in British Politics*, Longman, 1982

Postgate, R. W., Wilkinson, E., and Horrabin, J. F., *A Workers' History of the Great Strike*, Plebs League, 1927

Potts, C. R., *The GWR and the General Strike (1926)*, Oakwood Press, 1996

Renshaw, P., *The General Strike*, Eyre Methuen, 1975

Symons, J., *The General Strike: A Historical Portrait*, first published London, 1957; Cresset Library, 1987.

Taylor, R., *The TUC from the General Strike to New Unionism*, Palgrave, 2000

Thompson, E. P., *The Making of the English Working Class*, Penguin Books, 1991

Biography, Autobiography, Memoirs and Diaries

Bell, A. E., ed., *The Diary of Virginia Woolf*, vol. 3, *1925–1930*, Hogarth Press, 1980

Bennett, A., *The Journal of Arnold Bennett*, vol. 3, *1921–1928*, Doubleday, 1933

Boyle, A., *Montagu Norman: A Biography*, Cassell, 1967

Brown, G., *Maxton*, Mainstream Publishing, 1986

Bullock, A., *The Life and Times of Ernest Bevin*, vol. 1, *Trade Union Leader 1881–1940*, Heinemann, 1960

Childs, W., *Episodes and Reflections: Being some records from the life of Major-General Sir Wyndham Childs, KCMG, KBE, CB*, Cassell, 1930

Citrine, W., *Men and Work: The Autobiography of Lord Citrine*, Hutchinson, 1964

Cole, M., ed., *Beatrice Webb's Diaries 1924–1932*, Longmans, Green & Co. 1956

Jenkins, R., *Asquith*, HarperCollins, 1988

Koss, S. E., *Lord Haldane: Scapegoat for Liberalism*, Columbia University Press, 1969

Marquand, D., *Ramsay MacDonald*, Richard Cohen Books, 1997

Middlemas, K., ed., *Thomas Jones: Whitehall Diary*, vol. 1, *1916–1925*; vol. 2, *1926–1930*, Oxford University Press, 1969

Middlemas, K., and Barnes, J., *Baldwin: A Biography*, Weidenfeld & Nicolson, 1969

Morgan, K., *Harry Pollitt*, Manchester University Press, 1993

Nicolson, H., *King George V: His Life and Reign*, Constable, 1952; paperback, 1984

Pimlott, B., ed., *The Political Diary of Hugh Dalton 1918–1940, 1945–1960*, Jonathan Cape, 1986

Rhodes James, R., *Memoirs of a Conservative: J. C. C. Davidson's Memoirs and Papers, 1910–1937*, Weidenfeld & Nicolson, 1969

Rhodes James, R., *Churchill: A Study in Failure 1900–1939*, Penguin Books, 1981

Rose, K., *King George V*, Phoenix Press, 1983

Samuel, Viscount, *Memoirs*, Cresset Press, 1945

Sitwell, O., *Laughter in the Next Room: An Autobiography*, Macmillan, 1958

Skidelsky, R., *Oswald Mosley*, Macmillan Papermacs, 1981

Skidelsky, R., *John Maynard Keynes*, vol. 2, *The Economist as Saviour 1920–1937*, Macmillan, 1992

Squires, M., *Saklatvala: A Political Biography*, Lawrence & Wishart, 1990

Stuart, C., *The Reith Diaries*, Collins, 1975

Taylor, D. J., *Orwell: The Life*, Chatto & Windus, 2003

Taylor, S. J., *The Great Outsiders: Northcliffe, Rothermere and the Daily Mail*, Phoenix Giant, 1998

Thomas, H., *John Strachey*, Eyre Methuen, 1973

Wheen, F., *The Soul of Indiscretion: Tom Driberg, Poet, Philanderer, Legislator and Outlaw*, Fourth Estate, 2001

Williamson, P., *Stanley Baldwin, Conservative Leadership and National Values*, Cambridge University Press, 1999

Wilson, A. N., *Hilaire Belloc*, Hamish Hamilton, 1984

Index